# ADORNO AND THE

'Hammer is to be congratulated for presenting a lucid and consistent case for the significance of Adorno's political thought, doing justice to its complexity while situating it within its specific historical context.'

Howard Caygill, *University of London*

'Clearly written, well-structured ... It is a remarkable achievement to have attained this level of clarity about a topic that is this difficult and obscure.'

Raymond Geuss, *University of Cambridge*

Interest in Theodor W. Adorno continues to grow in the English-speaking world as the significance of his contribution to philosophy, social and cultural theory, as well as aesthetics, is increasingly recognized. In this lucid book, Espen Hammer critically considers and investigates Adorno's political thought.

Espen Hammer examines Adorno's political experiences and assesses his engagement with Marxist as well as liberal theory. Looking at the development of Adorno's thought as he confronts fascism and modern mass culture, Hammer then analyzes the political dimension of his philosophical and aesthetic theorizing. By addressing Jürgen Habermas' influential criticisms, he defends Adorno as a theorist of autonomy, responsibility, and democratic plurality. He also discusses Adorno's relevance for feminist and ecological thinking. As opposed to those who see Adorno as someone who relinquished the political, Hammer's account shows his reflections to be, on the most fundamental level, politically motivated and deeply engaged.

*Adorno & the Political* is an invigorating exploration of a key political thinker and also a useful introduction to his thought as a whole. It will be of interest to scholars and students in the fields of philosophy, sociology, politics, and aesthetics.

**Espen Hammer** is Reader in Philosophy at the University of Essex. He is the author of *Stanley Cavell: Skepticism, Subjectivity, and the Ordinary*.

# THINKING THE POLITICAL

General editors:
Keith Ansell Pearson
*University of Warwick*
Simon Critchley
*University of Essex*

Recent decades have seen the emergence of a distinct and challenging body of work by a number of Continental thinkers that has fundamentally altered the way in which philosophical questions are conceived and discussed. This work poses a major challenge to anyone wishing to define the essentially contestable concept of 'the political' and to think anew the political import and application of philosophy. How does recent thinking on time, history, language, humanity, alterity, desire, sexuality, gender and culture open up the possibility of thinking the political anew? What are the implications of such thinking for our understanding of and relation to the leading ideologies of the modern world, such as liberation, socialism and Marxism? What are the political responsibilities of philosophy in the face of the new world (dis)order?

This new series is designed to present the work of the major Continental thinkers of our time, and the political debates their work has generated, to a wider audience in philosophy and in political, social and cultural theory. The aim is neither to dissolve the specificity of the 'philosophical' into the 'political' nor to evade the challenge that the 'political' poses the 'philosophical'; rather, each volume in the series will try to show it is only in the relation between the two that the new possibilities of thought and politics can be activated.

Volumes already published in this series are:

# ADORNO AND THE POLITICAL

## Espen Hammer

Routledge
Taylor & Francis Group

LONDON AND NEW YORK

First published 2006
by Routledge
2 Park Square, Milton Park, Abingdon, Oxon OX14 4RN

Simultaneously published in the USA and Canada
by Routledge
270 Madison Ave, New York, NY 10016

*Routledge is an imprint of the Taylor & Francis Group*

© 2005 Espen Hammer

Typeset in Sabon
by Taylor & Francis Books

Printed and bound in Great Britain by
TJ International Ltd, Padstow, Cornwall

*British Library Cataloguing in Publication Data*
A catalogue record for this book is available from the British Library

*Library of Congress Cataloging in Publication Data*
Hammer, Espen.
Adorno and the political / Espen Hammer.
p. cm. -- (Thinking the political)
ISBN 0-415-28912-2 (hardcover : alk. paper) -- ISBN 0-415-28913-0 (pbk. :
alk. paper) 1. Political science--Philosophy. 2. Adorno, Theodor W., 1903-
1969. I. Title. II. Series.
JA71.H273 2005
320.53'22'092--dc22
                                          2005005628

ISBN 0 415 28912-2 (hbk)
ISBN 0 415 28913-0 (pbk)

T&F informa
*Taylor & Francis Group is the Academic Divison of T&F Informa plc.*

FOR KRISTIN

# CONTENTS

CONTENTS

# ACKNOWLEDGMENTS

In writing this book I am indebted to my colleagues and students in the Philosophy Department at the University of Essex whose intellectual support has been invaluable. Much of the material in it has benefited from comments made by the participants of my graduate seminar in continental philosophy. In particular, my research students have offered much good debate and input. The Philosophy Department at the University of Essex granted me generous research leave at the time when I most needed it.

My gratitude also goes to the Humboldt Foundation, which financed my research in Frankfurt. Without that research, and without the stimulus provided by the Research Colloquium in the Philosophy Department at the University of Frankfurt, it would have been much more difficult for me to have written this book. I would especially like to thank Axel Honneth, Ståle Finke, Rahel Jaeggi, Jay Bernstein, Simon Critchley, and Rainer Forst for discussions of issues related to this project.

Peter Dews commented on portions of the manuscript, for which I am sincerely grateful.

Material from the book has been presented at various conferences. I would like to thank the audiences for their useful comments.

I would also like to express my deepest debt of love and gratitude to my wife Kristin Gjesdal, without whom this book would never have been.

**Note:** the English translations from Adorno's collected works in German, *Gesammelte Schriften*, are my own.

# INTRODUCTION

Theodor W. Adorno was one of the most politically acute thinkers of the twentieth century. Indeed, it is difficult to think of a major intellectual figure from this period for whom the attention to, and formation of, political judgment has had more deep-seated implications than in his case. Not only do his individual theoretical contributions and cultural interpretations display a keen awareness of the socio-political subtexts that pervade every symbolic exchange, but the manner and style in which he wrote, down to the very texture and rhetoric of his well-crafted, intellectually challenging sentences, testify to an uncompromising willingness to engage with the political in all its complexity and historical specificity.

To be sure, Adorno never developed anything like a theory of politics. His writings contain very little that, at least directly, would qualify as a genuine contribution to discussions, say, of representative government, international relations, legitimate forms of dissent, and so on — that is, the institutionally recognized *topoi* of current political philosophy. As one of the last great representatives of Western Marxism and the most famous luminary of first-generation Critical Theory, his accounts were geared, rather, towards disclosing mechanisms and systems of domination, as well as towards the possibility of rational resistance and subversion within them. The interest that consistently guided his research was emancipatory: as opposed to simply interpreting the social phenomena within the relevant framework, it aimed at diagnosing the present with a view to anticipating a more liberated, humane and rational future.

Given his explicit desire not only to read off repressed and sedimented social meaning from manifestations of culture, but to resituate philosophy in a contentious political space and indeed make it a placeholder for what he saw as an otherwise absent praxis, it is chastening to note that Adorno, more than perhaps any other radical theorist of the twentieth century, has been accused of betraying the critical heritage within which he theorized. In the eyes of the militant students of the late 1960s, and orthodox Marxists more generally, as well as in the analyses offered by Jürgen Habermas and other representatives of second-generation Critical Theory,

1

Adorno's thinking unwittingly slides into a kind of mandarin academicism with little to offer but a sterile and potentially reactionary critique of mass culture combined with a compensatory investment in modernist art. As a result, so these critics argue, of his pessimistic philosophy of history, according to which the exercise of human rationality is essentially and inevitably driven towards self-destruction, there can be no room, in this account, for an emancipatory politics. What Adorno represents is rather a conservative, quietist position from which the Hegelian–Marxist scheme of inevitable, or at least possible, progress has been replaced by a peculiar version of original sin — that is, the formation of a one-sided disposition towards formal-instrumental or purposive rationality.

No serious interpreter can easily dismiss this objection. According to Adorno, Western modernity has radically forfeited the claims and promises with which it emerged and separated itself from pre-modern arrangements. Due to a fateful dialectic of enlightenment, whereby the urge towards liberation transformed itself into ever-widening circles of domination and social control, it has lost sight of its own grammar or deep meaning. Contemporary society, as Adorno viewed it both from his American exile and from his position as celebrated intellectual in the post-war German Federal Republic, seems to have entered a phase of complete intransparency and irrationality, culminating not only in Auschwitz and the Gulag as the apex of identitarian violence, but with the general commodification of all aspects of interpersonal relations under late capitalism. To show why and how this is so, as well as to demarcate and defend cultural forms that, in his eyes, oppose what he regarded as a false totality, became the defining features of his life-long project.

Any attempt, such as this, to invent, map out and deploy markers for a revaluation of Adorno's relevance within contemporary debates on the Left must take into account the horizon from within which his interventions were made. Adorno was eminently a thinker of the present, and he engaged in a philosophical critique of the present; thus his philosophy, like the art works he so passionately defended, is itself mortal: it cannot be ripped out of context and applied wherever and whenever it may seem suitable to do so. Yet this book would not have been written had I been convinced that the interest his works may provoke is merely historical. On the contrary, in the late postmodern age of corporate globalization, of a dwindling public sphere, of a widespread loss of historical and social awareness, of political newspeak and TV docudramas, of a seemingly irreversible technization of the lifeworld and an ever more pervasive commodification of all areas of human engagement, a period in which nothing — nature, labor, subjectivity, art, collective praxis, the Unconscious — seems capable of figuring as sites of subversion and difference, Adorno appears not to have lost his relevance. As Fredric Jameson (1996: 5) casually remarked in 1990, Adorno's version of Critical Theory, "which was no great help in the previous periods, may turn out to be just what is needed today."

As already mentioned, Adorno adamantly resisted the traditional interpretation of the Marxist dogma of a unity between theory and praxis as entailing the demand for immediate political action. In his view, the theory/praxis constellation needs to be speculatively reconfigured. Since praxis in the sense of immediate collective action seems to have become unavailable, or at least fraught with difficulties, the claim to social reconfiguration implicit in the concept of praxis must be transposed to the level of theory — not theory for its own sake, but theory that has detached itself from immediate political concerns in order to stand back and be able to reconnect politically from other and more profound angles than those which are normally associated with critical theorizing. Indeed, under current conditions, he claims, theory is the only true form of praxis. Moreover, in order to have a genuine political purchase, theoretical reflection must avoid the simple taking up of positions; indeed, theory must stop communicating with people's beliefs and instead aim at a more hermetic language of images, parables and dialectical reversals. In a letter to Walter Benjamin in 1934, in which he responds to material from the Arcades Project, we thus find Adorno (1999a: 54) writing that "No one is more aware than I am that every single sentence here is and must be laden with political dynamite; but the further down such dynamite is buried, the greater its explosive force when detonated." To many, such irruptive qualities may hardly be imaginable as the result of theoretical work, and for the radical Left of the late 1960s and 1970s, such pronouncements were more than enough to make Adorno seem unappealing. Today, however, some thirty or forty years later, when organized Marxism in the West is close to extinction, a second look at Adorno's reasons for holding on to alternative and more unseasonable conceptions of politics may indeed be felt as pressing. Although theory became the major vehicle for the articulation of social awareness and for the exercise of autonomy, Adorno never retracted his commitment to radical political change and the uncovering of rational forms of practice. A central aim of this book is to provide a sense of the nature and scope of that commitment.

## Difficulties of Adorno's work

Although his work in a deep sense responds to a rather limited set of intellectual concerns, Adorno is notoriously difficult to place and engage with within the standard interpretive grids of most commentaries or studies in philosophy. There are many reasons why this is so. One is the sheer abundance of writers, artists, cultural phenomena and social tendencies with which he takes issue. Very few, if any, readers of Adorno will be equally at home not only with the majority of Central European philosophers, authors and composers since Kant, Goethe and Beethoven, but also with debates in mid-twentieth century German and American sociology, theories of fascism, advanced musical analysis, the German romantics, theories of film and mass culture, early developments of surrealism, the history of Western Marxism, the research undertaken by the Frankfurt School, the many social and intellectual contexts to which Adorno was exposed — just to mention some of the many areas one ideally ought to master in order to understand his thought. Faced with this over-abundance of material, the critic is all too often left with the displeasing trilemma of silence, explicit exclusion or just plain old charlatanism.

A second difficulty, related to the first, is that Adorno's work seems to resist every effort to categorize and define it. Is Adorno a kind of Nietzschean Marxist? Or is he a modified Hegelian with a Kantian sense of finitude and limitation? How pervasive is the influence of Lukács and Weber? And what effect does the Judaic impulse, mediated by Rosenzweig and Benjamin, actually have? Is he perhaps a failed avant-garde artist who turned to philosophy and sociology? Or is his work best seen as an anticipation of Foucauldian or Derridean poststructuralism? Questions of this sort do not admit of any quick and easy answers — indeed, the further into it one gets, the more difficult it becomes to determine what kind of work this actually is. Like the art works he defended, it is as if his texts transcend every straightforward interpretive efforts. Rather than systematic reconstruction, what they require is a combination of constructive reading and self-reflection.

The difficulty is reinforced at the level of rhetoric and style. From his first publications and throughout his writing career, Adorno displayed a penchant for the essay and the aphorism over the thesis and the academic paper, and even his largest and most ambitious works, *Negative Dialectics* and *Aesthetic Theory*, can be read as extended elaborations and variations on the tangential method of the essay. As he explains in the first essay of *Notes to Literature*, the essay, while informed by theory, is less oriented towards the development of general categories and regimented, logical entailment-relations than it is towards allowing the object under scrutiny to reverberate in its non-identity with its generic term.[1] Like literary art works, its neighboring but not identical genre of discourse, or Kantian reflective judgments, it seeks to interpret (social) totality, the universal, on the basis of the author's subjective response to the fragment in its singularity. Rather than explaining, justifying, and drawing stable conclusions, it aims at provoking and stimulating the reader's own reflection — not infrequently by means of paradox and indirect forms of communication. The appeal to intersubjective verification procedures and *a priori* rules for the linking of theoretical phrases has for Adorno itself become suspect: systematic philosophy is no longer possible.

## Approaches to Adorno

The remarkable influence of Adorno's writings on late twentieth century European and American intellectual culture, especially since the collapse of the Communist bloc, and the way in which his work seems to have affected nearly every field in the humanities, is far from easily understandable. With some important exceptions, he seems to have been virtually oblivious to the concerns of postcolonialism, including race, discrimination, and imperialism. His blunt Eurocentrism, focused as it was on Germany and Austria in particular, predisposed him to reject, or at least view with suspicion, forms of cultural expression — notoriously jazz — that did not fit into his own framework. It also led him to stake most of his claims for the role of art as embodying an alternative form of rationality on forms of aesthetic high modernism that since the mid-1960s have largely lost their attraction and relevance. In the current poststructuralist climate of continental critical theory, his Hegelian vocabulary of negation and mediation, of appearance and reality, as well as his (however complex and qualified) defense of the subject, may well seem dated and difficult to put to use.

Adorno's work requires active and creative reading. His dialectical critique of the concept, and of reification, has inspired feminists interested in articulating sexual difference. His modernist construction of the advanced work of art has been extended to apply to post-auratic, conceptualist art of the 1980s and 1990s. Postcolonialists have made use of Adorno's reflections in *Minima Moralia* on exile and social difference. His negative dialectics has been brought into dialogue with contemporary approaches in the philosophy of language.

Very provisionally, readings of Adorno since the 1970s can be divided into at least six different categories:[2]

a) Poststructuralist readings, represented by Wolfgang Welsch (1990) and Rainer Nägele (1986), have downplayed the idealist (Kantian and Hegelian) background and related Adorno's work to those of Foucault, Derrida, Lyotard, and Lacan. In this configuration Adorno is seen as a radical critic of Western logocentrism and a spokesman of singularity, rupture, difference, and paradox — in opposition to any form of (Hegelian) synthesis. Such readings take Adorno to be aiming to deconstruct all forms of totality, including the identity of the subject and the progressivist, teleological construction of history. Of central interest to this line of interpretation is the relationship to Benjamin, whose work has widely been seen as manifestly anti-Hegelian and therefore conducive to poststructuralist appropriation.

b) Partly related to such readings are the more overtly Heideggerian approaches to Adorno, represented by commentators such as Ute

Guzzoni (1981) and Hermann Mörchen (1981), for whom Adorno maintains the necessity of a thinking that can anticipate a reconfigured, less violent relationship to nature. In their view, which bears affinities with central dimensions of deep ecology, Adorno's work should be read as calling for a *Besinnung* with regard to the technoindustrial mode of social and material reproduction itself.

c) At the opposite end of the spectrum stand the approaches offered by Jürgen Habermas (1987), Albrecht Wellmer (1991), Axel Honneth (1991), and other representatives of second- and third-generation Critical Theory. On their accounts, Adorno's analyses of systemic intervention in the lifeworld, his critique of instrumental reason, his defense of the value of human autonomy (*Mündigkeit*), and his search for alternative, non-instrumental forms of rationality within the framework of a critical theory of modernity, have been sources of great inspiration. Their most serious objection, however, is that his work suffers from a normative deficit which they see as related to an outmoded representationalism. At the end of the day, Adorno repudiates much of the modernist impulse of the early Frankfurt School in favor of an aesthetically inspired investment in sources of authority beyond the range of what the subject can be held rationally accountable for. Ironically, Adorno thus ends up becoming an anti-modern Nietzschean.

d) More explicit Marxist readings have taken many forms, ranging from downright negative ones, especially in the 1970s, to current attempts, exemplified by critics such as Fredric Jameson (1996) and Robert Hullot-Kentor (1989), to re-estimate the relevance of Adorno in a contemporary context. The debates here are complex, reflecting the shifting positions and allegiances of different groups and individuals committed to some form of Marxist interpretation of society. The critique presented by the New Left in Germany and the United States has been focused on a number of concerns, including Adorno's rejection of the primacy of class struggle, his hostility towards the Communist regimes in the East, his lack of an immediate political commitment, as well as his skepticism with regard to attempts to identify a social macro-subject. While Jameson brings out essential elements of this critique in his chapter on Adorno in *Marxism and Form* (1971), arguing that a work such as *Negative Dialectics* fails insofar as it tries to save philosophy itself, his more affirmative 1990 text *Late Marxism* seeks to define Adorno's writing as *the* legitimate form of Marxism for the postmodern condition of the 1990s. According to Jameson, Adorno's characterization of late capitalism as a totality offers a potent framework for analyzing the current state of global commodification. Engaged in a more "orthodox" reconstruction, we find Hullot-Kentor who is less interested in actualizing

6

Adorno within a postmodernist, culturalist approach than he is in returning to a dialectical and materialist account of society. For Hullot-Kentor, any *rapprochement* with either deconstruction or postmodernism is likely to misrepresent the nature of Adorno's project.

e) From a less Marxian and more openly Hegelian angle, Jay Bernstein (1992, 2001) has produced a series of powerful interpretations that focus on Adorno's account of the status and implications of cultural differentiation. For Bernstein, Adorno's work is grounded in a perception of modernity as bifurcated between the claims of particularity and the claims of universality and generality. Whereas the former are located within the realm of the aesthetic (and to some extent the ethical), the latter appear in science, technology, administration, and formal morality. According to Bernstein, Adorno is involved in conducting a remembrance of the price agents pay for the process of cultural differentiation. In contrast to Habermas, who regards the differentiation of cultural value spheres mainly as a cognitive achievement, a chance for the different spheres (science, morality/law, art/art criticism) to cultivate their own autonomous logics, for Bernstein it signals a problematic loss of meaning. In a wholly disenchanted world, the advanced art work appears as an oblique representative of serious ethical and political claims. While Bernstein has thereby defended the continuing importance of the legacy of high modernism, his most recent book, *Adorno: Disenchantment and Ethics* (2001), articulates an Adornian ethic of proximity and care.

f) Unlike Bernstein's reading, which in many ways reiterates Adorno's distinction between high and low, linking this opposition to the fragmented world of late modernity, the postmodernist approach to Adorno's work, which has tended to be rather negative, takes issue with its apparent nostalgia for what its critics see as an idealized notion of bourgeois elite culture. Focusing on the culture industry chapter of *Dialectic of Enlightenment*, Jim Collins (1987) has argued that Adorno and Horkheimer's interpretation of mass culture is oversimplified and distorted: rather than displaying a fundamental unity and cohesiveness, the mass culture of the twentieth century has been impure and marked by plurality. In insisting on a distinction between high and low, Adorno fails to account for the democratic impulse of contemporary culture, thereby preventing its many emancipatory potentials from emerging. Although the pioneering character of Adorno's political analysis of culture has hardly been called into question, within the field of cultural studies a similar criticism has been put forward against Adorno's defense of philosophy. Inspired in part by Althusser's critique of its alleged ideological status, many practitioners of cultural studies have rejected philosophy in favor of micro-oriented analyses of mass cultural phenomena.

My own approach does not fall easily into any one of these interpretive paradigms. Even though I critically engage with representatives of all of them and adopt some of their respective orientations, the Adorno I find politically relevant will neither be a poststructuralist critic of the subject, determined to identify with the ever-changing flux of being, nor an anti-modernist Heideggerian who seeks to reject the notion of rationality altogether. My Adorno does not think that the espousal of a theory of communicative rationality can lay claim to a genuine inheritance of the critical energies of the first-generation Frankfurter theorists, nor does he think that his traditional Marxist roots can be sufficient to come to terms with the new tensions and contradictions of late (postmodern) capitalism. Finally, the Adorno I would like to consider does not find himself in a position of being able to distinguish an untainted ethical life from the effects of cultural differentiation, and does not draw a clear-cut division between items of high and low culture. While resisting the relativism of postmodern cultural theory, his critical interventions will always be local and unassured, motivated by singular experiences of negativity rather than pre-given appeals to universality.

The validity of Adorno's approach to politics cannot be separated from the "success" of each of his critical interventions. If his social theory is bleak indeed, the ethically informed, micro-interruptive operations that make up the bulk of his philosophical entries are models of responsible exercise of autonomy in the societies that today are called democratic.

## Overview of the argument

As I want to show in this book, Adorno's thinking is alive and well worth exploring within the parameters of a contemporary political context. While his insistence on totality, the universal system of mediation in late capitalism, is relevant in order to theorize the phenomenon of globalization, his search for its non-identical other represents a timely rejoinder to the postmodernist celebration of appearance, post-historicity, and unrestricted social constructivism that has dominated so many theoretical debates over the last two decades. The reading I provide will thus insist on the need to reconceptualize and reassess certain normative notions of truth, rationality, responsibility, and commitment.

More consequential, however, for the position I end up with as a whole is the recontextualization I provide of aspects of Adorno's work within the framework of ordinary language philosophy. Whereas Habermas, in an attempt to offer a rational foundation for Critical Theory, has offered an account of reason by developing the work of Austin and Searle in the direction of a general theory of communicative competence, the philosopher I bring into dialogue with Adorno, while building on Austin, has himself extended ordinary language philosophy to be able to address wide areas of cultural and political engagement. In the writings of Stanley Cavell, I find an account of ethical and political perfectionism that, if brought to bear on selected Adornian problematics, seems eminently suited to bring out the distinctive character of Adorno's notion of the intellectual's responsibility. By viewing Adorno as a perfectionist thinker along Cavellian lines, I hope to gain a better understanding of how political withdrawal from one's community, as we see in Adorno's refusal of politics in the direct or immediate sense, can result in a more appropriate reconnection with it. To those who instinctively balk at bringing Adorno's austere negative dialectics together with contemporary work in ordinary language philosophy, I should say that it does not mean that I think Adorno's work can be exhausted by such a procedure. It should rather be thought of as local operations — or perhaps as the creation of constellations — that aim to stimulate new readings of highly selected moments in the critical theorist's writings.

Chapter 1 deals with Adorno's own political experiences and his theoretical response to them. I argue that by contrast to the popular view of him as an unpolitical aesthete, Adorno was strongly engaged in a number of political issues, and that his work must be understood while bearing his response to them in mind. Central to Adorno's experiences is his sense that contemporary politics is in a deep crisis. I suggest that the way he construes this crisis has far-reaching consequences for his own philosophical thinking. Chapter 2 situates Adorno within the Marxist tradition and explores the impact of Lukács and Benjamin. I argue that his mature assessment of modernity, while Marxist in certain respects, should be understood as a materialist inscription of Benjamin's thinking about history. Of central interest here is the chiastic relationship between progress and regress, and how the subject itself is constituted. Chapter 3 provides an analysis of Adorno's thinking about fascism and anti-Semitism. I critically discuss his employment of Marxist and Freudian models, and argue that his experience with fascism deeply influenced his thinking about the relationship between theory and practice. I also discuss some ambivalences in his notion of pedagogy. Chapter 4 approaches the culture industry and discusses the concepts of ideology, experience, and cultural criticism. I argue that the distinction between high and low, while less abstract than it seems, may prevent a productive understanding of popular culture's political potential. I also compare Adorno's work to postmodern theories of culture, in particular that of Baudrillard, and defend his insistence on depth and universality. Chapter 5 excavates the political dimension of Adorno's negative dialectics. In addition to analyzing his approach to Hegel and Heidegger, I focus on the notion of freedom, which I relate to the writings of Nancy and Badiou. Chapter 6 returns to Benjamin and reconsiders Adorno's aesthetics in the light of the former's criticisms of an autonomy-based account of art. I argue that Adorno's advanced art-work models a form of ideal politics that critically engages with the present through the register of the sublime. Chapter 7 addresses Habermas' influential criticisms of Adorno. In particular, I suggest that, as opposed to Habermas' interpretation, Adorno should not be viewed as a philosopher of consciousness, and that he has a more nuanced and positive conception of intersubjectivity than what Habermas ascribes to him. I also argue that Adorno would think the political in terms of antagonism and conflict. Chapter 8 situates Adorno's philosophy within the broader context of contemporary political debate. I argue that his work can be applied to problems of liberal political theory, and I also contend that while unstable, his anti-essentialist conception of radical, sublime critique may productively be brought to bear on contemporary feminist theory. In a final section I relate his thinking about nature to questions of environmentalism. I suggest that Adorno's thinking may help to bring environmentalism to a better and more coherent conception of itself. In particular it is objected against the holism and anti-humanism of deep ecology.

# 1

# PERMANENT EXILE
## Adorno's political experiences

The development of Adorno's political thought is inseparable from the historical experiences he, as a male German of Jewish ancestry, had — from the Weimar Republic to Nazi Germany, from the United States of the New Deal Era to the Federal Republic of Germany. As opposed to the widespread view of Adorno as devoid of political interest, a closer reading of his work reveals a wealth of political references that often, especially after the return to West Germany in 1951, serve as direct interventions in current state of affairs. Although he neither formulated a political program nor advocated any form of activism, he engaged theoretically in trying to resist the identitarian regimes that block the realization of freedom and happiness.

In this chapter I outline the history of Adorno's political experiences, highlighting his early years, his period of exile in the United States, and his encounter with the Student Movement in the late 1960s. I argue that while his vision of the conditions of democratic political activity is extremely bleak, the desire to resist and anticipate change remains a constant focus throughout his life.

## From liberalism to Marxism

Like many European intellectuals of the same generation, Adorno experienced the First World War as the end of the old world of bourgeois certainty and the beginning of a new and dark world whose meaning could only be approached adequately through experimental, avant-garde art practices. The First World War led to the downfall of the traditional liberal order, yet it also involved a near complete shattering of the political hopes for a better future. After the failed revolutions in Germany in the aftermath of the war, the young Adorno tended to sublimate his desire for change into a quest for the aesthetically or even religiously absolute. In Ernst Bloch and Franz Rosenzweig he found thinkers ready to translate political struggle into artistic or theological terms, leaving politics to become a matter of reading off utopian potentials from an otherwise oppressive and decadent social reality.

11

The fact that the First World War represents such a watershed in Adorno's perception of contemporary Western history may have been a reason for his nostalgic, though highly ambivalent, assessment of liberalism. The war, with all its destruction and bloodshed, is what separates Adorno and his contemporaries from the old order and makes unproblematized cultural transmission impossible. While his approach to liberalism will be discussed in more detail in Chapter 8, it is worth noticing that, like virtually all the other neo-Kantians of the day, Adorno's earliest political orientation was predominantly liberal, though vaguely tinged with a sympathy for socialism.[1] Even in his most Marxist phases, he never repudiated his basic subscription to a liberal (or Kantian) concern for the autonomy of the individual. Although he viewed the formation of human individuality as dependent on the social structures in which it is embedded, the interests of the social group or collectivity as a whole should never be satisfied at the expense of the freedom of any single human being.

Adorno viewed liberalism as the ideology of a more humane order that has come to pass and disintegrated. Rather than calling for a return to past certainties, however, the correct relation to liberalism would be to retain its promises of human freedom and dignity while radically rethinking their meaning. Although the bourgeois family structure may have permitted the formation of stronger egos, and market relations may have been more transparent and less mediated by corporate structures, Adorno was enough of a Marxist, even in the early 1920s, to view the self-representation of the early liberal state as ideological: its freedoms and rights, though pronounced universal, predominantly served the interests of the burgeoning bourgeoisie.

Adorno often speaks as though the categories of liberal thought have suffered a decay. Failing to actualize what they promised, they no longer enjoy any historical right to claim simple, straightforward validity. In some early texts, following Horkheimer, the decay is related to the post-1848 demise of bourgeois liberalism, in others to the social upheavals and concentrations of capital in the 1870s, and, in yet others, to the First World War. The decay has particularly hit what Adorno considers to be the arch-bourgeois vision of a continuity between reason and reality. In his *Antrittsvorlesung* from 1931, "The Actuality of Philosophy," he claims that "The *autonome ratio* [*autonomous reason*] — this was the thesis of every idealistic system — was supposed to be capable of developing the concept of reality, and in fact all reality, from out of itself. This thesis has disintegrated" (2000a: 25). In the classical entrepreneurial phase of early capitalism, the active representatives of the bourgeoisie were able to conceive of themselves as epistemically and morally self-authorized: they were "self-made men" facing a social world not yet entirely dominated by systemic imperatives. As ownership of capital was concentrated in fewer hands, and state and economy lost their former independence from one another, the early bourgeois claim to a harmony between reason and reality collapsed, leaving philosophers and intellectuals with the need to design more overtly compensatory ideological systems. According to Adorno (2000a), the Marburg School of Neo-Kantianism, with which he was once, following his teacher Hans Cornelius, in great sympathy, represents an example of such a compensatory stance.

There can be no doubt that Adorno's political views were radicalized in the late 1920s under the influence of Marxist thinkers and friends such as Lukács, Benjamin, Horkheimer, Löwenthal, and Marcuse. However, unlike several of the associates of the Institute for Social Research, including especially its first group of researchers under the directorship of Adolf Grünbaum (Karl August Wittfogel, Richard Sorge, Henryk Grossmann, Franz Borkmann, Friedrich Pollock, and Felix Weil), he was never attracted to Leninism, and after the Moscow trials in 1934 he persistently rejected the authoritarian practices of Eastern communism. In light of the late realization on the part of many Western intellectuals on the Left of how oppressive Soviet communism actually was (in France it did not become a major political issue until the publication of Solzhenitsyn's *Gulag Archipelago* in the early 1970s), it is in retrospect admirable that Adorno grasped the nature of Leninism and Stalinism as early as he did. Of course, the repudiation of Eastern-style communism was conditioned by the peculiar fact that, for someone whose political commitments were eventually shaped so heavily by Marx's *Capital* and Lukács' *History and Class Consciousness*, he neither had any connection with, nor took any direct interest in, the labor movements that formed the outlook of the German Social Democrats in the 1920s and 1930s. While Jameson's claim (1996: 7) that Adorno's dismissal of Moscow (as well as his lack of sympathy or understanding for Third World revolutions) was determined by class is unduly crass, his distance from the actual political struggles of the day, which to a large degree were inspired by Leninist internationalism, could hardly have been greater.

But was Adorno in the radical years before and immediately after 1930 in any way committed to a socialist revolution? According to Müller-Doohm (2003: 121–2), while he was convinced that the pre-war bourgeois world had come to an end and that capitalism was corrupt, he was so repelled by collectivist ideologies that he was never prepared to join the Communist Party, let alone take part in activities that would demand obedience to leaders or principles of any kind. There is, however, no doubt that his political views gradually became shaped by socialist ideals, and that he considered the problems of contemporary society to be largely caused by the antagonistic dynamic of capitalism itself, a dynamic which, according to standard Marxist interpretations of history, was predetermined to come to an end.[2] Although the historical development had been stalled by war as well as the shift from a liberal to a more organized social and political order, its immanent meaning pointed towards the overcoming of social antagonism in a classless society. As in the last decade of his life, Adorno faced what he saw as a conflict between theory and praxis: while a theoretical analysis showed society to be objectively in need of radical social transformation, the praxis that could bring it about was missing. In the light of this cul-de-sac, Adorno chose to focus on the theoretical dimension, using philosophy of history, political theory and historical materialism to both diagnose the present and to uncover the potentials for change.

## Political experiences in the United States

I discuss Adorno's specific response to the Nazi takeover in Chapter 3. Moving further forward in time to Adorno's political experiences in the United States after leaving Oxford in 1938, the context that met him was largely defined not by a Marxist–socialist activism, but by an altogether diminishing commitment to radical social reform. However important it may be to consider Adorno's perception of this trend in the light of his negative assessment of American culture as a whole — its alleged standardization, its interweaving of high and mass culture, and so on — it is likely that it reflected a larger geopolitical transformation. According to Pels (1985: 76f.), whereas in the years following the crash of the stock market the political climate in liberal and left-wing circles had an explicitly Marxist or even communist bias, aiming to overcome injustices stemming from the existing capitalist system of distribution, the Moscow trials and the rise of fascism forced many to reconsider their allegiances. This reaction was precipitated further by the outbreak of war in 1939 and the rapid advancement of Hitler's troops, culminating in the attack on the Soviet Union and the Japanese onslaught at Pearl Harbor. At stake, it seemed to many, was not simply the concern for social justice but the protection of the relative freedoms still enjoyed by the American citizenry. The correct response, even among those who had previously subscribed to the radical goals of the Popular Front, seemed to be to support Roosevelt's New Deal policies and to use whatever means deemed necessary to defend American democracy.

The New Deal represented a shift from traditional liberal concerns with civil rights and individual freedoms, toward a greater emphasis on social interventionism and a closer collaboration between state power and corporate capitalism. What Roosevelt saw as the solution to America's internal social problems was a more organized and planned economy in which government agencies more actively than ever before used fiscal incentives in order to try to influence and ultimately control the running of major capitalist enterprises. While initially based on stringent federal control of

14

credit, the Roosevelt administration's strategy, extending the directing and regulating powers of the Treasury Department, intensified to involve large-scale extensions of federal authority and especially of presidential power to counter the effects of the crisis on industry and employment. The New Deal led to a greater concentration, if not of capital, then of power, and while on the whole agreeing with the Roosevelt administration's foreign policies (especially its decision to commit troops in order to curb fascist expansionism), both Adorno and Horkheimer argued that this process had as its consequences an increasing bureaucratization and a weakening of participatory democracy, yet with no discernible benefits to the working class. From employing totalizing terms mainly in the context of philosophical analysis, Adorno now started to extend the notion of totalization explicitly to social phenomena, speaking of "totally administered societies" [*totalverwaltete Gesellschaften*], as if such societies no longer leave any scope for individual deliberation, critique, and autonomous participation.[3]

In late modernity, Adorno argues, politics is under constant threat of being colonized by competing sub-systems of purposive-rational action, in particular the techno-administrative complexes, for which the demand for responsible and autonomous decisions is devalued in favor of strategic calculation and end-indifferent, instrumental intervention. Although he neither presents a detailed analysis of such processes, nor any theoretical model by which they can be fully understood, Adorno views modern complex societies as under the spell of a mechanized, regimented system of social integration for which no one is accountable. While political action should be free and relatively uninhibited by external constraints, administrative action is formal, highly codified and in every respect constrained by the system's internal requirements.

The thesis about the rise of totally administered societies is both simple and seductive, and in Adorno's later work it arguably takes the form of a dogma. There can be no doubt, however, that it generates many significant questions that are never fully addressed. The most glaring difficulty with it may be that it fails to differentiate adequately between the systemic integration taking place in a totalitarian regime and that taking place in a liberal democracy.

The parallel being drawn, for example, in the *Dialectic of Enlightenment*, between Goebbels' highly organized and targeted propaganda machinery and Hollywood productions, while perceptive in that both seek to establish allegiance by exploiting the economy of subliminal desire, is far too dismissive of the differences between these two forms of rhetoric, especially with regard to the masochistic submissiveness which Nazi propaganda wants to instill in its listeners as opposed to the hedonistic and narcissistic appeal of advertisement and consumerism. In general, it seems unlikely that an analysis such as this can retain much explanatory power when made to cover both totalitarian societies and liberal democracies.

In order to better understand how he arrived at such a view, it is worth keeping in mind that, like Horkheimer, he increasingly viewed the advanced capitalism of the United States and the fascist totalitarianism of Nazi Germany as political systems that are similar in that both, each in their own way, complete a more general world-historical passage towards greater abstraction, rationalization, and repetition — that is, the aggressive unfolding of a logic of identitarian reason that is being traced in the *Dialectic of Enlightenment*.[4] Nazi Germany realizes this operation by enacting, on a grand scale, an administered regression into a political myth of national foundation, excluding anyone who does not fit in with their exclusionary narrative; American capitalism realizes it through the culture industry and the ever more insidious manipulation of the everyday by means of advertisement and consumerism: both are for Adorno aspects of total administration.

For contemporary purposes the perhaps most weighty critique of the thesis of a totally administered society is that while at least partly valid in the classical industrial phase of capitalism, it fails to capture the emergence, in postmodernist consumer society, of new forms of individualism that radically overturn the older relationship between the private and the public sphere. According to Bauman (2000), today's Western societies are not integrated through highly organized and centralized social-control mechanisms. It is not true any longer that the public sphere invades and subjugates the private sphere. On the contrary, what marks late (postmodern) capitalism above all is the extraordinary extent to which public life is usurped by private initiative and consumer attitudes.[5] The individual should not, as in Adorno's conception, be viewed as "outer-directed" and heteronomous; rather, the individual finds itself in a rapidly changing environment in which, without communal backing or assurance, it is necessary to constantly make choices, and in which the readiness for self-invention, self-transformation and self-renewal becomes imperative. For Bauman, the most pressing political task facing Western societies today is to restore politics (and the public sphere in general) as a space in which questions of the *common* good (as opposed to individual preference and interest) can be raised and dealt with.

In response to Bauman, it can be argued that while Adorno's thesis of the victory of the society and the universal over the individual and the particular may today appear somewhat anachronistic, it does not follow from the apparent individualism of late capitalist societies that the systemic integration is less intense than in classical industrialist capitalism. In his theory of the culture industry, for example, Adorno allows for a considerable degree of individual choice. In contrast to Bauman's position, however, the exercise of autonomy is according to Adorno mainly apparent: the consumerist attitudes which guide such choices do not reflect a genuine capacity for autonomous deliberation and action but are ultimately created and maintained by the individual agent's identification with the commercial imperatives of mass advertising. It should also be pointed out that Adorno obviously does not castigate the public sphere as inherently threatening to the individual; rather, it is the perversion of public life, the transformation of participatory politics into pure administration, which is the target of this critique. Adorno would therefore be just as interested as Bauman is in seeing the public sphere being accorded its proper significance.

Standardization of life practices is thus another aspect of Adorno's political experience in the United States. *Minima Moralia*, his collection of aphorisms, is replete with the twin Adornian laments over the loss of individuality and the withering of experience. Although I return to these themes in my discussion of the culture industry, the speculative figure underlying these reflections is that objectivity — the administrative apparatuses, the social structures, and the exchange relation as such — threatens to eradicate subjectivity. While in liberal capitalism the subject once enjoyed a relative freedom, in monopoly capitalism it largely conforms to the demands of the system. The capacity to respond autonomously to social norms and expectations, as well as the ability to experience particulars that have not already been subsumed and abstractly determined by universal mechanisms of exchange, are seen to have more or less disappeared. For Adorno, even the landscape appears alienating and strange, a material allegory of lifelessness and destruction, reflecting not just the despair of the *émigré* but an otherworldly coldness stemming from the universal reduction of things and men to their exchange value, leaving culture and nature to merge indistinguishably with each other:

> The shortcoming of the American landscape is not so much, as romantic illusion would have it, the absence of historical memories, as that it bears no traces of the human hand. This applies not only to the lack of arable land, the uncultivated woods often no higher than scrub, but above all to the roads. These are always inserted directly in the landscape, and the more impressively smooth and broad they are, the more unrelated and violent their gleaming track appears against its wild, overgrown surroundings. They are expressionless. Just as they know no marks of foot or wheel, no soft paths along their edges as a transition to the vegetation, no trails leading off into the valley, so they are without the mild, soothing, unangular quality of things that have felt the touch of hands or their immediate implements. It is as if no-one had ever passed their hand over the landscape's hair. It is uncomforted and comfortless. And it is perceived in a corresponding way. For what

17

the hurrying eye has seen merely from the car it cannot retain, and
the vanishing landscape leaves no more traces behind than it bears
upon itself.

(Adorno 1974a: 48)

Although Adorno's experiences in the United States, while undoubtedly
colored by mandarin attitudes, may not have been as bleak as this passage
from *Minima Moralia* suggests, his insistence on the fundamental mone-
tary indecency with which North Americans have disconnected themselves
from European modernity's promise of freedom, equality, and utopian
social renewal has recently returned with a vengeance to haunt relations
between Europe and the United States. In view of the current globalization
of corporate capitalism and the concomitant weakening of the nation-
state, it may look as though Adorno's analyses have acquired a belated
relevance. Organized capitalism has arguably never been more deregulated
and powerful than today. It is worth pointing out, though, that Adorno
never considered late (and in his case American) capitalism as in need of
further regulation. Indeed, the capitalism he witnessed under the New Deal
appeared to him to be too regulated for the consumers' own good. In
current terminology, it was the Fordist model of highly organized capitalism that informed not only the account on offer in the *Dialectic of
Enlightenment* but his postwar writings on the nature of contemporary
capitalism as well. While today he may have worried about the anarchy of
the international stock markets and the impact a highly flexible and
dynamic corporate capitalism has on the Third World, creating stupendous
social and economic differences between North and South, in the 1930s
and 1940s he argued that capitalism, by overcoming the divide between
state and economy, thus absorbing and apparently eliminating economic
conflicts, was authoritarian in its essence. There is great irony in the fact
that what then appeared to him as highly threatening and problematic,
namely a significant degree of state intervention in the economy, is on
today's European and American Left seen as a necessary remedy in order
to control the effects of rampant capitalist expansion.

## The student movement

Adorno's return to the newly created Federal Republic of Germany after
the war involved a considerable alteration of socio-political environment.
From the *emigré* position of relative intellectual and political obscurity, he
quickly became a leading thinker and critic, a major figure in some of the
most consequential political debates of the first decades of the postwar
republic. As will be discussed later, Adorno raised severe doubts about the
extent to which the FRG had broken with its authoritarian past; he
became more explicitly opposed to communism (especially in its Soviet

form but also in the more intellectually refined versions offered by Lukács and Sartre) than before; and he criticized the positivism of current German sociology. Yet the most complex and important political challenge — a challenge which shaped as well as distorted much of the legacy of his thought — was the encounter with the German student movement.

Although united by a strong anti-authoritarian impulse, a renewed interest in sexual, social and political experimentation, and a hostility towards the war in Vietnam, the student movement, viewed as a world-wide phenomenon, was rather diverse. While the American scene, concurring with the rise of the civil-rights movement, combined a strong social and political pluralism with a pronounced orientation towards bohemian living, the French was more explicitly revolutionary, aiming, if necessary with violence, at replacing the centralized state apparatus with a more democratic, and in some cases anarchistic, social formation. Both in San Francisco and Paris, the creation, liberation, and cultivation of new desires went hand in hand with a strong critique of consumerism (including its passivity, its consequences for the environment, its implied retreat into the private sphere), though with remarkably little awareness of the risk, often pointed out by Adorno, that the former activities may actually be co-opted by the very same capitalist system that the students sought to resist.

Perhaps the most distinctive feature of the German student movement was the way in which the rejection of Germany's Nazi past shaped its political outlook. The German students rebelled not only against consumer capitalism but against their fathers and the continuities they perceived between fascism and contemporary culture; thus their struggle was arguably more oedipally structured than in any other Western society at the time. If capitalism was corrupt, then it had just as much to do with the belief that fascism had been a response to the crisis of capitalism in the first decades of the twentieth century, and that fascism and capitalism are politically kindred, than with the sense that the bourgeois notion of the free market was ideological per se. Although the *Wirtschaftswunder* had created new prosperity and helped stabilize the new democracy, the failure to come to terms with, or even approach, the past made the new order seem suspect, potentially harboring deep-seated conservative and authoritarian attitudes. While student radicalism concerned itself with the alleged democratic deficit of many important German institutions, in particular the universities, it was also critical of what many saw as an illegitimate instrumentalization of vital areas of human interaction — in higher education, in public life, and in relation to nature.

All of these were issues with which Adorno not only sympathized but had long since crucially incorporated into his own theorizing. Indeed, given the widespread interest among students in writings such as the *Dialectic of Enlightenment*, *Minima Moralia*, and *Prisms*, it may be argued that the political profile of the German student movement was to a considerable extent influenced by Adorno's work: theoretically, what many of the students did was to reflect, in however crude terms, the views espoused by the leading figure of Critical Theory. (Marcuse's meteoric rise to prominence in the late 1960s confirms this view insofar as his most cited work, *One-dimensional Man*, largely rehearses the Adornian critique of instrumental reason, albeit in a more popular form than in the *Dialectic of Enlightenment*. As opposed to Adorno, Marcuse sympathized not only with the aims but also with the methods employed by the students.)

One occasion upon which the affinities between Adorno and the students came out in the open was the killing, by the police, of Benno Ohnesorg, a student of literature, in the summer of 1967. After a period of political unrest focusing on the lack of parliamentary control over the executive and the planned "Emergency laws" (*Notstandsgesetze*) that were seen to be weakening democracy, a demonstration against the visiting Shah of Iran ended with violent clashes with the police. In trying to escape, Ohnesorg was shot in the back and killed by a police officer. The apparent execution of a student who was exercising his democratic right to demonstrate and the unreflective support for the police showed by the right-wing Springer press led Adorno to remark that to some extent the students had taken over the role of the Jews.[6] They were victims of similar authoritarian mechanisms — the police, the bureaucracies, the press — to those which had once been used to oppress the Jewish population. A few days later, referring not only to Ohnesorg but to the Six Day War between Egypt and Israel as well, he introduced his seminar on aesthetics with the following words:

> It is impossible for me to begin my lecture today without saying a word about the situation in Berlin, no matter how much it is overshadowed by the terrible threat to Israel, the home of so many Jews who fled the terror. I understand how difficult it is to form a just and responsible opinion of even the simplest facts, since all news that reaches us is already manipulated. But that cannot prevent me from expressing my sympathy for the student whose fate, no matter what is reported, stands in no relation to his participation in a political demonstration. Regardless of which of the contradictory reports of the terrible events is correct, one can in any case observe that Germany is still ruled by the official habit of higher powers, incompatible with the spirit of democracy, to cover up the actions of (in the double sense of the word) subordinate organs ... Not only the urge to gain justice for the victims but also the concern that the nascent democratic spirit in Germany not be strangled by hierarchic practices make it necessary to demand

that the investigation in Berlin be conducted by officials who are not organizationally linked to those who shot and swung their batons, and who cannot be suspected of having any interest whatsoever in the outcome of the investigation. That the investigation proceed in full freedom, expeditiously, and without authoritarian tampering, in accordance with the spirit of democracy is not my private wish but one that is rooted in the objective situation. I suspect you share it.

(Kraushaar 1998: II, 123)

Being concerned with threats against democracy, criticizing the unaccountability among public servants, showing sympathy for the protesting individual and for the students' cause in general — these are hardly compatible with the stereotypical view of Adorno as indifferent to the political struggles of the day. Moreover, by contrast to the common perception of his work at the time as advocating mainly subjective change in education and psychology, rather than objective social change (which presumably was deemed impossible) of the dominating institutions, he intervenes publicly and calls for an impartial investigation. The goal, clearly, of such an investigation would be, through the consequent introduction of more effective regulation, to abolish certain authoritarian practices in the police force.

Adorno's engagement in the Ohnesorg case continued a few months later when Karl-Heinz Kurras, the officer who had shot the student, was acquitted in court. In one of his aesthetics lectures in November 1967, Adorno criticized the brutal police methods in Berlin and demanded that those responsible for arming the officers who patrol student demonstrations should be investigated and held responsible. Adorno reacted in particular to Kurras' apparent indifference to what he had done. In a television interview, Kurras had employed expressions such as "Unfortunately a student lost his life." For Adorno,

The emotional poverty of that "unfortunately" condemns him as much as the impersonal "a student lost his life." That sounds as if on June 2 some objective, higher power had appeared and that it was not Mr. Kurras, whether he aimed or not, who had pulled the trigger. This language is frighteningly similar to the one heard in the trials against torturers in the concentration camps. Mr. Kurras did not even manage to say, "I am unhappy that I killed an innocent man." The expression "a student" in his remark is reminiscent of the usage of the word "Jew" still today in the trials and the press that reports them. Victims are treated as examples of a species.

(Kraushaar 1998: II, 324)

There can be no doubt that Adorno acted as a publicly engaged intellectual, especially in the second half of the 1960s. He signed petitions, he spoke at demonstrations (most famously on May 28 1968 against the "Emergency Laws"), he appeared in numerous radio discussions, and he took part in activities, some of them organized by Jürgen Habermas and Ludwig von Friedeburg, aimed at university reform. For a while he even participated in informal exchanges with members of the German Socialist Student Group (SDS) about the relevance of Critical Theory for political praxis and related issues, pleading for restraint against the temptation to use violence.

While many of these occasions bear evidence to the solidarity that existed between Adorno and the protesters, the topics that divided them regularly came to the fore. Among them were, first, Adorno's dismissal of revolutionary Marxism which he continued to find unrealistic and potentially authoritarian. Although adamant that history, despite its self-destructive logics, was teleologically developing towards a more humane and emancipated society, under present circumstances Adorno could neither identify a legitimate revolutionary strategy nor a genuine subject of radical action. Besides, no social revolution would ever safeguard against the emergence of new forms of oppression.

Second, Adorno embodied a rather pro-American attitude. Following Horkheimer, he was skeptical of the aggressive anti-Americanism that had evolved in the FRG in the wake of the civil unrest in the South, the assassination of Martin Luther King, and the prolonged war in Vietnam. Not only was Germany, for its liberation from fascism, still indebted to the United States, but American democracy, which he previously had condemned, was itself to be admired. Unlike Horkheimer, however, Adorno refused to defend the American intervention in Vietnam, referring in his 1965 lecture course on metaphysics to the war as a sign that the "world of torture" (*Welt der Tortur*) which had begun in Auschwitz was continuing.

A third and more damaging divide between Adorno and the students started to make itself felt in the last few months of 1967, culminating in a lecture he gave in Berlin on "The Classicism of Goethe's Iphigenie" on the occasion of which some members of the audience confronted him with a huge banner on which it was written: "Berlin's left fascists welcome Teddy, the classicist." The reference, in this rather icy, ironical display, to fascism alluded to Adorno's gradual support for Habermas' view that political resistance in the form of direct and possibly violent provocation against the state power would reflect a "voluntarist ideology" that could collapse into a "left fascism" (Kraushaar 1998: I, 258). By coining the provocative formula "left fascism," Habermas and Adorno had wanted to warn against the danger that violent and authoritarian dispositions, which they believed prevailed in the FRG, would

22

return under the cloak of calls for greater democratization: the left should not think itself automatically innocent of those dispositions.

The fact that the defense against such an aggressive branding of the activists would require irony and humor should not come as a surprise. By using such steely rhetoric, the older, established academics, though entirely unprepared for it, had, it would seem, invited a situationist type of rebuttal. In addition to the reference to left fascism, it is telling that the students would refer to Adorno as a "classicist," thereby complaining about his supposed retreat into the Ivory Tower of uncontaminated high culture. The banner thus highlighted two issues of continued dispute: first, whether political praxis could take an immediate, activist form; and, second, whether theory could have any relation to praxis. While a majority of the radical students were ready to engage in more direct forms of protest, Adorno insisted that political resistance necessarily had to be exercised in the medium of theory. Not only did he deem "theory a form of praxis" (1998b: 261), he also equated false praxis with no praxis. Counterattacking his accusers in the late essay "Resignation," he argues that activism inevitably regresses into pseudo-activity, "the attempt to rescue enclaves of immediacy in the midst of a thoroughly mediated and rigidified society" (1998b: 291). Such attempts are bound to fail, he continues, because praxis without theory is blind and reactive, imitating the false identity of subject and object while perpetuating the principle of domination that posits identity. "People locked in desperately want to get out. In such situations one doesn't think anymore, or does so only under fictive premises. [...] Only thinking could find an exit ..." (1998b: 291).

The episode, on January 31, 1969, when Adorno decided to call the police in order to protect the Institute for Social Research against striking students is famous yet does not reveal much of interest about the political nature of the clash except that Hans-Jürgen Krahl, the students' leader, by choosing this building for their sit-in, wanted to pay his respect to the thinkers who had shaped his intellectual outlook. In a note, probably authored by Adorno, the directors of the Institute justified their decision on the grounds that they rigorously opposed criminal action among the extra-parliamentary political groups.[7] A simpler and more convincing explanation is perhaps that they lost control of the situation and did not know what better course of action to take. Of greater significance is another confrontation, less than four months before his death on August 13, 1969, in which Adorno, before an auditorium of almost 1,000 students, was approached by two men who, accompanied by encouraging shouts from the back benches, demanded that he, in Stalinist style, criticize his own decision to evacuate Krahl and his companions from the Institute. When Adorno responded by suggesting that his "attackers" should be given five minutes to decide whether the lecture was to continue or not, three female students appeared on the podium and threw flowers at him while uncovering their breasts and putting on a display of erotic pantomime. Adorno then finally left the auditorium with an "expression of desperate anxiety [*verzweifelter Angst*] written on his face" (Müller-Doohm 2003: 723).

The episode has been interpreted in different ways. The attacking women could be construed as theatricalizing a return of the repressed — the claim of nature against culture to which Horkheimer and Adorno had ascribed a utopian significance in the *Dialectic of Enlightenment*. Their dance would intimate the eroticism of the Sirens that Odysseus, the "proto-bourgeois subject," sails past in spite of their promise of happiness. The moral of the episode would be that Adorno had forfeited the utopian dimension of his own theory and needed some sort of re-education. Adorno's fear is the fear felt by an encounter with the Freudian uncanny — with that which is more familiar than anything else (since this is what he has desired), yet entirely strange (since the ego principle rejects it). On such a reading, there would be an unspoken solidarity between the students and the teacher. In however stark terms, the students would be reminding the teacher of his own doctrine. Of course, the happening could equally well be considered as an attempt to ridicule both Adorno and his thinking altogether. On this less edifying, and in my view more plausible, interpretation we would be faced with an exercise in what Sloterdijk (1987) would call cynical reason, involving a wholesale dismissal of the apparent primacy of theory and rationality, and a Dadaist rebellion against the belief that right action always has to base itself on a reasoned stance. The unity of theory and practice would not, as in Adorno, itself be mediated by theory; rather, theory and practice would form an immediate unity: thinking and acting would be united in the transgressive political event.

Even if this was the intention, Adorno (1973–86: XX (1), 402) did not see much else in it but *petit bourgeois* amusement:

> Even with me, who has always opposed all forms of erotic repression and sexual taboos! To mock me and send three women dressed up as Hippies at me! I found that abhorrent. The amusement effect which was thereby achieved was indeed that of the narrow-minded bourgeois who giggles when he sees women with naked breasts. Obviously this idiocy was calculated.

By refusing — perhaps out of a genuine fear of crowds and the horror felt at what he considered to be the possible resurgence of fascist authoritarianism on the left — to grant the action any real political relevance, Adorno's judgment may seem a little too harsh. Although the "flower power" intervention in his lecture could easily be dismissed as both naive and embarrassing, its misplaced attack on a left-wing professor a perfect testimony to the confusion and failures of the 1960s student movement, there is a danger that Adorno's position could be employed to condemn all forms of expressive, non-discursive political action. Indeed, the fact that Adorno, as mentioned, did participate in some such activities indicates that his response was more fine-grained and specific to the nature of the intervention at stake.

As Berman (2002: 111) rightly suggests, it may be useful to keep in mind that the image, which has haunted his legacy since the 1960s, of Adorno as an unpolitical aesthete is entirely predicated upon the belief that "progressive politics must be easy" and that anyone who points out the difficulties should be demonized. While the student movement brought about many progressive changes — among them a more democratic university, greater equality between the sexes, a new awareness of racial inequality, and so on — positions such as that of Marcuse's revolutionism, with its immediate guides to action, failed spectacularly. Disagreeing mainly with their methods, Adorno, although rejecting the dream of a post-historical state of reconciliation as potentially authoritarian, certainly did sympathize with the overall goal of the movement of achieving a more just and humane society. Unlike the students, however, his account of late capitalism was such that it permitted no direct translation of theory into enlightened political practice. For resistance to be possible, it needs the autonomous media of art and philosophy. (On the basis of this judgment, it is highly ironic that, when the violent actions of the Red Army Faction threatened the inner stability of the FRG in the mid-1970s, the accusation leveled at Adorno's work was that the Marxist terrorists had simply adopted his theory. However, while Ulrike Meinhof's knowledge of the *Dialectic of Enlightenment* cannot be doubted, the peculiar combination of romantic decisionism and cruelty, characterizing most of the individuals participating in violent action, finds no resonance whatsoever in Adorno's writings.)

The old picture of Adorno's distance from political thought and engagement must be corrected. Not only did he participate in, and reflect upon, a number of contemporary debates, ranging from Soviet and American politics to West German debates, he also constructed his critical, dialectical, and aesthetic positions so as to analyze and respond to them. In an age in which politics has been threatened by the loss of even its relative claim to autonomy, Adorno invented new ways of articulating political promises. If classical politics in the republican sense is dead, then theory and art, he wagers, may have become its placeholders. The question for the rest of the book is whether a migration of politics to such placeholding media, as well as its strategic transformation into what can be called an ethics of resistance, can coherently be conceived.

25

# 2

# ADORNO'S MARXISM

Adorno's work comes out of, and responds to, the tradition of Western Marxism, and its relationship to Marxism in general is largely mediated by Adorno's position within this tradition. As this is the most immediate historical and theoretical subtext of Adorno's thinking, it is necessary to take some steps toward mapping this disorganized landscape. Very roughly, Western Marxism, represented by figures such as Georg Lukács, Karl Korsch, Ernst Bloch, and Antonio Gramsci (and later by Maurice Merleau-Ponty, Lucio Colletti and, arguably, Louis Althusser), arose as an attempt to reformulate Marx's intellectual legacy in order to understand the social and political conditions in Central Europe during the 1920s. Its main concern was to provide social and philosophical analyses of its own societies with a view to uncovering their emancipatory potential; its intent, in other words, was diagnostic as well as anticipatory.

The rise of fascism is the overshadowing political event of this decade. However, with the popular turn towards the Right, the Marxist prediction of a historically unavoidable and imminent proletarian revolution had to be drastically revised. As Perry Anderson (1976: 92) writes, Western Marxism was "born from the failure of proletarian revolutions in the advanced zones of European capitalism after the First World War."[1] In the eyes of the Western Marxists, this failure — and with it the sudden gap that had opened between theory and practice — needed to be accounted for, yet neither the economist (Karl Kautsky) nor the vanguardist (Lenin, Trotsky) versions of Marxism, the two main competitors laying claim to the Marxian heritage at the time, seemed to be in a position to do so. While the determinism of Kautsky's evolutionary reformist economism was incapable of explaining the non-occurrence of social revolution, the voluntarist vanguardism of Lenin and Trotsky, which had been so effective in Russia, seemed too dogmatic and authoritarian to be applied in a more liberal Western context. A new and different approach seemed to be called for.

Numerous theoretical and interpretive conflicts surround the term "Western Marxism," and its historiographic meaning has been highly dependent on commentators' intellectual interests and commitments.[2] In the following I use Lukács' 1923 text *History and Class Consciousness* as the paradigmatic expression of this tradition, and I approach Adorno by relating his central notion of reification to similar concerns in Lukács and Benjamin.

## The imprint of Lukács

The history of Adorno's engagement with Lukács is complex, involving a number of different attitudes, ranging from near devotion to downright rejection. In the spring of 1921, he discovered Lukács' early work *The Theory of the Novel*, an essay which exerted a tremendous impact on the young Adorno and which to a considerable extent was instrumental in forming his future view of both history, aesthetics, and politics. Like Hegel, Lukács sought to uncover the various historic forms of epic literature, arguing that whereas the Greek, classical forms were objective, the modern forms were subjective, reflecting the alienation of modern man from the absolute. Reformulating Schiller's distinction between naive and sentimental poetry within an essentially Hegelian framework, Lukács claimed more specifically that whereas the classical epics were concerned with the "transcendental home" of a world filled with gods and with purpose, the novel was concerned with the problematic culture of a world in which such sources of orientation no longer were available. According to Lukács, the loss of meaning is best described in terms of a claim about how time is experienced in these two forms of narrative. In the epics, on the one hand, the life immanence of meaning is so strong that it abolishes time: the heroes of the Homeric world do not undergo inner changes; and despite the hardship they suffer, their self-understandings remain in harmony with the generalized role expectations that are generated within a well-functioning ethical life. In a modern novel like Flaubert's *Sentimental Education*, however, the hero no longer finds his essence provided by the normatively structured social world, thus a radical split occurs between his self-understanding and his social role, and time no longer serves to unify past, present, and future. Indeed, since the hero is radically alienated from his environment, reality breaks into "separate fragments" and time gets experienced as a succession of contingent "now-points" without any deeper connection with the hero's identity or projects.[3]

Like many of the other attempts to combine a pessimistic diagnosis of the present with a panoramic view of Western history (using the fine arts as a psychosocial barometer and being scornful of scientific rationalism) that were published in the immediate aftermath of the First World War, including Bloch's *The Spirit of Utopia* and Kracauer's *Sociology as Science*, *The Theory of the Novel* represented a reaction against what Kracauer called "a metaphysical suffering from the lack of deep meaning in the world."[4] Indeed, at the time of writing his book on the philosophical implications of epic narrative, Lukács not only rejected Bolshevism on moral grounds but even flirted with a kind of spiritualism inspired by Dostoevsky. Needless to say, from the vantage point of the later Lukács, this was a politics of bourgeois despair, amounting to little more than a feeble conservatism incapable of effecting social change. Soon afterwards, however, in 1919, he became a member of the Central Committee of the Hungarian Communist Party and a staunch defender of Marxism; and in 1922, being in conflict with the dogmatic policies of the Executive Committee of the Comintern, he wrote *History and Class Consciousness*. In order to understand this work it is necessary to keep in mind Lukács' ambition, which was to conceive of Marxism as a project concerned with dissolving what he viewed as the objectified, "soulless" social forms of modernity and replacing them with concrete forms which did have a "soul." In contrast to what many commentators have interpreted as a radical break, there is a deep continuity between the Lukács of *The Theory of the Novel* and the Lukács of *History and Class Consciousness*; and in trying to combine a negative philosophy of history with a social analysis of the present, Adorno retrieves elements from both.

As is well known, Lukács' *History and Class Consciousness* (and in particular its central section entitled "Reification and the Consciousness of the Proletariat") combines the Weberian category of "rationalization" with the Marxian category of "reification." From Weber, Lukács borrows the view that essential to the development of Western modernity is the possibility — actualized most paradigmatically in the capitalist enterprise with its concomitant amalgamation of bureaucratic and legal administration — of rational calculation. Weber refers to the action-orientation corresponding to rational calculation as *purposive-rational action (zweckrationales Handeln)*, or what is often called instrumental or strategic action. On the practical level, purposive-rational action is a form of social action whereby the attainment of given ends is secured by "means of an increasingly precise calculation of adequate means" (Weber 1974: 293). According to Weber, rational book-keeping constitutes the most integral expression of such an orientation and sets the modern type of capitalist production radically apart from prior sorts of capitalist activity such as usury or adventurer's capitalism. Moreover, in the introduction to his essays on the world religions, Weber stresses that such attainment would be impossible without precise and abstract concepts, as well as universally applied rules, laws, and regulations; thus to the purposive-rational action corresponds a cognitive attitude whereby reality is to be controlled and predicted on the basis of abstraction. Indeed, purposive-rational action seeks both technical control of nature and strategic control over other humans by means of applying calculable, homogeneous, and impersonal rules. As a result, the phenomena become knowable not in their individual specificity but in terms of their potential for being procedurally subsumed under higher-order terms, categories, or classes. Abstraction and domination go together to form the destructive-productive unity that Adorno comes to associate with the notion of "administered societies," from which the non-identical, and indeed the very possibility of the new, has been successfully exorcised.

Central to Lukács' reception of Weber's work, however, is his view that the analysis of rationalization needs to be complemented by a consideration of what Marx called the commodity form. It is the commodity form which, in the final instance, explains, in both Lukács, Benjamin and Adorno, the deformations of contemporary social reproduction. Intimately linked, though, with the notion of the commodity, or of commodity fetishism, is the more general notion of reification, which has a long history in modern German philosophy, going all the way back to Herder, Schiller, and Hegel's respective critiques of their contemporary societies.[5] In the early Hegel's essays on religion, for example, the notion of reification, or what he calls "positivity" [*Positivität*], was used to characterize allegiances to doctrines or value-systems that were imposed from the "outside," merely "posited," as opposed to being rationally adopted.[6] Later, in essays from his Jena period, Hegel generalizes the term "positivity" to become the defining moment of enlightenment modernity itself.[7] By conceptualizing modernity in this way, Hegel means that enlightenment Reason, rather than being fully accountable for its own possibility and conditions, has fallen apart into a number of discrepant principles, each of which, while grounding a field of value (art, science, morality, and so on), are reliant either on dogmatic premise or faith, causing bifurcations (*Entzweiungen*) between form and content on all levels of society. Hegel's diagnosis is of a society that is radically self-alienated, its members fixated on objectifications for which they cannot recognize themselves as their rational authors. In Adorno's view, which has its source in Hegel and the Jena romantics, the ultimate consequence of reification is nihilism, the progressive replacement of genuinely motivating rational authority with naked coercion.

Marx's appropriation of the theme of positivity (reification), which Lukács, Benjamin, and Adorno, each in their own way, seek to inherit and renew, arises out of his attempt, mainly in *Capital*, *Theories of Surplus Value*, and the *Grundrisse*, to formulate a theory of value.[8] Central to this theory, which aims to explain how the capitalist system of commodity production operates, is the distinction between use-value and exchange-value. Every commodity, Marx states, has a two-fold aspect: on the one hand, a *use-value*, which "is realized only in the process of consumption" (1971: 20), referring to the structure of needs that define agents in their status as natural beings; on the other, an *exchange-value*, which fixes the value a product has when offered on a market in exchange for other products. Without wanting to rehearse Marx's complex theory of value in much detail, the difference between use-value and exchange-value (and between concrete and abstract labor) is so important to Lukács, Benjamin, and Adorno that it is necessary to pause for a moment in order to consider, at least roughly, what Marx actually does with these categories.

For an item to be a commodity and hence enter into an exchange relationship, it is necessary that it be commensurate with other items. Considered exclusively in terms of its use-value, an item is precisely incommensurate; there is no common measure of value by means of which the exchange can take place. Since use-value is no basis for commodity exchange, Marx postulates that every commodity, in addition to having a use-value, must have an exchange-value. The question, though, is how the exchange-value gets constituted. In classical neo-liberal economic theory, it is the laws of supply and demand which account for the actual exchange-value of a given item. According to Marx, however, who follows Smith and Ricardo in tracing all value back to human labor, it is "abstract general labor," measurable in terms of the amount of time expended by the worker in the production of the commodity, that determines exchange-value. Whereas concrete labor, the specific set of human operations that go into the production of an item, determines its use-value, it is the amount of hours, a quantifiable variable, that it takes to produce it which makes the item commensurate with other items.

Thus, corresponding to the distinction between use-value and exchange-value is the distinction between concrete and abstract labor, and since labor power itself is a commodity it follows that the exchange-value of labor can be identified with the socially necessary labor time that goes into producing the necessities of life for the worker. By purchasing labor power at its exchange-value, which seems perfectly fair, the employer succeeds in procuring for himself a commodity that generates surplus value. What explains this is that the worker's activities in advanced industrial production makes it possible to produce commodities whose exchange-value exceeds the cost of maintaining the worker at the subsistence level. The difference between surplus and necessary production can then be appropriated by the employer. Capitalism thus screens the operation by which workers are exploited: what looks like fair exchange is in essence unfair.

For both Lukács and Adorno, what is particularly striking in Marx's analysis of value is how use-value, under capitalism, can only be expressed in terms of exchange-value, thus effecting a misidentification that extends all the way into human consciousness itself. What is in fact an unequal relation between the capitalist and the worker, for example, appears as an equal relation between the amount of labor it takes to produce an item and the wages paid by the owner. More generally, the logic of commodification itself allows a thing to appear only insofar as its use-value — which for Adorno becomes a cipher for everything that can possibly contain a utopian promise: difference and heterogeneity, otherness, the qualitative, the radically new, the corporeal, in short what he calls "the non-identical" — becomes subordinate to its exchange-value. The processes which the early Marx, in the 1844 *Economic-Philosophical Manuscripts*, described as the *alienation of labor* are thus in *Capital* analyzed in terms of *Realabstraktion*, the transformation of social and concrete relations and processes into frozen and quantifiable properties of things.

The fact that the social characteristics of human labor take on the appearance of "objective characteristics of the products of labor themselves, as the socio-natural properties of these things" (Marx 1976: 164–5) is what Marx famously calls "commodity fetishism." Something becomes a fetish when an inanimate object gets invested with magical, seemingly inscrutable powers, by its worshipper. In another passage of *Capital*, Marx (1976: 165) notes the same aspect, though with a different emphasis, claiming that "It is nothing but the definite social relation between men themselves which assumes here, for them, the fantastic form (*phantasmagorische Form*) of a relation between things." From the point of view of the exchange itself, one commodity is as good as another, if the values are equal. Its concrete social determination becomes at best an appendix to its market value.

Given the significance of this concept, Marx himself had little to say about the social, cultural, and intellectual consequences of commodity fetishism. For him, the theories of surplus value and crisis became much more important and deserving of elaboration. Indeed, the dialectic of commodification, expounded in the opening chapter of *Capital*, only serves as a prolegomenon to his analysis of the exploitation of labor. For Lukács, by contrast, the commodity is the universal structuring category of capitalism, and it is the commodity which accounts for the high level of reification in contemporary society: commodification leaves its mark on all human capacities (the subject, or subjective), and on all objects and relations between men (the object, or objective). Most significantly, labor itself is wholly subsumed under the laws of capitalistic exchange. In Lukács' conceptual edifice, the question thus becomes how capitalism, with its fateful combination of instrumentalist rationalization and commodification, as well as its alienation of labor, can be overcome. Is there an agent of historical change, and if so, how can that agent be brought to awareness of its own status and be prompted to act?

This is the point at which Adorno and Lukács radically part ways. Drawing on Hegel, Lukács helps himself to a definition of the industrial proletariat as the universal class of late capitalism. Just as Marx, in the *Economic-Philosophical Manuscripts*, had postulated the worker as the most immediate representative of man's *species-being*, a species-being which is alienated as a result of the externalization of labor under capitalism, so

Lukács views the proletariat, the agent of production, as embodying an objective interest in emancipation. Through collective revolutionary activity, the wage-laborer is capable of reappropriating his own labor and its products, and thereby to abolish reification. For Lukács, this process can be modeled on the basis of a simple subject–object dialectic: the (collective) subject, having experienced the burden of its own dismemberment in the alienated otherness of abstraction, returns to itself as the identical subject–object of history. Lukács believes this is possible because the proletariat possesses a privileged epistemological standpoint: that of practice itself. Contemplative, theoretical awareness of reification, while useful to the theorist, generates no revolutionary disposition. On the contrary, it is practice itself, the experience of the effects of the discrepancy between the alienation of labor, on the one hand, and the interrelated claim to be the subject of one's own life, on the other, which ultimately motivates emancipatory activity.

Adorno's grievances against Lukács' belief in the self-overcoming of social totality are well known, anticipating as they do much post-Marxist theory (Lyotard, Lefort) of the 1970s and 1980s. For one thing, Adorno is deeply suspicious of the notion of a self-identical subject–object of history. Any such notion inevitably seems to presuppose some form of Fichtean or Hegelian idealism — the identity of thought with its object, which can only be anticipated from the standpoint of redemption, and not from within history itself. Rather than serving an emancipatory purpose, the concept of an absolute subject of all historical genesis, ready to untie the riddle of history, stands in danger of affirming *status quo*. This is related to Adorno's complex stance towards the very notion of totality, which, as Jay (1984b) argues, is likely to have made up the most central theorem within Western Marxism. While Adorno retains this notion as an epistemological key to the analysis of contemporary society, he refuses to apply it as a social-ontological category. Contemporary society may be considered a *false* totality, yet from the vantage point of theoretical reflection it reveals itself as atomized, contradictory, and recalcitrant to teleological interpretation. As Jay (1984b: 255) succinctly puts it,

> for all of Adorno's interest in Lukács and Hegelian Marxism, for all his fascination with the concepts of reification, mediation, and second nature, for all his attraction to the totalizing methodology of Horkheimer's Institute, he stubbornly maintained that under present circumstances, the anti-holistic lessons he learned from Kracauer, Benjamin, and Schoenberg were of equal, if not greater, value.

Indeed, when pushed to its logical extremes, Lukács' position, while unyielding in its materialism, unfolds an essentially Hegelian philosophy of history, including a progressivist belief in the historical immanence of reason and a concomitant espousal of the notion of historical necessity. For Adorno, who adopts, as we will see, a version of Benjamin's deliberately melancholic *Verfallsgeschichte*, and for whom the notion of progress always threatens the redemptive moments of history with oblivion, any such humanist philosophy must be rejected. For something to count as a cipher of possible redemption, it would have to be located outside the scope of universal progressivist history in the Hegelian/Lukácsian sense.

Second, Adorno is dismissive of the (Fichtean) idea that the proletariat should be capable of transforming its reified interpretation of itself into a class consciousness that can dispose it for authentic class praxis and revolutionary action. In his view, the proletariat is so thoroughly under the sway of the structural laws and forms that regulate social totality that no injection of Hegelian dialecticism is ever going to release its stifled ability for self-determination. Adorno, moreover, who in a sense defends the contemplative attitude against Lukács' belief that it can be dialectically overcome in revolutionary praxis, is profoundly unsympathetic towards the classical Marxist problem of organization, believing that only the isolated, if not asocial, intellectual, rather than the collaborating worker, can embody any form of genuine resistance: "For the intellectual, inviolable isolation is now the only way of showing some measure of solidarity" (Adorno 1974a: 26). Under present circumstances, that is, as long as "society precedes the subject," mass or group behavior ought *in general* to be viewed with suspicion.

The more adequate attitude, which will be discussed more closely in Chapter 8, is expressed by the specific exercise of civic virtue that Adorno sees embodied in what I would call a "citizen intellectual" willing to risk her established place in the social realm for the preservation and achievement of republican liberty, civic equality, and a more humane system of social reproduction. One may argue, however, that Adorno goes too far: if all forms of group solidarity (and not just manifestly oppressive ones) are said to inevitably threaten the exercise of autonomy, then rational collective will-formation seems impossible. It would follow that progressive social movements (labor movements, civil rights movements, and so on), while capable in certain cases of promoting social change, are devoid of "philosophical" or "ethical" legitimacy. This is a large and potentially damaging issue which has haunted Adorno's legacy. Suffice it to say, though, that Adorno's apparent hostility towards collectivities of all sort must be viewed as a response to totalitarianism. His qualified support for some of the student uprisings in the late 1960s speaks against the view that he had no tolerance whatsoever for political group behavior. Rather than acts of solidarity and the explicit identification with shared political interests as such, it is predominantly conformism — the destruction of citizenship and man's capacity for independent thinking and judgment — that for Adorno threatens the political.

Third, Adorno was adverse to Lukács' emphasis on labor. Although he, in the late essay "Marginalia to Theory and Praxis" and elsewhere, argues that praxis "arose from labor" (1998b: 262), he remained skeptical of Lukács' identification of praxis with social labor. In Adorno's account, praxis, involving an emphatic claim to freedom, transcends the sphere of labor. While praxis may articulate itself in ways that we would count as restricted, it cannot be tied to labor except on pains of forfeiting any possible claim to freedom. Aware of the *causal-genetic* relation between labor and praxis, he thus insists on the irreducible *essence* of praxis: there is an ethical imperative, unknown to labor, which applies to the sphere of action. Whereas for Lukács (following the young Marx) a rational society entails the emancipation of labor in its externalized form, for Adorno emancipation entails the dispensation of labor altogether.

Yet what exactly does this mean? The claim becomes clearer by distinguishing between mental and material labor, where only the latter is to be transcended in a more rational order. "The fact that some live without material labor ... indicates that this possibility exists for everyone" (1998b: 267). This optimistic yet rather naive remark is substantiated by appeal to the technical forces of production. Although in conflict with some of his negative remarks about the dehumanizing effects of technology and mass production in the *Dialectic of Enlightenment*, Adorno generally subscribes to the view that the rational use of technology within a well-organized society could make material labor redundant. Unlike Marcuse and Horkheimer, however, who flirted more openly with a technological utopia of this kind, Adorno never develops this argument in any detail. Indeed, as the notion of a "humanized," "soft" technology, presumably allowing for the widespread abolition of material labor, seems to have reached its ironical apogee in the age of information, there is reason to believe, first, that such technology, however mental, does not diminish the strains of labor but rather in many cases intensfies them, and, second, that labor is hardly less alienated today than it was in the classical industrial era.

Adorno is however deeply skeptical of "hard," industrial technology, associating technological progress with the administration of mass societies and an ever-growing objectification and control of living subjectivities and nature. While some passages in Adorno seem to suggest a Marxist sympathy with the notion of technological development and change as the motor of historical development, it is often argued that technological society encourages standardization both of behavior and social environment. Even the crucial Marxist invocation of an "unleashing of productive forces" is feared by Adorno (1973b: 306–7) for its "affinity to the violent domination of nature ... The very word 'unleashed' has undertones of menace."

Remarkably uninterested in emphasizing Marx's distinction between abstract and concrete labor, Adorno finally refuses to follow Lukács in initiating the discussion of reification on the basis of the way men's productive activity becomes alien and objective to them under capitalism. On the contrary, rather than deriving a theory of value from the alienation of labor, the analysis of commodification becomes restricted to the level of exchange itself, thus ignoring how the commodity form emerges in production. In conjunction with the dismissal of what he calls Lukács' "wishful image of unbroken subjective immediacy" (1973b: 374), he also distances himself from Lukács' belief that reification can be surmounted as the result of a change of consciousness. Reification, he argues, is not a result of "a subjectively errant consciousness, but objectively deduced" (374). If anything, it should be treated as an objective-philosophical category, descriptive of the social *a priori* of the exchange process.

Adorno's difference from Lukács in these matters, and in particular his unwillingness to mobilize Marx's distinction between abstract and concrete labor for the purpose of analyzing the extraction of surplus value, may seem to weaken Jameson's claim for "the essential Marxism of this thinker" (1996: 230). Indeed, as Rose (1978) and others have argued, Adorno's Marxism is at best highly selective, leaving much of the apparatus of Marx's analysis of capitalism's injustices in the background while emphasizing the more Weberian elements of Lukács' account in which late capitalism represents the victory of the forces of rationalization with the effect of freezing social relations and ultimately replacing them with the subject-transcendent mechanisms of systemically enforced exchange (the bureaucracies, the market, and so on). Having downplayed both notions of class and class struggle (every society is class ridden, yet class is not the fundamental problem of modern society), as well as the narrative of historically inevitable liberation, operative in both Marx's theory of falling rates of profit and Lukács' more humanist call for the proletariat to reappropriate its own labor, the great challenge for Adorno is how a progressivist political agenda can continue to be sustained. That is, as the agent of historical change (i.e., the proletariat) drops out, and as a readily identifiable victim of oppression becomes difficult, if not impossible, to locate, it seems as if the impulse that would animate social criticism gets irretrievably lost.

In an open letter to Horkheimer (quoted in Buck-Morss 1977: 67), Adorno acknowledges this issue, suggesting that the primary difference between their approaches can be traced back to their diverging accounts of judgmental validity. In Horkheimer's case, critical judgments are to be formed with reference to concrete forms of injustice, in particular as they evolve out of structural asymmetries in the bourgeois society that he was attacking. For Horkheimer's ethically informed engagement, Critical Theory can claim to embody an emancipatory interest because it aims towards addressing hurt and suffering. As Buck-Morss (1977: 67) puts it, "The transcendent element of idealism which allowed a moral distinction to be made between what is and ought to be remained essential to Horkheimer." Her point is reflected in Adorno's letter to Horkheimer, in which he states that "With you the primary thing was indignation over injustice."[9] Horkheimer, Adorno contends, was in this regard influenced by the Judaic ethics of his family as well as bourgeois Enlightenment principles of equality and respect. One could add to this the fact that Horkheimer, throughout his career, was deeply indebted to Schopenhauer, adopting not only his belief in the universality of human suffering but also the desire to see the ethical demand as arising from acts of empathy with the victims of hurt and domination. While bourgeois ethical principles can be used to confront bad bourgeois practices (of injustice, irrationality, monopolization, and so on), the experiential value of these principles stem from the sense in which the theorist, in applying them, is able to give misery a voice and bring it, as it were, to principled attention, thus calling for social change.

By contrast, Adorno, in the letter to Horkheimer, describes himself as primarily oriented towards the notion of truth. It is truth, he writes, which is the foundation on which a Critical Theory must rest: truth rather than justice constitutes the touchstone of judgmental acceptability.

When Adorno asserts a priority of truth over justice, what he refers to is not truth as correspondence between representation and reality. Rather, the notion of truth-content (*Wahrheitsgehalt*), which plays a prominent role throughout Adorno's career, is of Platonic and Hegelian origin: it implies that truth consists in the negation of appearance. Truth is the antithesis of illusion or appearance (*Schein*); it ineluctably embodies a metaphysical moment aiming to transcend the immanence of appearance. Transposed to a less Platonic register and keyed to the theme of reification, what this means is that Adornian Critical Theory seeks to criticize claims to immediacy or objectivity that in effect screen their actual social and historical mediation. Reification, though intimately connected with the domination of the exchange process, is the general process whereby social and historical meaning get hypostatized and transcoded such as to be presented in terms of first principles, that is, as static, invariant, and self-identical.

Now the truth-content Adorno is looking for in philosophy and art would by implication carry an emancipatory promise. The moment of truth occurs when a crack shows up in the otherwise seamless web of illusion that, on the most general level, following Lukács and Weber, is linked to the notion of abstraction (economic, psychic, social, and philosophical), yet which in a more determinate sense leads on to a constellation of other critical concepts: "fate," "myth," "phantasmagoria," "second nature," and "identitarian reason." Adorno, it might be argued, turns to meta-

36

physics not to find meaning in a world of pure transcendence but to undo the claims, reflected in Lukács (and behind him Hegel), for the totality of immanence. While Lukács provides Adorno with most of the basic terms of his social analysis, it is ultimately Benjamin who inspires the construction of his "critical" or "negative-dialectical" response to this analysis. Although Adorno rarely makes the connection between metaphysics (understood as a determinate negation of immanence) and politics explicit, the claim that he renounced the emancipatory interest of Marxist thought must be viewed in relation to this turn towards theory. In an essay on Hegel, "Skoteinos, Or How to Read Hegel," he interestingly draws such a connection, arguing that "Hegel's logic is not only his metaphysics; it is also his politics" (1993b: 94). If Hegel's logic can be his politics, then Adorno, modeling his work on Hegel's account of dialectical experience while rejecting its drive towards synthesis and finality, is claiming to be in a position to offer a complete reconceptualization of the Marxist doctrine of the unity of theory and practice. Politics (and practice) becomes the work of theory.

## Benjamin and natural history

Benjamin's influence on Adorno is nowhere more explicit than in his two early essays, "The Actuality of Philosophy," first presented as his 1931 inaugural lecture in Frankfurt, and "On Natural History," a speech given in 1932 to the Kant Society in Frankfurt.[10] In both essays, Adorno attacks the appeal to totality and immanence and calls for a replacement of idealist thinking (defined in terms of belief in a synthetic unity of subject and object) with a program of philosophical interpretation. It is worth noticing how strongly Adorno's friends at the Institute — among them Horkheimer — objected to these talks. Wiggershaus (1998: 94) says of "On Natural History," in which human history is viewed as petrified, repetitive social reality and nature as historical and disruptive, that "none of them liked it." Apart from the extreme density of their mode of presentation, it seems clear that they all felt that Adorno, especially in "On Natural History," had been venturing into precisely the kind of metaphysical speculation that Horkheimer, with his interdisciplinary program of materialist research, involving the collaborative efforts of philosophy and sociology, had wanted to exclude from the Institute's activities. A closer look at these texts reveals, however, that Adorno is not in the business of reverting to a dogmatic metaphysics; on the contrary, the central concern, arguably, of these essays is to develop a notion of *Darstellung* — of philosophical *presentation* or *representation* — that can free thinking from its traditional dependence on conceptual continuity and generality. Adorno doesn't call for knowledge that extends to an alleged realm of noumenal or subject-transcendent reality so much as he aims to construct a method, culminating in his inheritance of Benjamin's notion of constellation, that allows the theorist to unravel illicit claims to totality. To see how this takes place it is worth recalling some of the results of Benjamin's famous "Epistemo-Critical Prologue" [*Erkenntniskritische Vorrede*] to *The Origin of German Tragic Drama*.

In stark contrast to the Lukács of *History and Class Consciousness* as well as the later Benjamin of the Arcades project, the Prologue does not for a moment communicate with the Marxist tradition. While far from oblivious to politics, Benjamin's engagement with it had at the time of composing *The Origin of the German Tragic Drama* been restricted to his disillusioning affiliation with the German Youth Movement, whose romantic anti-capitalism transformed itself, for him, into a strong moral imperative with reference to which the contemporary world seemed decadent and corrupt. If anything, this piece of philosophical writing continues the efforts Benjamin had made more than ten years earlier, in the 1916 essay "On Language as Such and on the Language of Man," to develop a theory of knowledge. In a letter to Gershom Scholem of February 1925, written when his work on the *Trauerspiel* study was in its final stages, he remarks that the Prologue is "an immeasurable chutzpah — nothing more or less than a prolegomena to the theory of knowledge; thus a second — I know not whether better — stage of the early work on language, which, as you know, appears as a theory of ideas."[11] As the title suggests, "On Language" is best approached as a theory of language, or rather of the relationship between language and world. By using the biblical narrative of the Fall as a foil for expressing his views, Benjamin daringly argues that language and world, representation and reality, must be considered as separated by a void that came into being with man's expulsion from the Garden of Eden.[12] He further dramatizes this speculative conception by imagining a collapse from an original Adamitic language, a divine language of names that were grounded in God's presence and then bestowed by man on a mute creation, to a human language of concepts and predication. While the former had a foundation *de re*, reflecting the order of the divine so as to be expressive of world as it is in itself, the latter, though a means of communication, ceased to be an immediate expression of the things themselves, leaving post-lapsarian nature mute and alien. When applied with a predicative intent, concepts from then on allow identification of an object's general features, the "object *qua* something;" they do not, however, reveal the thing in its ultimate (divine) reality, thus language deteriorates into what Kierkegaard, in *The Concept of Anxiety*, calls prattle:

> The knowledge of things resides in name, whereas that of good and evil is, in the profound sense in which Kierkegaard uses the word, "prattle," and knows only one purification and elevation,

to which the prattling man, the sinner, was therefore submitted: judgment.

(Benjamin 1978: 327)

Drawing on Hamann, Hölderlin as well as strands of Jewish mysticism, Benjamin's argument is in part directed against Kant and the neo-Kantian tradition, for whom objectivity was effected by the synthetic activities of the transcendental subject. Benjamin strongly argues that Kant's position represents a perversion of the ideal of truth and that truth has to be divine in origin — ontologically superior, that is, to the finite functions of categorical determination. However, it is also directed against a progressivist view of history. In Benjamin's deliberately melancholic view, what appears as progress is in fact the indefinite return of sameness, of fallen, profane time, imprisoning the self in ever-widening cycles of guilt, evil, and decay. Any possible redemption from the empty time of the "always-the-same" (*das Immergleiche*) requires the interference of Messianic, discontinuous time, an interference which Benjamin refers to as "now-time" (*Jetztzeit*) in order to emphasize its singular, irruptive quality. Since the moments of history that are charged with such explosive particles of now-time tend to be brushed under the carpet by the historian who looks for continuity, Benjamin proposes the figure of a counter-historian whose task it is rescue and salvage — not by constructing but by deconstructing and destroying. As Wolin (1994: 48) puts it,

> For Benjamin, the philosophy of history becomes *Heilsgeschichte*, the history of salvation, and the task of the critic ... is that of rescuing the few unique visions of transcendence that grace the continuum of history, the now-times [*Jetztzeiten*], from the fate of oblivion which incessantly threatens to consume them.

In the Prologue to the *Origin of the German Tragic Drama*, Benjamin continues to rethink the Kantian distinction between cognitive knowledge and noumenal truth. Like Kant, he distinguishes between concepts, which stand on the side of appearance and knowledge of appearance, and ideas, which stand on the side of the absolute. Yet whereas Kant, in the transcendental analytic, restricted objectivity to the knowledge of appearances, Benjamin seeks to make the "contemplation of the ideas" available as a humanly possible access to truth in the non-empirical, absolute sense. The basic task of philosophy, he claims, is the representation (*Darstellung*) of ideas, which will only be possible through the tracing of constellations.

The philosophical key to Benjamin's extraordinary exposition is his claim that the representation of ideas, rather than demanding some form of direct intuition of the absolute (which both Kant and Benjamin reject), must take place from out of empirical reality itself. Philosophy, in the form of "experience" (*Erfahrung*), redeems the phenomena by breaking them down into elements that can be decoded and read as a script. In contrast to the traditional Platonic construction of ideas as eternal, transcendental forms, Benjamin envisions the absolute as transitory, fragmentary, and particular, and the idea articulates the phenomenon as eternal truth. For this to be possible, however, the intentional control of everyday conceptual appropriation must give way to the unintentionally organized alterity of elements that arise in such an experience. According to Benjamin, the ideas must be viewed as composed of clusters or groups of concepts, and just as constellations of stars reveal meaning in the apparently meaningless night sky by forming a kind of relational system, so is the idea the result of a constellative writing — the solution to the problem of *Darstellung* — in which concepts are configured together. Any attempt to violently yoke concepts together in the regimented form of a system would return them to the mere status of arbitrary empirical concepts, providing no more than cognitive knowledge in the restricted sense. When Adorno, in the late 1920s, worked to adapt the *Trauerspiel* theory to a Marxian, materialist framework, it was the moment of interpretation — the construction of ideas as constellations — that became the central object of focus:

> Interpretation of the unintentional through a juxtaposition of the analytically separated elements and illumination of the real by the power of such interpretation is the program of every authentically materialist knowledge ....
>
> (Adorno 2000a: 32)

While Adorno worked hard to bring out the anti-idealist strands of Benjamin's theory — a theory he always feared would put philosophy in the service of theology, rather than the opposite — there can be no doubt that Benjamin, regardless of how one assesses the speculative thrust of its most extravagant moments, had developed an account of truth that would haunt the rest of Adorno's work, including the *Negative Dialectics*. Of tremendous significance for Adorno is, first, the investment in the particular and the fragment as opposed to the general and universal — that the former represents the absolute and needs to be redeemed; then, second, the idea that truth only appears through the relationship between phenomena or between the concepts of phenomena, which for Adorno translates into the principle that truth can only be the result of negation; and, finally, the emphasis on a method of philosophical representation, for Adorno the essay, that resists regimentation, systematicity, and linear argumentation.

We are now in a position to see how the allegorist, Benjamin's melancholy figure in the *Trauerspiel* study, by viewing history as a piling up of ruins, a grand regressive movement characterized by inevitable decay and disaster, finds himself able to break the spell of the congealed, repetitive self-sameness that history has become and redeem its explosive moments of alterity. Whereas the Hegelian-Marxist tradition would look to the immanent development of social history in order to uncover the potential for change, the allegorist seeks to disrupt that development and locate the "intentionless being" that is buried underneath it. The future can thus only be rationally configured through a redemptive critique of the past; history itself, if considered in isolation from the latent promise of this otherness, is meaningless, indeed catastrophic.

In "On Natural History," Adorno adopts this allegorical strategy, arguing that the subversive potentials of the present must be read off, in constellations, from the past. Yet just as the present can only be redeemed by the past, so must also the past be viewed in terms of the emancipatory interest that guides the present. Just as history must be considered as nature, self-perpetuating cycles of pure violence and domination, so must nature be viewed as the transcendent other of history, a promise of change and difference. There is a strategic pessimism at work here, aiming to create images of the present so bleak and devoid of meaning that they unravel and reveal fragments of redemptive "now-time."[13] In both Benjamin and Adorno, allegorical truth content can thus be connected to the image of sacrifice. However, unlike Benjamin's more overtly Messianic construal, in which the event of reconciliation would be located entirely beyond history, Adorno, following Hegel's philosophy of religion, tends to link sacrificial death and resurrection with the utopian potential inherent in the social world as such. As I will explore later, however, Adorno's insistence on conceiving transcendence exclusively from within is not without difficulties. If Benjamin, necessarily viewing now-times as exceptions, stands in danger of becoming politically quietist and resigned, Adorno, who never fully disconnects himself from the Marxian promise of identifying general historical tendencies capable of anticipating a state of reconciliation, seems politically torn between, on the one hand, a stoic attitude of indefinite waiting and inaction and, on the other, a desperate search for socially relevant ciphers of reconciliation. I return to this issue in Chapter 5. For now, however, I want to turn to the *Dialectic of Enlightenment*.

## The eternal recurrence of the same

Although the continuity of Adorno's thought from his first published book, *Kierkegaard: The Construction of the Aesthetic* (1933), to his posthumously published *Aesthetic Theory* is truly remarkable, it is the *Dialectic of Enlightenment*, co-written with Max Horkheimer near Los Angeles and published in 1947, that finally marks his full breakthrough as a philosopher. Of course, the *Dialectic of Enlightenment* presents the reader with very little of what he or she ordinarily would expect of a major work in philosophy. Originally entitled *Philosophical Fragments* (*Philosophische Fragmente*), the book contains no theory, no sustained, linear argument, and no apparent center that would indicate the direction of future research. It is deliberately written in accordance with Adorno's claim, in "The Essay as Form" and elsewhere, that philosophy after the demise of idealism has to aspire to the qualities of the essay — anti-systematicity, the rejection of methodology, and deliberate fragmentation. From Adorno's refusal to let his work be thematized and reified, it does not follow, however, that the *Dialectic of Enlightenment*, while incapable of providing ideas that may guide hypothesis formation in empirical social theory, is best thought of as a piece of literary writing. To distinguish strictly, as some critics do, between the cognitive sphere of theory and the non-cognitive (albeit disclosive) sphere of literature involves, at least implicitly, a commitment to the old positivist divide between justification and discovery, a divide which post-positivist, post-Kuhnian philosophers of science have vigorously drawn into question: there simply is no sharp line to be drawn between the hypotheses that are formulated with the purpose of being systematically tested and the vocabularies that are being used to disclose a given field of research.[14] On the other hand, to follow Richard Rorty (2000) in trying to extract from the book a set of simple and independently verifiable theses would lead to equally unwarranted consequences. In Rorty's reading, the *Dialectic* amounts to little but a rambling display of tortuous and incoherent cultural pessimism, all of which can quickly be dismissed as "false." For the moment, we will have to accept that its formal discontinuity makes up just one dimension of Adorno's more general effort to analyze and attack the identity form.

Just as "The Actuality of Philosophy" and "On Natural History" were written as attempts to inherit certain central features of *The Origin of the German Tragic Drama*, so, while aspects of Lukács' *History and Class Consciousness* arguably make a late return, especially in the chapter on the culture industry, the *Dialectic of Enlightenment* draws heavily on the work of Benjamin. It is crucial, though, to recall the situation in which it is written — the Second World War as viewed from the authors' exile in California and the attempt to come to terms with Benjamin's tragic suicide on the border between France and Spain while trying to escape Nazi persecution. Especially formative in this respect is the impact of Benjamin's late *Theses on the Philosophy of History*, which were published by the Institute for Social Research in a small memorial volume in 1942. In the *Theses* Benjamin introduces the notion of a complete reversal between historical development and myth, arguing (1969: 257) in the famous entry on Paul Klee's painting "Angelus Novus" that history, as seen from the vantage point of its redemptive other (the angel which is blown backwards out of paradise), should be viewed as a progressive piling up of catastrophes. Adorno and Horkheimer continue this thought by envisioning a vast panorama of historical events, from the epic dawn of mankind to the present, all of which display a reversibility between enlightenment (liberation from the powers of necessity) and myth (the perpetuation of the *Immergleiche*).

Before we look closer at this remarkable exercise in redemptive criticism, it seems worthwhile to distinguish the project in the *Dialectic of Enlightenment* from what I consider as some standard misinterpretations. It is often claimed, most notably by Habermas, that the *Dialectic* should be read as a study of the destructive consequences of the historical predominance of "instrumental reason." The central argument of the book would then tend to take the form of demonstrating that human reason necessarily is calculative, oriented towards efficiency and obtaining the best and most precise means to achieve given ends, but that it contains no intrinsic conceptual resources for deliberating about ends. On this reading, the book extends Weber's thesis concerning the predominance of purposive-rational action in the most rationalized societies of the West to world history in general. It is important to realize, however, that while instrumentality certainly plays an important role in the overall assessment that Adorno and Horkheimer make with regard to reason as such, it is not *the* central term of the book.[15] The central term, if any, is *identity*, which is played out and rotated in an often confusing, although ultimately quite consistent manner. Indeed, the term "instrumental reason" does not even appear in the *Dialectic*, and it hardly makes itself felt in any of Adorno's other writings. It was on the contrary Horkheimer, in works such as *Eclipse of Reason* (carrying the German title *Kritik der instrumentellen Vernunft*), who coined the term and, together with Marcuse, made it into the kind of catch-word that in the 1960s was so often employed to denounce the alleged evils of rationalized late modernity. In the excursus entitled "Juliette or Enlightenment and Morality," there are, however, sentences that come close to expressing the instrumentality thesis: "Reason is the organ of calculation, of planning; it is neutral in regard to ends; its element is coordination" (1979: 88). It must be noted, though, that this chapter was mainly written by Horkheimer. In the sections that are authored by Adorno, the excursus on *The Odyssey* and the chapter on the culture industry, the critique of reason is inscribed in a much more complex dialectic, involving not just the anthropological identity of domination and reason but also a larger and more speculative claim about repetition and the compulsive return of the same.

Another noteworthy tendency in the reception of the *Dialectic* is the idea that its argument must necessarily be politically conservative. Indeed, the claim that the enlightenment, especially in its late, techno-scientific configuration, has reverted into myth, and hence into something inherently dangerous and unwanted, may seem to reverberate strikingly with the deliberately conservative views espoused by writers such as Jung,

Klages, and (albeit in extremely complex ways) Heidegger. In all of these thinkers, civilization itself suffers from a tragic fault; thus the only acceptable stance consists in rejecting the values of the Enlightenment (progress, freedom, emancipation, technology, secularization, equality, and so on) in favor of that which it somehow threatens or suppresses (for Jung, an archaic, subconscious and collective unity; for Klages, a motherworld of primeval life-forces; for Heidegger, Being (*Sein*) as opposed to enframing (*Gestell*)).

Needless to say, a politics based on a global critique of civilization may take many different forms, ranging from stoic despair (an attitude frequently associated with Adorno), abstaining from any interventionist activity, to a desire to retrieve symbolic authority (as in Stefan George and Hermann Broch), or even, in its most extreme expression, to an apocalyptic will to destruction and sacrifice (as in Ernst Jünger). The sense of the *Dialectic* as being a work of political conservatism is closely related to the thesis, developed by Jay and adopted by Habermas, that it entirely transcends the epistemic horizon of the Institute's previous research. Whereas most of the empirical research that went on in the 1930s under Horkheimer's leadership had been geared towards ideology critique as well as uncovering the psycho-social mechanisms responsible for the rise of fascist totalitarianism, proposing that the ultimate political solution to the ills of the present consisted in some version of socialist transformation, the *Dialectic*, according to Jay, represents a wholesale abandonment not only of a Marxist construction of universal history (based on the progressive dialectic between forces of production and relations of production) but also of its implicit hopes for liberation from capitalist oppression.

In response to these claims, it is, first, useful to note that the discontinuity thesis, while applicable to Horkheimer, is not true of Adorno. As already indicated, there is a strong continuity between Adorno's early work, from around 1930, and the *Dialectic*. Though undeveloped and abstract in comparison with the later work, all the basic ideas that structure the argument in the *Dialectic* are present in "On Natural History." More importantly, Adorno, unlike his conservative opponents, is not in the business of rejecting the enlightenment but rather of reconsidering it in the sense of *Besinnung* (mindful consideration). Indeed, neither Horkheimer nor Adorno had ever wanted to repudiate enlightenment thinking as such. On the contrary, as Wiggershaus (1998: 326) notes, "Both of them has at one time been enthusiastic supporters of enlightenment. Horkheimer had endorsed the French Enlightenment as exposing social hypocrisy and injustice, while Adorno had endorsed the idea of clarifying and elucidating everything instinctual and obscure, insensate and subconscious. Both of them had endorsed Marx's clarification of the socio-economic preconditions for human emancipation." As they write in the introduction to the *Dialectic*:

The dilemma that faced us in our work proved to be the first phenomenon for investigation: the self-destruction of the Enlightenment. We are wholly convinced — and therein lies our *petitio principii* — that social freedom is inseparable from enlightened thought. Nevertheless, we believe that we have just as clearly recognized that the notion of this very way of thinking, no less than the actual historic forms — the social institutions — with which it is interwoven, already contains the seed of the reversal universally apparent today.

(1979: xiii)

The insistence on defending "enlightened thought" against the actual enlightenment sets Adorno and Horkheimer's project radically apart from conservative critics of modernity. Modernity (or what Habermas, following Weber, calls *cultural modernity*, in order to separate the normative content of modernity from its *de facto* realization) is by its very nature wedded to a set of promises that so far have either been misinterpreted or misapplied. The task, then, for Adorno and Horkheimer (as it was for Kant and Hegel) is to come up with a more adequate set of principles by which moderns are invited to legislate themselves.[16]

The argument of the *Dialectic* has nearly been beaten to death by the amount of commentators who, to the detriment of other and less famous texts, have focused exclusively on this work. Since its highly speculative anthropology is not immediately relevant for an assessment of Adorno's dialectical and political thinking, I will restrict myself to reminding the reader of its most consequential moves. Inspired by the radical, if not cynical, naturalism of Schopenhauer, Nietzsche, and Freud, Adorno and Horkheimer fundamentally claim that reason must be conceptualized in the light of a basic drive for self-preservation. Human rationality in general, as well as language itself, is shaped by the overall purpose of securing the individual's survival. As a result, thinking, with its use of conceptual language, is geared towards identifying, controlling, and organizing a hostile and potentially dangerous environment. To think, and hence to liberate oneself from nature, is to identify and reduce complexity.

Linking Adorno and Horkheimer's position more specifically with writings such as Nietzsche's "On Truth and Falsity in an Extra-Moral Sense" and Benjamin's "On Language as Such and on the Language of Man", the fundamental imperative of self-preservation transforms linguistic behavior into a strategy of survival. By subsuming a particular (or set of particulars) under generic terms or class terms, judgments effect a synthesis between particular and universal that ultimately fails to express what is proper to the particular as such. Indeed, predication itself, by reducing the determinations of the particular to the universal determination implied by the predicate term, distorts and mystifies the particular by omitting its *differentia specifica* and imputing to it a higher-order reality of which it knows nothing. As a result, language, or at least simple predicative (affirmative) sentences, makes us prone to disregard the infinite potential for experience and intuition that is proper to *this* particular object, or what Adorno and Horkheimer would call the non-identical.

Throughout the course of history, however, human beings have liberated themselves from the fear and temptation of uncontrolled nature (including their own inner nature) at a high price: for at the end of this process, they have identified nature with that which the identitarian regimes of natural science and technology, each in their own way, aim to make comprehensible and masterable, thus causing nature to become disenchanted and stripped of meaning. Ultimately, the world (the world of the abstract identity of the merchandise), reduced to a correlate of the procedures and instruments according to which instrumental knowing is produced, no longer forms a basis for restricting human claims to objective knowledge; the acceptability of judgments becomes conditional upon their place in the framework of accepted beliefs, yet the framework itself seems increasingly to lack external pressure and friction. Idealism, conceived as the (however false because violent and reductive) identity between subject and object, thus becomes the truth of this false totality.

As a result of a fear of everything amorphous and potentially uncontrollable, the individual is forced to sacrifice his or her immediate claim to happiness (which paradoxically is connected to the nature repudiated) and orient calculatively towards the future. "The history of civilization is the history of sacrifice. In other words: the history of renunciation" (1979: 55). By exclusively serving the purpose of self-preservation, reason is itself a piece of nature, and subjectivity becomes a function of self-preservation. The great and deliberate dialectical *Umschlag* of the *Dialectic* arises from the fact that that which was to be preserved through sacrifice itself becomes an object of sacrifice. Rather than liberating itself from nature in accordance with the demands of enlightened thinking, the subject, which has no existence apart from the relationships of domination into which it must enter, itself becomes an object of sacrifice and hence a piece of nature.

This point largely explains the reversibility between myth and enlightenment. In explicit opposition to the traditional eighteenth- and nineteenth-century narratives of *mythos* and *logos*, of enlightenment thinking as a more or less complete liberation from the operations of the mythical mind, Adorno and Horkheimer argue that myth and enlightenment are necessarily implicated with each other. Just as myth, by intending "report, naming, the narration of the Beginning, but also presentation, confirmation, explanation" (1979: 8), ultimately enlightens, so does enlightenment itself, by its reduction of every phenomenon to the powerful logic of repetition, totality, and identity, *which themselves are the subjective principles of the mythical imagination,* inevitably succumb to the tranquil, nature-like realm of myth. Behind the panoramic thesis of historical reversion, however, the principle of self-preservation effects an absolute closure of the relationship between subject and object; for implied by this account is a complex notion of self-destructive violence and rage: against external nature, which is gradually disenchanted, stripped of subjective qualifications, and subjected to the subsumptive regimes of enlightenment thinking and technology; against internal nature, which is reified and ultimately sacrificed so as to be responsive to the objective demands of purposive reasoning; and against all conceptions of reason that resist a reduction to abstraction.

> Man's domination over himself, which grounds his selfhood, is almost always the destruction of the subject in whose service it is undertaken; for the substance which is dominated, suppressed, and dissolved by virtue of self-preservation is none other than that very life as functions of which the achievements of self-preservation find their sole definition and determination: it is, in fact, what is to be preserved.
>
> (Adorno 1979: 54–5)

By forgetting and repressing its own partaking in nature, the subject, as categorically detected in the sundering effects of Kant's formal conception of transcendental subjectivity, ends up destroying itself and its own substantiality. Under the conditions of late modernity, Adorno and Horkheimer contend, the subject is virtually liquidated.

It is crucial to note, though, that Adorno and Horkheimer never purport to dismiss the independent legitimacy of instrumental reason. Their genealogical point, rather, is that reason as such has become purely instrumental, and, hence, in Kant's terminology, that categorical rationality is now hypothetical rationality as an end in itself, implying that the pre-history of this predicament involves a violent metonymic displacement whereby one part of reason is taken for the whole, that is, as exhaustive of what reason can be. A central aim of the *Dialectic* is therefore to anticipate a more complete conception of reason.

Clearly, such a conception would focus on the notion of mimesis, which the authors never spell out in detail. Whereas, in Benjamin, mimesis refers to the domain of correspondence, a non-instrumental appropriation of the object which, over the course of history, has degenerated from sensuous immediacy to non-sensuous, linguistic mediation, in Adorno and Horkheimer mimesis becomes an anthropological component of man's relationship to nature. However, they never conceive of mimesis as an alternative to discursive rationality. Despite what many commentators have claimed, there is no "mimetic rationality" that can be dealt with separately and opposed to the narrow rationality of enlightenment thinking. On the contrary, from the very dawn of humanity, mimesis, especially in magic rituals whereby the practitioner seeks to influence the object by imitating it, became inscribed in rational procedures. Today, as Adorno argues in the *Negative Dialectics*, mimesis reappears as the qualitative moment of cognition — the ineradicable appearance of *haecceitas*, thisness, without which no scientific judgment would even be possible. However, the most radical and challenging form in which it appears is in the advanced work of art.

Epistemologically, the point of introducing the concept of mimesis is to re-think the Kantian notion of intuition in terms of an imitative disposition of a self toward the object. Rather than being appropriated by being brought under a universal, the subject responds non-subsumptively to the object by likening itself to it, thus exploring what Adorno and Horkheimer call the affinities between its own concepts and that for which they stand. In *Aesthetic Theory*, Adorno (1997a: 54) describes mimesis as "the nonconceptual affinity of the subjectively produced with its unposited other."[17]

I will return to the notion of mimesis in my discussion of *Aesthetic Theory* and elsewhere. In the next chapter I want to extend the argument of the *Dialectic* to examine Adorno's approach to fascism.

# 3

# APPROACHES TO FASCISM

No attempt to understand the political dimension of Adorno's work would qualify as serious unless it takes into account his response to fascism. The experience of fascism is the great political trauma to which Adorno always keeps returning. It makes itself felt on all levels of his intellectual activities: in his letters, in his private recollections, in his anthropological, political, and social-psychological theorizing, as well as in his metacritical analyses. With regard to the event of Auschwitz, Adorno even sees the need to postulate the occurrence of a radical historical break.[1] What Auschwitz entails, he argues, is the complete failure of culture, including its capacity to generate images of meaning and transcendence. After the fact of industrialized mass murder, any narrative of progress, emancipation, and liberation will sound hollow, and existence as such becomes a "guilt-context."

In this chapter I want to elaborate upon the ways in which Adorno approaches fascism — as political reality and as ideology. As we shall see, these approaches take various shapes, ranging from relatively traditional Marxist accounts to Freudian ones, as well as reflections that take their lead from anthropology, rhetoric, pedagogics, and even theology. I start by analyzing Adorno's political strategies in the 1930s. I then go on to discuss his theoretical take on fascism, and in particular his use of Freud's theory of group behavior. The final parts of the chapter deal with his perception of Auschwitz and the political situation in West Germany in the 1950s. While I point out several ambiguities and weaknesses, especially in his approach to the relationship between remembrance and pedagogy, my overall impression is that Adorno's writings on fascism are both powerful and important.

## The paradoxes of resistance

Hitler's accession to power in 1933 had an immediate impact on Adorno's life. Being of Jewish descent, he soon lost his *venia legendi* (the right to teach at a German university) as well as a number of other rights and entitlements. However, whereas most of his friends at the Institute for Social Research went into exile within a year after the Nazi takeover, Adorno decided to stay. In his eulogy at Adorno's burial in the Central Cemetery of Frankfurt on August 13, 1969, Horkheimer recalls how his attempt to persuade him to leave had been brushed aside with the following reply: "No Max, we have to stay here; we have to fight" (Kraushaar 1998: I, 457).[2] The discrepancy between this remark and the routinized disparagement, in the 1960s and later, of Adorno as an unpolitical aesthete, the lonely inhabitant of an ivory tower of endless theoretical negation, seems striking. Yet what kind of action is Adorno actually recommending?

It is clear that his political involvement in this period did not involve any illegal, underground action, at least not any that is known.[3] Indeed, as a result of the ruthless efficiency and brutality of the SA, SS, and the Gestapo, there was in general little direct or violent resistance in Germany, and when it did occur, its effect was highly limited. Nor did Adorno ever seem to have had much patience with positions which, like Jean-Paul Sartre's wartime celebration of the heroism and authenticity of pugnacity, sees the purity of individual will as the goal of political action. Inoculated, perhaps, by Heidegger's 1933 flight to official Nazi prominence, the very link between heroism and politics — in paragraph 74 of *Being and Time*, as well as in the infamous 1933 rectoral address — is completely alien to Adorno's thinking. For Adorno of the mid-1930s, the task of the anti-fascist intellectual consisted mainly in protecting existing culture from destruction. To fight against the Nazi *Gleichschaltung* (the attempt to replace the public sphere and the world of art with a centrally organized system of propaganda and nationalist symbolism) became a moral and political imperative.

In view of the great importance cultural politics had for the regime, while orienting one's efforts to the sphere of culture may at first glance seem unimpressive if considered as a form of resistance, it can hardly be characterized as easy or non-committal. Indeed, such activities may in some cases have had greater repercussions for the regime than many of the more "activist" forms of rebellion, most of which were quickly crushed anyway, and which too easily played up to the government's need to profile itself against concrete enemies. It also formed the basis for Adorno's later conception of how the activities of intellectuals can have practical influence. In the late "Marginalia to Theory and Praxis" (1998b: 277), for example, we find Adorno writing that "Wherever I have directly intervened in a narrow sense and with a visible practical influence, it happened only through theory." This is about the intellectual entering a public space in order to side with a given cause. But what happens to theory as soon as it starts to negotiate its way into the social field as a means towards some political end? Indeed, how far will Adorno allow theory to venture into the crude lawlessness of politics, and indeed even totalitarian politics?

In order to approach these questions, we need to look closer at what Adorno actually committed himself to during those difficult early years after the Nazi takeover. Having recently published his monograph on Kierkegaard, which appeared on the day that Hitler took power, most of his output in 1933 and 1934 consists of music criticism. During the 1920s, he had written for, and edited, influential journals of musicology and new music such as *Anbruch* and *Die Musik*, and he continued, in 1933, to publish in *Die Musik* even after it had been taken over as an official organ of the Nazi youth organization. Particularly instructive of the difficulties and paradoxes Adorno faced in trying to hibernate through everything that was going on is a review he contributed to *Die Musik* in 1934.[4] In it, he praised Herbert Müntzel, a composer Adorno felt the need to support, for having written a cycle of songs, *The Banner of the Persecuted*, that "was marked out as consciously National Socialist." The cycle, he continues, whose texts were selected from poems by the Nazi leader, Baldur von Schirach, evokes "the image of a new Romanticism ... perhaps of the type which Goebbels has defined as 'Romantic Realism'" (Adorno 1973–86: XIX, 332).

Shocking as it no doubt is to come across this passage in Adorno's *Gesammelte Schriften*, the impact this review had when quoted in an attack on him in *Diskus*, the student newspaper at the University of Frankfurt, in 1963, was considerable. Suddenly there seemed to be reason not only to ascribe opportunism to Adorno but to dismiss his position as a critic of fascist and anti-Semitic potential in West Germany. On the basis of the lack of charity with which many of Adorno's most hostile critics in the 1960s assessed his work, it could even be construed as an Adornian version of the Heidegger affair. Finally, on a more general level, it seemed to weaken Adorno's claim to seriousness. If the seriousness of an ethical belief is in part a function of whether the claimant avoids hypocrisy, then the ethics of anti-adjustment, of radical intellectual autonomy, which runs through all of Adorno's postwar writings, appears to be thrown into doubt. Put differently, if autonomy turns out performatively to be a principle that applies only *prima facie* and in accordance with strategic considerations, then Adorno has forfeited his right to be a moralist or teacher.

In his reply, Adorno rejects the charge of opportunism.[5] While regretting aspects of the review, in particular the (more or less implicit) endorsement of von Schirach's lyrics, the defense he offers is well worth quoting in some length:

Whoever reads my essay without prejudice is able to see my intention: to defend modern music; to help it survive the Third Reich; as I recall, Müntzel's very talented work was a good place to start. My emphasis alone on internal compositional legitimacy in contrast to the pressure "to be comprehensible and immediate" leaves no doubt about my goal. I wrote this at a time when anything like this was denounced as cultural bolshevism; they gave me special treatment in the exhibit on "Degenerate Music." If anyone wants to suspect me of trying to appease the new powers, my reply is that I would not have come to the public defense of the denounced music.

(Kraushaar 1998: II, 168)

Despite the unfortunate insinuations in *Diskus*, there can be no doubt that Adorno's review in no way, whether rhetorically, culturally or politically, allows comparison with Heidegger's notorious 1933 rectoral address, in which the Freiburg thinker not only defends the *de facto* regime but purports to uncover its essence as expressive of the destiny (*Geschick*) of the German people.[6] In the case of Heidegger, the charges involve more than simple opportunism or lack of principle: in 1933 he appears to have been an enthusiastic and deeply convinced National Socialist. Moreover, if Adorno can be said to have been opportunistic, then this would not have been because promoting Müntzel would offer much personal gain. The decision to stay in Germany had temporarily ended his chances of making an academic career, and there is little reason to conjecture that someone who had been branded by the regime as inferior would be able to help himself, whether financially or in terms of finding another position, by writing reviews of this sort. His opportunism (if this is the right word) or partial lack of principle is much rather to be understood if we take into account Adorno's belief, in the first couple of years after Hitler's accession to power, that the Third Reich could not possibly last very long. Strangely, at this point in modern history when pessimism, especially on the part of the European Left, was easier than ever to succumb to, the otherwise so apparently gloomy Adorno was quite optimistic.[7] The Nazis, he believed, would probably not hold on to power for very long:

> The genuine error lay in my incorrect evaluation of the situation, or, if you will, in the foolishness of someone for whom the decision to emigrate was very difficult. I believed that the Third Reich could not last long, and that one should stay in order to save whatever was possible. This and this alone led me to my naively tactical phrases. Against these phrases stands everything that I have written during my life, before and after Hitler took power. Anyone who reviews the continuity of my work cannot compare me with Heidegger, whose philosophy is fascist into its innermost cells.[8]

(Wiggershaus 1998: 87)

The Müntzel text poses a number of questions, and its significance cannot be reduced to a univocal lesson in the perils of social critique. It certainly exemplifies the application of Adorno's later so pronounced idea that politics can and should be pursued through art and criticism, that is, through the defense and interpretation of advanced cultural expressions. Of course, the question then becomes *how* this happens. For those of a slightly cynical bent, for whom interventions in the public sphere are mainly to be evaluated on the basis of instrumental criteria, the text may appear as a shrewd exercise in "parasitic" social criticism. Appealing to the ideals of the enemy (Goebbels' romantic realism, etc.) while simultaneously subverting them (by defending Müntzel's music), it contributes to the protection of culture from the politics of totalitarian co-optation. To others it may seem objectionable in its entirety. Yet the false empirical basis on which it was produced, namely that political change was more or less imminent, together with the uncomfortable compromises it involved, may have marked Adorno irrevocably. According to Kraushaar (1998: II, 673), his later vision of society as a closed, negative totality and his corresponding view of social criticism as demanding radical autonomy, allowing no compromises to be made, no *Mitmachen* to occur, can be traced back to his memory of the futile and intellectually dishonoring attempt at individually resisting Nazi Germany. I would agree, though, with Berman's (2002: 114) rejoinder to Kraushaar that while the experience of fascism undoubtedly shaped Adorno's views about the limits and difficulties of direct political intervention, it cannot simply be extrapolated to, and help to explain, Adorno's perception of politics in the postwar context. In addition to fascism, a complex constellation of factors, involving the rise of Stalinism, new and more insidious forms of social integration in the West, a traditional Marxist skepticism towards the public sphere, as well as a romantic investment in the model of aesthetic education, privileging the aesthetic over the political sphere while resisting their complete separation, must be taken into account. It should finally be stressed that the Müntzel text highlights a deep dilemma, not only for Adorno, but for the intellectual in general who seeks to resist an oppressive regime. On the one hand, it would seem that radical criticism must enter the vocabularies of those it seeks to correct, for otherwise it has no effect; on the other hand, as soon as it has entrenched itself in those vocabularies, it would seem that its critical edge stands in danger of getting lost. Adorno is remorseless in his fury against those, such as the later Lukács, whom he believes have relinquished the ideal of autonomy.[9] Yet there is clearly a sense in which the critic has to define his or her stance within the parameters set by his or her own culture. There is no definitive answer to this dilemma in Adorno's work. As we will see, the best place to look is in his aesthetics, in which critical autonomy becomes a function of the art work's capacity to negate immediate cultural intelligibility and transmissibility.

## Interpreting fascism

There is no unified approach to fascism among the members of the Institute for Social Research. While some, including Adorno in the first years after the National Socialist takeover, leaned towards the standard Marxist account — that fascism must be viewed as a response to the crisis of monopoly capitalism — others, such as Franz Neumann, Otto Kirchheimer, Friedrich Pollock, Horkheimer, and the Adorno of the war years and later, advocated a multi-faceted approach which appealed to explanatory mechanisms borrowed from economy, anthropology, psychology, and theories of culture.[10] One contribution in particular, Pollock's article "State Capitalism: Its Possibilities and Limitations" (Pollock 1941b), made a huge impression on Adorno and reinforced his sense of contrast between liberal and administered capitalism.[11] In this article, which was published in the final issue of the Institute's journal, Pollock argued that Western societies had undergone a transformation from private to state capitalism, and that state capitalism, most conspicuously in National Socialist Germany, was in its essence totalitarian. The term "state capitalism" is meant to suggest that this formation is "the successor of *private* capitalism, that the state assumes important functions of the private capitalist, that profit interests still play a significant role, and that it is not socialism" (1941b: 201). Theoretically, the implication of this view of society was that the Marxist account of the market, including its potential for crisis and change, had become irrelevant. In the new order prevailing especially in Nazi Germany, the economic laws that had previously governed the market-based coordination of production and distribution were replaced by a system of state manipulation and control. "Freedom of trade, enterprise and labor are subject to governmental interference to such a degree that they are practically abolished. *With the autonomous market the so-called economic laws disappear*" (1941b: 201).[12] According to Benhabib (1986: 159), the consequences of Pollock's theory for a critical theory of society are threefold. First, state capitalism is inherently static: it neutralizes all economically generated conflicts by transforming them into other forms of conflict. Second, the widespread etatization of society precludes the possibility of offering an analysis of its institutional structure that is grounded in political economy. Third, just as the freedom of exchange which characterized the self-understanding of agents in liberal capitalism disappears, so do the normative aspirations — of individualism, freedom, and equality — which accompanied this exchange erode. The system of state capitalism implies that the function of ideology changes. From now on a critic cannot simply point to the discrepancy between ideal and reality; the "truth-content" of classical ideological belief-formation has been demolished.

Pollock's account of state capitalism influenced Adorno and Horkheimer's rejection of traditional economic analysis in the *Dialectic of Enlightenment*. While not referred to directly, it makes itself in all sorts of oblique ways. It also plays a role in Adorno's 1942 essay "Reflections on the Theory of Class" and the important 1968 piece "Late Capitalism or Industrial Society." However, while its formative role is beyond doubt, there is reason to believe that the Marxist in Adorno took issue with some aspects of it, in particular the manner in which Pollock envisioned a non-antagonistic economy. In a letter to Horkheimer responding to an early version of Pollock's paper, Adorno expressed doubts about Pollock's "undialectical assumption that a non-antagonistic economy might be possible in an antagonistic society."[13] Although economic antagonism *appears* to have been eliminated, the fact of social antagonism unavoidably created non-apparent, though highly real, forms of economic antagonism. No extensive analysis of National Socialist Germany is needed in order to validate this point: despite widespread state interference in the economy, conflicts of interest between workers and owners, rather than being eliminated, were suppressed under a screen of totalitarian consensus-making.

It can also be objected to Pollock's distinction between private and state capitalism, and hence to Adorno's frequent use of it. As many critics have pointed out, Pollock idealizes both categories. There has never been a purely private capitalism devoid of etatist elements, nor does the late capitalism of corporate or state-based monopoly completely drive out the market-place as the focal point of exchange. Thus, while Adorno tends to paint a too rosy picture of capitalism in its pre-organized phase, occasionally seeing the market as a humane and rational space of social integration, he equally, and to some extent unjustly, demonizes post-organized capitalism.

In his 1942 study *Behemoth: The Structure and Practice of National Socialism*, another member of the Institute, the political sociologist Franz Neumann, presents a less claustrophobic view of National Socialist Germany. According to Neumann, the new German order, far from involving a complete abolition of economic antagonism, was bound to compete ideologically against the strong, objective interest of German workers. Although Neumann accepted that the German economy under totalitarian conditions was largely monopolistic, he believed, following Marx, that production itself is a rational process, involving inherent claims to the abolition of alienated labor. Insofar as the magical order of National Socialism — an order whose authority was sustained by means of intense propaganda and the cultic celebration of charismatic leadership — could not promise a *real* overcoming of the self-alienation of suffering workers, it was intrinsically unstable. Indeed, in the early 1940s, Neumann even believed that German workers were on the brink of collectively recognizing how wide the gap actually was between their own interest and the proclamations of National Socialist ideology, and hence that a socialist counter-revolution was within reach.

Although Adorno, in the 1969 lecture course *Introduction to Sociology*, recommends Neumann's study as the most accomplished analysis available of National Socialism,[14] *Behemoth* proved a lot less consequential for his own work than Pollock's account of the closed system of state capitalism. The reason for this is not surprising. In Adorno's view, Neumann, when observing the German regime, was far too optimistic about the possibility of distinguishing between myth and enlightenment, or magical delusion and rational interest. What distinguished Pollock's contribution was precisely its implicit appeal to a dialectic of enlightenment: that in modernity, enlightenment has become indistinguishable from myth, and thus that no interest can present itself as purely rational or uncontaminated by ideology. For Adorno, the system of symbolic exchange that we think of as National Socialism should be thought of as a unified, seamless totality: it is illusionary because it radically misrepresents the real interests of its citizens, yet its illusory character cannot be isolated and made transparent as easily as Neumann believes. In National Socialist Germany, Adorno argues, illusion has become second nature and thereby an essential dimension of social reality.

## Reappropriating psychoanalysis

Adorno's objections to Neumann does justice to Arendt's (1973: 459) famous assertion that twentieth-century totalitarianism meant that "everything is possible." Because the National Socialist order — with the greatest intensity in the camps, but also more generally — constituted a space wherein its inhabitants, especially its workers and its "internal enemies" (Jews, gypsies, communists, and so on), were stripped of their rights and political status, it transformed politics into biopolitics: the direct creation, manipulation, and destruction of man as a living being. In its lack of regard for the individual, totalitarianism reduced its subjects to the status of either resource or enemy.

One may think of this as a political operation — or perhaps rather as the end of politics. Yet Adorno's analysis is also about the functioning and effect of naked power. How entitled are we, however, to believe that power, in these circumstances, applies directly and without any subjective mediation? Is Adorno too strongly wedded to the image, familiar from Chaplin's *Modern Times*, of man as a cog in the wheel, a merciless extension and complement of the social machinery? Does he have an account of how individuals, inside such regimes, came to identify with power and subject themselves to it?

In the 1951 essay "Freudian Theory and the Pattern of Fascist Propaganda," Adorno tries to tackle this issue through a reading of

Freud's writing on mass psychology, developing, as we shall see, a theory of the relation between the individual and fascist society based on the neighboring concepts of narcissism and identification. Unlike Fromm, however, the Institute's officially designated theorist of psychoanalysis who in the early 1930s had toyed with the idea that psychoanalysis could illuminate the origin of fascism, Adorno (1991b: 130) limits its explanatory scope to the elucidation of its integrative achievements: "Psychological dispositions do not actually cause fascism; rather, fascism defines a psychological area which can be successfully exploited by the forces which promote it for entirely non-psychological reasons of self-interest." While objecting to the notion that psychoanalysis can refer to the causes, he insists on its theoretical necessity: "Without psychology, in which the objective constraints are continually internalized anew, it would be impossible to understand how people passively accept a state of unchanging destructive irrationality and, moreover, how they integrate themselves into movements that stand in rather obvious contradiction to their own interests" (1998b: 271).

When Adorno wrote the essay on fascist propaganda, more than twenty years had passed since he completed *The Concept of the Unconscious and the Transcendental Theory of the Mind*, his first major work on psychoanalysis from 1927. Among the motives that constantly accompany his approach to Freud is the Kantian problematic of *Mündigkeit*, the attempt to "think for oneself" and to fashion one's life in accordance with rational, self-chosen imperatives. In contrast to the general orientation of individuals in authoritarian societies, to be *mündig* means to be capable of resisting the claims of heteronomous, dogmatically adopted sources of authority. What Freudian psychoanalysis can offer with regard to the analysis of such societies, he argues, is a sustained set of reflections on ego-weakness, yet it also contains suggestions concerning the social conditions under which strong egos may develop. Essentially, a strong ego, which Adorno typically (and problematically) associates with early liberal capitalism, presupposes a successfully integrated super-ego. However, if the super-ego, as envisioned in Kantian moral theory, comes to dominate the psyche and thus exerts its aggression in ways that are detrimental to the integrity of the ego, then the result is a loss of freedom. There can be no freedom without some measure of spontaneity, and too much self-control may in fact stifle and rigidify the self.[15]

A sense of profound ambiguity about the notion of ego-strength runs through all of Adorno's writings. On the one hand, he defends it passionately, pointing to it as a condition of social resistance and deploring its demise in late modernity. Indeed, thinking itself, insofar as it involves a moment of identification and logical stringency, presupposes a coercive moment of self-discipline; thus the need for an effective incorporation of strong ego-ideals becomes subservient to the higher goal of enlightenment.

On the other hand, and in stark contrast to the celebration of ego-strength, "the identifying principle of the subject is itself the internalized principle of society" (Adorno 1973b: 241). In a society organized around the production of exchange value for its own sake, the individual finds herself entirely under the spell of compulsory identity, hence the identitarian dimension of the self is ultimately false. In Freud, this insight was articulated in terms of the essentially alien character of the super-ego: "The Freudian School in its heroic period ... used to call for a ruthless criticism of the super-ego as something truly heteronomous and alien to the ego. The super-ego was recognized, then, as blindly, unconsciously internalized social coercion" (1973b: 272).

In trying politically and speculatively to face up to this predicament, Adorno (1973b: 281) posits the utopia of the end of compulsory identity, the reconciliation of ego and id: "The subject's nonidentity without sacrifice would be utopian." A reconciliation of this kind would collapse the distinction between primary and secondary processes, pleasure principle and reality principle, that is, the antagonisms which on Freud's account give rise to psychic suffering, and bring about the conditions of true happiness. As in all of Adorno's intimations of utopia, however, a reconciliation in a false society would itself be false. In light of the antinomy of ego-strength and the utopianism of a reconciled ego, he therefore opts for the "coldness" of the former. The price agents pay for their autonomy may well be high, but as Freud himself argues in *Civilization and its Discontents*, no historical alternative seems available, thus Adorno's preferred option centers on anamnesis of the non-repressive and the non-coercive, rather than revolutionary praxis.

However, Adorno's Freud is not simply a theorist of autonomy. Of great importance to him is also the ability of psychoanalysis to testify to conflict or non-identity — between nature and culture, and between individual and society. As opposed to later attempts by Karen Horney and others to revise psychoanalysis and make it more amenable to direct social critique, Adorno insists, in his essay "Revisionist Psychoanalysis," on its essentially "dark" and anti-progressivist aspects: psychoanalysis should not be viewed primarily in clinical terms, as if the aim of analysis was successful social reintegration, but rather as an expression of the dialectic of enlightenment. Whereas Horney downplays the moment of biologism and idealizes "love" as something altogether different from the unruly dynamics of Freud's libidinal cathexes, Adorno emphasizes the somatic element of drives, the compulsion to repeat, and the death-drive. Like de Sade and Nietzsche, Freud becomes one of the "somber bourgeois" writers who rejects false notions of harmony and progress.

Adorno's account of Freud's *Group Psychology and the Analysis of the Ego* is his most explicit attempt to use psychoanalysis in order to analyze the nature of fascism: "It is not an overstatement if we say that Freud, though he was hardly interested in the political phase of the problem, clearly foresaw the rise and nature of fascist mass movements in purely psychological categories" (1991b: 115). In order to do justice to Adorno's use of this material, it must be noticed at the outset that he dismisses the popular view of fascism as being simply a disastrous reoccurrence of archaic id energies that had been suppressed during the long process of man's liberation from the immediate powers of nature. While certainly regressive both politically and psychologically, fascism represents a *controlled* reproduction and return of repressed content: it is *an administered rebellion*, hence an explanation is called for as to why and how these powerful id energies allow themselves to be exploited for authoritarian purposes. How can these energies be co-opted so easily?

Following Freud, Adorno views mass behavior of the form displayed, say, in the Nuremberg rallies as involving an archaic decomposition of the ego. Masses represent the antithesis of individuality and individual accountability: they effect a blurring of the boundaries between ego and alter; members shed those qualities that would characterize them as distinctive; and, as Le Bon argues, they lead the aggregate collective to act as a unity. As expressed in Hitler's slogan "*ein Führer, ein Volk!*," the group acts as if with "one will only." The main problem with Le Bon's otherwise powerful pre-analytic account, which Freud uses as a foil against which to profile his own view, is its inability to explain how this sense of unity comes about. Unsurprisingly, for Freud it is libido which functions as the glue which holds the group together. By regressing to the position of the primal horde described in *Totem and Taboo*, the members replace their internalized ego-ideals — which are weak as a result of the weakened positioned of the father in a crisis-ridden, unstable economy — with a common ego-ideal which they find embodied in a charismatic figure who figures as the all-powerful primal father. Literally hypnotized by this figure, the mass, through identification, internalize his demands and make them their own. Of course, for Freud identification always presupposes a narcissistic disposition: as the ego identifies with the object and places it inside itself, object-cathexis gives way to a strangely ambivalent love of the self. On the one hand, the follower, or rather the part of the follower's libido that is attached to his own ego and has not been molded into the idealized leader image, is gratified by the feeling the identification gives of "enlargement," of belonging to something "bigger" than oneself. The follower increases his sense of authority. On the other hand, since the leader image appears omnipotent due to its collusion with the archaic father-image of the primal horde, it is only possible to have a passive-masochistic attitude towards it. Thus, the follower not only loves and reveres authority, he also fears and hates it. Exploiting the mechanism of archaic identification and the gratification it offers, fascist propaganda creates what Freud (1959: 76) calls "a thirst for obedience."

An interesting complication arises as soon as one brings into the picture the primary jealousy of each other displayed by the members of the psychological "brother horde." In this Oedipal structure, the father possesses the women each one of them desire, hence the unity of the group would seem to be threatened by an all-out war of all against all. According to Freud, the only mechanism that permits the members to counter-balance their jealousy of each other is their similar love for the same object, i.e., the introjected father-figure: thus their coherence should be interpreted as a reaction formation, resulting in ambivalence, against their mutual aggression. Not only does Freud thereby throw light on what Adorno (1991b: 126) refers to as fascism's "undercurrent of malicious egalitarianism, of the brotherhood of all-compromising humiliation," he also provides a conception of how hatred against out-groups — foreigners, refugees, Jews, and so on — is generated. Since the members of the in-group cannot admit their latent aggression towards each other, they project their negative cathexis upon the out-group. The members of the out-group become scapegoats whose sacrifice satisfy the unconscious wish to inflict harm on one's peers.

While Adorno's use of Freudian theory is striking in its ability to engage critically with central features of fascist propaganda and politics, it is not without problems of its own. First, it appears to be in conflict with his claim, familiar from the more overtly philosophical writings, that theory — even scientific theory — must be self-reflective. Although Adorno made steps towards a reflective appropriation of Freud in *The Concept of the Unconscious and the Transcendental Theory of Mind*, his very first work on psychoanalysis, in his later essays he tends simply to *apply* psychoanalysis to social phenomena. Unlike his metacritical adaptation of moments in theorists like Kant, Hegel, and Nietzsche, in which he painstakingly uncovers the concrete social experiences that determine and mediate their thinking, Freud's metapsychological categories are virtually left untouched. In this region of Adorno's thinking, there is no dialogue between the concept and the thing itself, and no attempt to read off the non-identity of concept and object by exposing the concept to an experientially sensitive critique. Instead, mirroring Adorno's own Hegelian critique of Kant, form and content remain essentially unmediated by one another, and experience in the emphatic sense of letting "thoughts that are true ... incessantly renew themselves in the experience of the subject matter" (Adorno 1998b: 131) ends up being thwarted. There is great irony in the fact that in the late 1960s Habermas, a non-dialectical thinker if ever there was one, became the first figure within the history of the Frankfurt School to provide a metacritical analysis of Freud's metapsychology.[16]

Second, Freud's *Group Psychology and the Analysis of the Ego* is in many ways a puzzling and theoretically unsatisfactory work. Only in conjunction with writings such as *On Narcissism: An Introduction*, *Beyond the Pleasure Principle*, and *Mourning and Melancholia* does it make full sense. For example, while Freud had introduced the death-drive the year before writing *Group Psychology*, it makes no impact on his reflections on mass behavior, despite its apparent capacity to illuminate the nature of human aggression. This omission is all the more strange in light of Adorno's belief in the validity of this concept. Also, as Ricoeur (1970: 219) points out, its treatment of archaic identification itself is problematic. Is Freud referring to a primordial identification preceding every object-choice, or to a derived identification arising from libidinal object-choice through a regression to narcissism? If it is the latter, then Freud needs to supplement his account of archaic identification with the theory of narcissistic identification expounded elsewhere.

Finally, the scope of Adorno's Freudian hypothesis, though specified so as to rule out any ambition to explain the origin of fascism, is unclear. In the essay "Freudian Theory and the Pattern of Fascist Propaganda," it refers exclusively to fascism. However, in a number of other essays, including "Marginalia to Theory and Praxis" and the late "Sexual Taboos and Law Today," it is used to address Western liberal societies in the 1960s. It appears regularly in connection with the discussion of the culture industry and seems to make up an intrinsic element of Adorno's account of it. The question therefore arises as to whether Adorno really is entitled to endorse the wider scope-claim. Can both fascism and a phenomenon such as the culture industry really be analyzed with exactly the same set of psychological tools?

According to Christopher Lasch, whose book *The Culture of Narcissism* revived the social-theoretic relevance of narcissism for contemporary debate in the early 1980s, it is imperative to distinguish the hard, authoritarian replacement of ego-ideal that Adorno and Freud dealt with from the soft, anti-authoritarian narcissism that arose in Western societies in the aftermath of the sexual liberation and exploding consumerism of the 1960s. Whereas the first type of narcissistic disorder is characterized by obedience, aggression towards out-groups, and repressed rivalry, the second is characterized by an explicit orientation towards the self, hedonism, open rivalry, and a marked predisposition for depression. In Lasch's account, the absence of a centralized system of symbolic authority with which to identify leads to a different type of atrophy of the self than the one we find in an overtly authoritarian society. Individuals today are more prone than ever to conjure their identity from a number of different sources, many of which are fleeting and non-substantial: hence the appeal of "postmodern" or "Nietzschean" celebrations of the multiple self. In view of the discrepancies between these two types of narcissistic disorder, Adorno's application of a theory of fascist authoritarianism to the conditions of postmodern consumerism seems less than convincing.

61

## The authoritarian personality

Adorno did however participate in another project aimed at uncovering the nature of the authoritarian personality. In 1944, he co-authored *The Authoritarian Personality*, an empirical study of fascist mentality that made up one volume of the more comprehensive *Studies in Prejudice*, the Institute's collaborative effort (together with a number of external researches) to understand the meaning and political function of anti-Semitism. For Adorno, ideology was always intimately related to, and for all practical purposes identical with, prejudice; thus, *The Authoritarian Personality* was designed as a study of the authoritarian mentality that underpinned fascist anti-Semitism. How does the average fascist think? How does he justify his hatred towards Jews? How does he understand himself and his place in society? Those were some of the questions Adorno and his colleagues Else Frenkel-Brunswik, Daniel J. Levinson, and R. Nevitt Sanford addressed in this work. As Adorno (1998b: 235) put it many years later:

> Our intention, similar to that of psychoanalysis, was to determine present opinions and dispositions. We were interested in the fascist *potential*. In order to be able to work against that potential, we also incorporated into the investigation, as far as was possible, the *genetic* dimension, that is, the emerging of the authoritarian personality.

By conducting extensive interviews in the United States and, later, in postwar West Germany, the two fundamental tasks allotted to the project was: (1) to chart the personality structure of persons susceptible to anti-Semitism, and (2) to develop a set of indicators capable of measuring susceptibility to anti-Semitism.

Among the most controversial aspects of the later so famous study (which largely established Adorno's reputation in the United States as an empirical sociologist) was the so-called F-scale (fascist scale), whose purpose it was to register the components — aggression, anti-intellectualism, conventionalism, cynicism, and so on — which according to the researchers distinguished the fascist mentality from the liberal-democratic one. As Wiggershaus (1988: 413) puts it, "In the eyes of the Berkeley group, the F-scale, with its non-ideological, purely 'psychological' items, offered virtually direct access to personality structure." By inventing questions that, when addressed to the interviewees, were supposed to be able to record their degree of conformity with some or all of these components, they hoped to uncover, both qualitatively and quantitatively, the structure of fascist mentality, as well as how this structure was influenced by additional parameters, researched in other sections of the interviews, such as family background, childhood, sexuality, social relations, and social and political views more generally. The results of the interviews are not particularly surprising, especially for someone who is familiar with Adorno and Horkheimer's remarks on the fascist character elsewhere. As one commentator glosses them,

> the essential traits of the fascist character were: a rigid commitment to dominant values, mainly conventional middle-class values such as outwardly correct, unobtrusive behavior and appearance, efficiency, cleanliness, success along with a pessimistic and contemptuous view of humanity, a readiness to believe that uncontrollable, dangerous events were taking place in the world and that sexual depravity could be detected everywhere; extremely hierarchical thoughts and feelings, with submissiveness towards idealized authorities in one's own group and contempt for outside groupings and everything deviant, discriminated against or weak; anti-introversion, i.e. defense against self-reflection, sensibility and fantasy, with a simultaneous tendency towards superstition and stereotyped misperception of reality.
>
> (Wiggershaus 1988: 414)

This is hardly original. What sets *The Authoritarian Personality* apart from many other studies of the same topic is the methodological, political, and philosophical assumptions that form, as it were, its epistemological background. A particularly thorny issue, obviously, is how the ideal fascist mentality was constructed. As many critics have noted, despite all its sophisticated theoretical discussion, the study contains a number of unthematized assumptions that may have pre-determined the choice of parameters as well as the questionnaires in which those parameters were interpreted and reflected. According to Jay, Adorno's ideal type of fascist mentality is arrived at "by simply inverting the features that define the (ideological) image of the liberal bourgeois individual."[17] Thus, as opposed to what Adorno seems to imply, his view of authoritarianism is uncritically inscribed within a network of unquestioned expectations regarding normality.[18] In my view, since the opposite of having a perspective or viewpoint would be to appeal to the fiction of a "view from nowhere," Adorno could concede this point without much damage to the project. There is no proper reason to think that he ought to have aspired to eliminate all unthematized assumptions. A related and, in all likelihood, potentially more hard-hitting objection, proposed by Jarvis (1998: 85), is that Adorno, in *The Authoritarian Personality*, gets himself into conflict with his own requirement that experience should be interpreted and not classified. The very rigidity of the criteria being used — their reified character — may easily prevent them from revealing historically complex and dynamic truths.

63

In more direct political terms, *The Authoritarian Personality* represents a break with the more or less explicit Marxist presuppositions that guided the Frankfurt School's empirical research in the 1930s. Certainly, the tendency to ascribe explanatory power to social-psychological categories when viewed in at least partial isolation from their socio-historical emergence is a strong indication of this tendency. While the study does relate the formation of mentality to specific dimensions of the social world such as the family, education, and so on, it conspicuously abstains from relating its "cultural" aspects to its "economic." The silence about Marxism and its central categories is consistent with the thrust of the *Dialectic of Enlightenment* on which Adorno worked simultaneously. It is, however, in conflict with much of the work that Adorno produced after the war.

## Anti-Semitism

In the recently published 1964/65 lecture-course *Zur Lehre von der Geschichte und von der Freiheit*, Adorno discusses nationalism with particular reference German history. While the early formation of nation-states in Europe can in general be viewed as a progressive event in that it made possible the dissolution of medieval theocracy and the establishment of a liberal political order in which technological and scientific progress became possible, the nationalistic frenzy in the nineteenth century, which accompanied the hegemonic struggle for colonial expansion, was largely regressive. In the Germany of the nineteenth and early twentieth centuries, nationalistic impulses were especially ferocious — a fact Adorno ascribes partly to its late establishment (the German nation was united in 1871), and partly to a fear and denial of the enlightenment values of cosmopolitanism and tolerance. The Hegel, he argues, of the *Lectures on the Philosophy of History* and the *Elements of the Philosophy of Right* — in Adorno's view his two most ideological writings — is highly illustrative in this regard. For even though Hegel wants to overcome every positivity, he not only leaves the category of the nation untouched by dialectical mediation but hypostatizes it to a point where it becomes a sacred entity, a representative, as Hegel famously writes, of God on earth.

A full understanding, however, of the blind commitment to the nation, which under Nazism was cloaked in quasi-biologistic and vitalist terms, requires that we take into account Horkheimer and Adorno's discussion of anti-Semitism in the *Dialectic of Enlightenment*. Even though their notion of anti-Semitism draws on the psychoanalytic and empirical investigations that we have already looked at, and in a sense is incomplete without them, it also contains a distinctly, though highly complex, anthropological component that now has to be addressed.

While Fascism, in light of the dialectical link between enlightenment and domination, can be seen as a kind of organized regression from rationalized society to a world of magic that allows a false or simulated version of mimetic behavior to take place (Adorno encourages his readers to think of "the skulls and disguises, the barbaric drum beats, the monotonous repetition of words and gestures" (1979: 185) that were prevalent in the fascist formula), anti-Semitism, more specifically, arises from the need for scapegoats. Like Sartre, in *Anti-Semite and Jew*, Horkheimer and Adorno deny that there is any intrinsic connection, causal or otherwise, between the Jew, or the Jewish people, as such and anti-Semitic hatred. On a deeper level, the Nazis did not target Jews *because* — or *only* because — they had certain features or represented certain interests. Rather, in the eyes of the anti-Semite, the Jew is a figure who simply embodies a specific role assigned to him or her by the nature of the scapegoat logic. But what is this logic? How does it come about that the search for scapegoats arises? According to Horkheimer and Adorno, as a result of their visibility in the sphere of economic circulation, the Jews were identified with this sphere; thus, due to the intransparency of capitalism with which they were associated, the Jews were seen as greedy capitalists whose cosmopolitan "rootlessness" was destructive of the immediate social relations characteristic of the constructed image of the *Vaterland*. However, this negative identification did itself come about as the result of a projection onto the Jews of a claim to be able to transcend the authoritarian order of identitarian exchange. The anti-Semite hated the Jew not because he or she was rich or powerful but because the Jew was seen to represent everything that the logic of domination — the dialectic of enlightenment — forced him to reject or dispel:

> No matter what the Jews as such may be like, their image, as that of the defeated people, has the features to which totalitarian domination must be completely hostile: happiness without power, wages without work, a home without frontiers, religion without myth.
>
> (1979: 199)

The figure of the Jew is thus closer to the anti-Semite than he or she would ever be prepared to admit; indeed, it is the anti-Semite's own impulses — the claims of nature, as it were, of everything that organized compulsion, the condition of both society and subjectivity, outlaws—that "are attributed to the object — the prospective victim" (Adorno 1979: 187). Consequently, the mere fact that a person is called a Jew becomes an invitation to violence — a violence which repeats the age-old sacrifice of otherness and mimesis on which civilization is predicated.

Adorno and Horkheimer's argument does not presuppose that the Jews succumbed to the logic of mimesis, and certainly not to the "bad mimesis" of fascist regression. Indeed, in the eyes of the anti-Semite, they have by no means transgressed the laws of civilization. On the contrary, the Jewish proscription on images, the taboo on mimesis, means that the Jews, while being defined by their mysterious relation to non-identity, in fact represent culture's triumph over nature. In other words, the Jews — and Judaic monotheism in general — are seen *both* as the epitome of the principle of civilization *and* as its Other. Persecuting Jews, then, becomes a form of revenge for civilization's triumph over nature. The Jews are those who have most perspicuously repressed or extinguished in themselves that which we all secretly long for.

Critics of the analysis argue that Adorno and Horkheimer naturalize anti-Semitism and construe it as an unavoidable and inherited mechanism of humanity. According to Anson Rabinbach (2002: 144), in their account "Antisemitism is not, as the conventional arguments go, either the result of Christian Jew-hatred or modern scientific racial thinking, but emerges at the threshold of human evolution." Considering the quasi-biologistic form in which the typical anti-Semite formulates his hatred, Rabinbach's point becomes all the more urgent. In Horkheimer and Adorno's defense, however, it must be noted that although they aim to provide an anthropological explanation of the phenomenon of anti-Semitism, it does not follow that its exercise is simply a matter of adhering to one's culturally deep-seated empirical inclinations. The anti-Semite is not a robot, or a mere by-product of civilization's tragic triumph over nature. Following Kant, human beings are for Adorno at least partly rational creatures. While principles and maxims of action are often accepted without much deliberation, no belief can become part of an individual's motivational set of beliefs unless he or she, in one way or another, chooses to adopt it and take some measure of responsibility for it. Rabinbach's point would only be damaging if Adorno was a thoroughgoing naturalist who rejected the existence of human rationality entirely.

Rabinbach (2002: 145) also suggests that the *Dialectic of Enlightenment* "ultimately holds the Jews accountable for their own fate." While there is some truth to this assertion insofar as Horkheimer and Adorno — and especially Horkheimer — occasionally attribute to the Jews an exceptionally strong inclination towards "civilizatory virtues" and argue that this is the real reason for their sacrifice,[19] it hardly follows that such virtues — provided that their ascription to the Jews as an ethnic group makes any sense whatsoever, which is doubtful — makes them accountable for their own persecution. For the Jews to be accountable in the sense Rabinbach outlines, they would have to have knowingly done something that they knew could cause "offense" to someone, or they would at least have to have been aware of the possibility that some of their actions could threaten the (however unconscious) interests of others. In this case, however, the very notion of such intentionally inflicted damage is inapplicable.

## Extreme evil and remembrance

The significance of Auschwitz for Adorno's thinking can hardly be exaggerated. Not only does it represent the negative culmination or fulfillment of history — the encapsulation, as it were, of the dialectic of enlightenment — it also changes for ever the conditions of human self-understanding. After Auschwitz, Adorno submits, culture itself, "including its urgent critique, is garbage" (1973b: 367). Human thought, especially in its most advanced conceptual articulation as negative dialectics, must from now on make sure that no theodicical content, or no immediate movement towards the Absolute, enters the terms and conditions of its practice.[20] Auschwitz places future generations in a relationship of unconditional responsibility: to make sure that it never happens again. If politics is to be possible, it must take place in a move against history, a confrontation of the totalizing horror of human history by a demand for justice that ultimately will remain non-political, vigilant, and highly vulnerable.

But how does Adorno understand the nature of the kind of events for which Auschwitz has come to stand as emblematic? What kind of analysis does he provide of the very phenomenon of industrialized mass murder? Surprisingly, perhaps, he never develops anything like a full-blown sociological or historical account. What interests him, rather, and which he discusses in the final and extraordinary chapter of the *Negative Dialectics*, "Meditations on Metaphysics," as well as in the recently published lecture-course on metaphysics, is what he can say as a philosopher about the extermination camps.

For Adorno, Holocaust appears as a systematic process, a machinery, aimed at one thing only: to ensure the complete destruction of individuals — or rather, the individuality of the individual. What took place in the camps, he writes, was that "The last, the poorest possession left to the individual [was] expropriated" (1973b: 362). The victims' moral worth and integrity were not allowed to be dependent on descriptions and predicates applying to them as individuals. All that mattered was the fact that, from the perspective of the system, one belonged to a certain category — Jew, Gypsy, and so on — a category whose membership was associated with inferiority. By stripping the victims of every individualizing item, including their clothes, family, habits, and professional activities, and by treating them as if they were strictly interchangeable, the perpetrators did in fact succeed, Adorno argues, in their aim of eliminating individuality, leaving physical death as the inevitable outcome. Thus, "in the concentration camps it was no longer an individual who died, but a specimen ..." (1973b: 362), that is, a sample or instance of a class, genus, or whole, where only the universal counted as ground for assessment.

In order to illustrate this claim philosophically, Adorno turns to Hegel, arguing that Hegel's closed system of absolute idealism can be seen to anticipate, or be complicit with, the world of the extermination camps. While the objection to Hegelian claims to totality has justifiably gained credence in much post-Auschwitz thinking and theology, including the work of Emile Fackenheim (who largely builds on Rosenzweig), it is not clear that it makes full sense on Adorno's construal. Indeed, since the association between Hegel and industrialized mass murder is based simply on the perceived similarity or analogy between the two (they both aim at achieving some form of integration), it doesn't follow that the integration taking place in Auschwitz was, in any sense, of the same nature as the integration that occurs whenever, as in Hegel's attempted identification of identity and non-identity, a particular is logically determined by a universal. In resting his case against Hegel on this claim, it would seem that Adorno risks either reducing the severity of Auschwitz or overestimating the (negative) significance of Hegel's thinking.

Another problem with Adorno's claim that "it was no longer an individual who died, but a specimen" is its disturbing ambiguity as between meaning that the victims were treated *as if* they were not unique and irreplaceable individuals (such that one important form of resistance would be to protect one's sense of being a unique person) and meaning that the *Endlösung* implied that the perpetrators succeeded in eradicating every possible perspective from which the victims could be viewed in terms of any other characteristic but their corresponding generic concept (i.e., their strict identity with other victims). From what is known about the Holocaust, the first interpretation seems prone to underestimate the efficiency of mechanisms of depersonalization in the camps and is inconsistent, moreover, with Adorno's emphasis on the absoluteness of integration (his stress on the absence of any remainder). The second interpretation is consistent with the claim to absoluteness but highly provocative, since it seems to call into question the intuition that those who died, even though they were not considered as such by the perpetrators, were indeed singular human beings with a unique and unexchangeable history and identity.

It is possible that Adorno did not consider this distinction. Equally possible, however, is it that he sought to retain the equivocation between *being treated in accordance with* and *being in effect reduced to* the general determination. Hannah Arendt (1973) famously writes about how totalitarian terror eliminates the individual (and the distance between individuals), although in her work this process is viewed in terms of a loss of the capacity for reflective thinking and judging more than in terms of a loss of criteria by which to individuate people. On the other hand, Agamben (2000), referring to the so-called *Muselmänner* who seem to have identified with the imperatives imposed upon them and paradoxically managed to stay alive as the result of doing so, emphasizes identitarianism as the key to understanding the extermination camps. According to Agamben (1999: 63), the *Muselmann* ... "is the site of an experiment in which morality and humanity themselves are called into question." In whichever way one chooses to approach Adorno's thinking about Auschwitz, it is evident that in order to be fully coherent his account needs to be spelled out in much more detail — sociologically as well as psychologically.

It should be added, though, that Adorno seems to have felt very strongly that there are limits to what can be said about Auschwitz. In his view, there is a sense in which Auschwitz remains in excess of the boundaries of intelligibility; indeed, only the advanced art work — Beckett's *Endgame* — is ultimately able to approximate the radical loss of meaning that industrialized mass murder represents.[21]

What are the implications of Auschwitz, and indeed of the Nazi period in general, for the postwar situation in Germany? Adorno addresses this question in two important essays: "The Meaning of Working Through the Past," from 1959, and "Education after Auschwitz," published in 1966 — both of which should be read and interpreted in conjunction with one another. Without explicitly mentioning his opponents, Adorno frames these essays by objecting to at least two views that were widespread during the Adenauer period. The first is the view, common to many in the liberal political establishment, according to which 1945 represented a more or less clean break in German history — a sudden shift from totalitarianism to a wholesale acceptance of Western values of democracy and freedom. The second is the more conservative view according to which there exists a deep cultural continuity — the German tradition — going all the way back to the medieval period that, while threatened by the Hitler regime, could be reactualized and cultivated after the war was over and the country back on track. Both of these views can be said to express complacency about the present; they both take *Vergangenheitsbewältigung*, the working through of the catastrophic past, to be irrelevant to the political health of the present; they both consider National Socialism to be a thing of the past.[22]

Adorno's most astonishing claim in these influential writings is that National Socialism should not be thought of as having abruptly come to an end in 1945. National Socialism "lives on" in the mind-sets and institutions of the Federal Republic. To think that it has been eradicated, and that the new German society has completely shed its authoritarian past, would be both irresponsible and unwise: "I consider the survival of National Socialism *within* democracy to be potentially more menacing than the survival of fascist tendencies *against* democracy" (1998b: 90). Democracy may well have a stronger foothold now than in the Weimar period, yet complacency could be fatal. Adorno's claim is both empirical and moral: not only is there a real risk that National Socialism could rise again, but at stake is also an obligation, stemming from the nature of the political crimes themselves, to which Germans, though not exclusively, stand in a special relationship. Ultimately, the survival of democracy depends neither on constitutional or republican patriotism, nor on the belief that a clear historical break with the past has been made, but on remembrance, on keeping the memory of the dead alive.

Remembrance, however, involves attentiveness to the present, as well as the relation between the past and the present; it is not enough simply to concentrate on the past and the bygone. "The past will have been worked through only when the causes of what happened then have been eliminated. Only because the causes continue to exist does the captivating spell of the past remain to this day unbroken" (1998b: 103). Unless the economic organization of society is changed such that the majority of people who are now treated as objects can step out of their state of political and psychological immaturity, there is little hope for a stable democracy. Political vigilance thus requires a persistent critical analysis of contemporary social phenomena. However, it also entails exposing culture to the memory of the death camps. If Auschwitz represents a catastrophe of meaning, art in particular must attest to this catastrophe by withholding meaning: "For the sake of reconciliation, authentic works must blot out every trace of reconciliation in memory" (Adorno 1997a: 234). Although Adorno refuses to elaborate upon its implications for politics, it ought to be clear that political action from now on has to relentlessly call itself into question, resisting the drive to reduce the distance between itself and the absolute. Politics should not, as in Hegel, Marx, or Lukács, be structured around the figure of an immanent realization of the absolute; rather, in order to keep faith with itself it needs, as Derrida (1999: 80) argues elsewhere, to exist in a state of perpetual disruption, interiorizing (yet without domesticating) the ethical transcendence and claim to non-identity that only art can intimate.[23]

Of particular importance is the connection Adorno draws, in "Education After Auschwitz," between politics and pedagogy. In a deliberately inverted relationship to the classic (Platonic) belief that the well-being of the *polis* requires that the exercise of political virtue is sustained by a successful program of education, Adorno introduces pedagogy as a means to avoid the worst: "All political instruction ... should be centered upon the idea that Auschwitz should never happen again" (1998b: 203). Both children's education as well as the intellectual, cultural, and social climate within which adolescents and adults orient themselves should promote anti-authoritarian behavior as well as the values of critique and *Selbstdenken*; and knowledge of the causes that led to the German catastrophe should be promulgated.

While some of Adorno's specific recommendations, such as rooting out many of the ancient German customs and initiation rites that, in the name of promoting hardness and self-discipline, inflict physical pain, have long since been realized in the Federal Republic and later in the post-1990 Germany, others may seem rather arbitrary. His diatribes against the coun-

70

tryside, for example, in which it is argued that the rural populace is less prone to "debarbarization" than that of any other social group and that "one of the most important goals of education is the debarbarization of the countryside" (1998b: 196) is hardly more than quaint. What is interesting about the essay is less its concrete recipes for an anti-authoritarian, anti-fascist Germany than the cautious optimism — so at odds with the pessimism of the culture industry thesis — being displayed in it. As opposed to the standard view of Adorno as being skeptical of *every* institution in late-modern society, holding that there is no place for macro-based social practices that can encourage and sustain individual autonomy, he does believe at the time of writing this essay that it is imperative that such a society invents something like a network of institutionally enforced apparatuses in order to discourage authoritarianism.

Now this obviously begs the question as to whether such institutions really are able to foster individual autonomy, or whether they simply involve new and more oblique forms of social domination. According to Foucault (1979), autonomy must always be viewed as an effect of the apparatuses that produce and regulate customs, habits, and productive practices. Autonomy or accountability is for Foucault always a by-product of normalization, the way in which disciplinary power rules by structuring the parameters and limits of thought and practice, sanctioning and prescribing normal and/or deviant behavior. While Adorno is right in drawing a clear distinction between acts of direct manipulation and social control (as in political propaganda, say, or perhaps, if we accept Adorno's alignment of the two, in certain manifestations of the culture industry), and acts of education aimed at releasing in its subjects the capacity for critical self-reflection, it is not clear that he is entitled to draw it as a distinction between authoritarianism *per se* and its antithesis. It is more likely that some of his claims about how the culture industry generally succeeds in manipulating *from within*, as it were, forming subjectivities, applies to the system of educational techniques as well. The danger with being too optimistic about the ability of modern educational institutions (nurseries, schools, universities, and so on) to create conditions for critical self-reflection in the Kantian sense that Adorno refers to is that it could prevent an awareness of how the disposition to form and respect apparently self-chosen norms of thinking and action may well be a result of practices that themselves are of a disciplinary nature. It is not that such practices are necessarily unwanted; it is that we need to understand how they work and how they generate consent and normality, and Adorno fails to provide such an analysis.

4

# THE POLITICS OF CULTURE

No concept in Adorno has been more influential than that of the culture industry. In penetrating detail, his approach to culture reveals how essential dimensions of a liberal conception of democracy — autonomous agency, a relative independence of culture from the systemically induced imperatives of economic and administrative reproduction, as well as the availability of a wide variety of interpretive models by which to engage critically with society — are deeply threatened in late modernity. Yet while its pioneering role within fields such as political theory, sociology, and media studies can hardly be denied, the concept of the culture industry has often been viewed as elitist or too reductive to be able to grasp the realities of modern mass culture. There seems to be a serious conflict between, on the one hand, Adorno's claim to speak in the name of a future, reconfigured culture, and, on the other, his extraordinary distance from cultural expressions that opponents of his work have deemed subversive.

The aim of this chapter is to rethink the political and ideological implications of Adorno's theory of culture. I argue against certain typical misreadings of it, and I seek to recontextualize it within the parameters of what could roughly be thought of as the postmodern. Although I question his strong opposition between high and popular culture, the central thesis that I seek to defend is that Adorno, if read so as to avoid some of his equivocations and false generalizations, presents a powerful alternative to the current dominance of postmodern modes of conceptualizing culture. While anticipating the postmodern presupposition of a wholly commodified sphere of cultural production, he insists on the need to question cultural totality in the name of its unpresentable other.

## The self-perpetuating character of late capitalism

On the most immediate level, the *explanandum* of the theory of the culture industry is the longevity of late capitalism. Adorno applies his radicalized version of Lukács' notion of commodification, or commodity fetishism, to the realm of culture, arguing that culture has now (in the twentieth and, by extension, twenty-first centuries) entered an era of self-perpetuating same-ness or identity, leaving virtually no room whatsoever for items or markers that point beyond the closed system of symbolic reproduction.

While bourgeois culture of the nineteenth century existed in a state of semi-autonomy, offering individual artists and writers the chance to produce work that was not determined by its exchange value, the culture industry, Adorno argues, imposes a thoroughgoing commodification. In line with the concomitant rise of monopolization and mass production for mass markets, cultural entities shed their claim to individuality, of being valued for their own sake and on their own terms, and become calculable *means* for profit: "The cultural commodities of the industry are governed ... by the principle of their realization as a value, and not by their own specific content and harmonious formation. The entire practice of the culture industry transfers the profit motive naked onto cultural forms" (Adorno 1991b: 86)

By inscribing the production and consumption of such entities into the logic of commodity fetishism, Adorno proposes that what Kant, in the *Critique of Judgment*, took to be the minimal yet necessary require-ment for an item to have cultural or artistic value, namely its capacity to elicit a disinterested pleasure, enabling its recipient to value it for its own sake and on its own terms, has now become irrelevant and impossible to apply: endowed with a false and compensatory sense of immediacy, autonomy, or aura, such entities can only generate pseudo value, hence valuing itself, the critical adjudication of markers of worth within culture, loses its rationale. Monopolized mass production saps culture of any possible claim to experiential reconfiguration and, in the final instance, disconnects it from utopian promises of any sort.

The theory of the culture industry is a theory of culture under the condition of late capitalism. Like the Marxist critiques of ideology it seeks to inherit and transform, it aims to explain why social and therefore historical forms seem to have petrified and congealed into reified struc-tures of apparent timelessness. On such a view, politics becomes neutralized and drained of genuine alternatives to status quo; and despite huge and manifest social problems, there is widespread political indiffer-ence. While democracies require plurality as one of their essential conditions, according to Adorno, contemporary Western societies have been progressively evacuated of dissenting voices.

However, the culture industry thesis does not only relate to capitalist societies in the West, it also seeks to come to terms with the rise of totali-tarianism in the pre-World War II Europe. When Adorno and Horkheimer introduced it in the second chapter of the *Dialectic of Enlightenment* (after the long excursions on Homer and de Sade), they contributed to a discus-sion that had been going on among members of the Institute for Social Research for more than a decade. The object of this discussion can be traced back to the Institute's negative reaction to the unsuccessful German revolution of 1918–19, yet also to the failure of the Weimar Republic to establish and consolidate a democratic culture in Germany, which for the Institute of the early 1930s was the overshadowing political phenomenon to be addressed and analyzed. In the cooperative research project *Studies on Authority and Family* (1935–6), as well as in Pollock's theory of state capitalism, which, as we saw in the previous chapter, directly influenced Adorno, we find attempts to theorize social and political regression — the collapse of individual accountability and the formation of non-democratic systems of social integration. Although the theory of the culture industry is historically indexed to the experiences Adorno (I concentrate on him from now on, to the exclusion of Horkheimer whose interest in culture was less pronounced) had in the United States before and during the World War II of the monopolization and commercialization of cultural production and transmission, its ramifications — namely the desire to grasp the nature of authoritarian societies *per se* — thus extend much wider.

Since the explanatory scope is so wide (indeed it is never clearly demarcated), it is hardly surprising that the hypothesis of the culture industry has seemed easily refutable. Indeed, Adorno's tendency to assimilate essential aspects of his perception of the capitalist culture industry to features of fascist propaganda does an obvious disservice to the articulation of the central intuitions behind his analysis.[1] To treat, as he occasionally does, the products of the culture industry as straightforward political propaganda does not do justice to their specific *modus operandi*. Conversely, a speech by Goebbels or any other symbolic artifact of fascist propaganda must be approached with different theoretical tools than those which Adorno employs in order to theorize capitalist mass culture. The equivocation between accounting for the commercialization of everyday life, on the one hand, and analyzing mechanisms of authoritarian consensus formation in totalitarian states, on the other, makes it difficult to locate his claims within a sufficiently specific mode of cultural transmission. I therefore stipulate that the theory of the culture industry should be restricted to Western democracies in their late capitalist phase. (Of course, exactly when this phase may be said to commence has been the focus of a lot of dispute within Marxist theory. Huyssen (2002: 29–56) plausibly argues that Adorno in effect draws on his work on mass culture in his analysis of Richard Wagner, thus extending its scope at least back to the last three decades of the nineteenth century. This conjecture is coherent with the standard Frankfurt School view, namely that the transition from a liberal to a more organized form of capitalism occurred in the 1870s.)

Adorno's interest in mass culture harks back to his essays on jazz, as well as the important "On the Fetish Character in Music and the Regression of Listening," all of which were written in the mid-1930s. However, it was not until his work on the Princeton Radio Project and the

74

later exposure to American sociology of mass culture — to social theorists such as Dwight MacDonald and C. Wright Mills — that his thinking about the fate of culture in late capitalism achieved sufficient systematicity to amount to a real theory.[2] While some of the existing material on mass culture was unblushedly elitist, rejecting technological media such as film and television out of hand, Adorno sought from the outset to avoid the simple binarisms of traditional cultural criticism.

He thus commences his discussion in the *Dialectic of Enlightenment* with a polemic against the widespread notion of a *de facto* cultural pluralism. For both conservatives and present-day multiculturalists, contemporary culture appears fragmented, chaotic, and differentiated: rather than a centralized structure of symbolic authority, there are numerous forms of semi-autonomous or wholly autonomous circuits and practices of symbolic interaction and exchange. Of course, while the conservative, in the name of unity, calls for a restoration or renewal of symbolic authority (the church, the family, the aristocracy, the classical work of art, and so on), the multiculturalist, in the name of plurality and difference, calls for the acceptance and celebration of cultural impurity and diversity. An instructive example of the clash between these two views is the so-called culture wars that occurred in the United States in the 1990s. At the center of these "wars" stood the cultural unity of the standard college curriculum and whether a return to "the Western canon" was preferable to a more liberal or new historicist dissolution of what critics saw as the traditional emphasis on "dead, white males." Adorno completely circumvents this type of debate. In his view, "culture now impresses the same stamp on everything. Films, radio and magazines make up a system which is uniform as a whole and in every part" (1979: 120).

Adorno's claim makes explicit use of a Hegelian figure: it presupposes a notion of totality, as well as the *false* reconciliation or identity between the general (the system of cultural exchange or capitalism as such) and the particular (the product and its consumption) within this (false) totality. Each particular — each manifestation of culture — not only expresses the general but embodies, or is stamped with, it completely. By violently subsuming the particular under the general, the particular, rather than achieving determinacy as the mediated particular in Hegel is supposed to do, gets obliterated: it only serves to affirm the socially enforced system of cultural exchange itself. The wholly commodified culture industry thus signifies the reign of totalitarian myth — a world of repetition and sameness from which notions of otherness, heterogeneity, difference, the qualitative, and the new have been expelled or liquidated: "The same babies grin eternally out of the magazines; the jazz machine will pound away for ever" (Adorno 1979: 148). In the eternal repetition of the same, the sheer self-presence of the commodity screens both nature and history: the advertisement on the billboard represents, and ultimately transforms, its object into an image, an exchangeable item, a signifier, for which there is no origin or narrative horizon of significance. The spectacular world of the culture industry is thus evacuated of meaning.

Although this thesis (about uniformity) is typically (but not falsely) interpreted as a claim about standardization and about how new technologies of mass distribution combined with more efficient networks of advertising and centralized control have amounted to greater cultural uniformity, it is important to note that it does allow for a great deal of surface plurality. There is obviously an extraordinary variety of cultural products, and new ones are continuously being presented for consumption. According to some of its critics, however, this variety seriously weakens the theory of the culture industry. Thus Hohendahl (1995: 143), for example, argues that "Contemporary mass culture does not confront us as a unified system speaking with one voice; its obvious variety in organization, recipients, style, and formal structures calls for a different explanation." While Hohendahl makes a valid point, he fails to engage with Adorno's view that part of the enormous influence wielded by mass-produced cultural consumption must be explained by the industry's capacity to cater for a huge number of preferences and tastes. The question is not whether this capacity leads to the creation of a great deal of consumer choice (it obviously does); rather, it is whether the production of such varied types of consumer goods sustain and reflect a genuine cultural plurality. Adorno never denies that the products on offer — the many channels and brands to choose from, etc. — display a great surface variety; instead, what he claims is that the differences on offer are illusory because no such product can be realized independently of the logic of commodification. According to this logic, which seeks to maximize revenue and ensure consumer loyalty, the effect each product is supposed to have on its addressee is calculated in advance: there is something for everybody, including those with the apparently most "exclusive" taste. One may think that the manifold at issue here is only horizontal, involving the difference, say, between two competing pop hits. However, even the vertical distinction between high and low culture, which Adorno so often has been indicted for defending, is within the framework of the theory of the culture industry seen as collapsing. In Adorno's view, the experience of someone attending an opera tends to be no less commodified than that of the consumer of soap-operas on the television. Or rather: there is nothing intrinsic to the opera, at least not in its traditional guises, that safeguards against co-optation by the culture industry.

The last point calls into question a line of criticism that has been directed against Adorno from an explicitly postmodernist position. According to Collins (1987), the early Frankfurt School's analysis of culture was marked from the outset by an untenable and unquestioned reliance on dividing cultural production into authentic art and inauthentic mass culture. By privileging so-called high culture along these lines, what they in effect did was to straitjacket the differences among cultural practices. Rather than celebrating the democratization of culture that was promised by mass production, someone like Adorno reverted to a conservative elitism. Like Collins, Eco (1986) argues that the division between high and low is at best an anachronism. At least since the late 1960s, high culture and entertainment have merged in all sorts of unruly ways, leaving approaches drawing on the old binarism of high and low incapable of providing new and exciting interpretations.

The problem with Collins' and Eco's critiques, which certainly are damaging to a traditional conservative view, and indeed, as I will argue later, to moments in Adorno as well, is that they fail to engage sensitively with Adorno's position. Adorno generally takes preciously little interest in defending the manifestations of bourgeois art over popular art, or in opposing the two along a scale of dogmatically set coordinates of value. In his essay on Bach, for example, "Bach Defended against his Devotees," he shows how the reception of Bach's music stands in danger of becoming just one more form of entertainment among many others. Only by being "rescued" from the widespread fetishism of original instruments and concurrent modes of seductive performance with their intimations of aura and exclusiveness can Bach's music be worthy our full attention. Likewise, in other essays, most notably "On the Fetish Character in Music and the Regression of Listening," from 1936, which was written as an indirect polemic against Benjamin's art-work essay, he points to the attention being paid by concert-goers to the conductor, rather than the music itself, as an example of reified aesthetic reception. In this way, he claims, the concert experience gets exclusively oriented towards the star-status of the director, rather than towards the singularity of the aesthetic event and its ultimate implications. While the art Adorno defended — the music, say, of the Second Viennese School or Picasso or Beckett — today may seem at the center of a "bourgeois" canon of twentieth-century modernist masterpieces, it is important to keep in mind how radical and undomesticated such art seemed to Adorno up until at least the 1950s. He did anticipate, though, especially in *Aesthetic Theory*, that even these works would be appropriated by the culture industry and lose their subversive capacity. Although Adorno's high modernism is staked on its refusal of culture as it stands, no work of art is automatically protected from the mechanisms of cultural industrialization.

Both "high" and "low" art lose their seriousness by being commodified. While there surely is a marked tendency in Adorno to want to denounce all forms of low art (and indeed mass culture in general), a closer look at some passages, especially in the late essay "Culture industry reconsidered," reveals a more nuanced position: "The seriousness of high art is destroyed in speculation about its efficacy; the seriousness of the lower perishes with the civilizational constraints imposed on the rebellious resistance inherent within it as long as social control was not total" (Adorno 1991b: 85). The notion that mass art contains a potential for rebellious resistance alludes to Ernst Bloch, for whom popular entertainment like the circus and the carnival function as ciphers of redemption in an otherwise reified social reality, yet it also connects with Adorno's own subterranean interest in the notion of happiness, pointing towards the anarchy of the human body and its unruly needs. The culture industry is corrupt not only because it prevents cultural items from actualizing their use-value but because, in doing so, it exploits people's genuine desires in order to profit from products that, rather than satisfying those desires, reconfigure them and offer substitute forms of gratification. This is why Adorno is so adamant that the culture industry is repressive: it never engages with real needs. On the contrary, it generates false need-interpretations and presents them to its audiences as though they were authentic. As a result, the traces of what Bloch considered to be subversive forms of low culture are perpetually being threatened by inclusion:

> The culture industry does retain a trace of something better in those features which bring it close to the circus, in the self-justifying and nonsensical skill of riders, acrobats and clowns, in the defense and justification of physical as against intellectual art. But the refuges of a mindless artistry which represents what is human as opposed to the social mechanism are being relentlessly hunted down by a schematic reason which compels everything to prove its significance and effect.
>
> (1979: 143)

The dialectical construal of the high–low distinction becomes even more pronounced in a letter that Adorno wrote to Benjamin in March 1936 in which he characterizes its poles as "torn halves of an integral freedom, to which, however, they do not add up" (1999a: 130). High art, rejecting the immediate claim to gratification which is on display in popular art, renounces happiness for the sake of happiness.[3] Such art exists in a mode of anticipation, owing its legitimacy to the false totality of the present. Popular art, on the other hand, aspires to articulate desire though fails to do so in an autonomous and true fashion. Only their unification, which would require radical social and political change, would permit the synergy of both autonomy and happiness.

## A theory of culture or of an industry?

According to Jameson (1996: 144), the theory of the culture industry "is not a theory of culture but the theory of an *industry*, of a branch of the interlocking monopolies of late capitalism that makes money out of what used to be called culture." On Jameson's account, because so-called Fordism, organized mass production, had not yet really started to be applied to culture at the time of Adorno's most influential work on mass culture, our contemporary level of acculturation of social life, in which everyday life, including fashion, lifestyle, and entertainment seems totally dominated by mass-produced images, symbols, and products, must simply have been inconceivable to him. What Adorno reacted to was a lot more tangible: the rise of the Hollywood studio system, jazz, the record industry, and so on. It would therefore be an anachronism, Jameson argues, to ascribe to Adorno a theory of culture cast in more thoroughgoing and total terms.

Jameson's construal of the culture industry thesis, which has gained a certain following in the critical literature, is difficult to square with aspects of it that he does not take into account. For one thing, as I have already mentioned, Adorno does in fact explicitly describe and analyze an intensi-fied and indeed total system of cultural exchange. His minute investigations not only of American magazines and advertising but (espe-cially in *Minima Moralia*) of things like material structures of everyday interaction (architecture and design), codes of behavior (ways of greeting one another for example), as well as people's self-understanding (the conflation of personal and economic-systemic identity), point to something much more pervasive and dominant than the appearance of certain indus-tries of cultural mass production and transmission. For another thing, it is historically inadequate to suggest that Adorno could not have had a proper inkling of Fordist methods of cultural distribution. It is unlikely that such a complex did not exist in Adorno's California of the early 1940s. Moreover, the fact that he retained most of the theory of the culture industry well into the 1960s speaks against the claim that he had no inkling of the image-society of postmodernity.

Although Adorno, as mentioned previously, occasionally presents the culture industry thesis in terms of a rather crude conception of more or less overtly delivered propaganda, it is clear that he also envisions the culture industry as capable of providing agents with models of self-interpretation, or what Pierre Bourdieu would later call a *habitus*. A habitus, Bourdieu suggests, should be thought of as "a system of dispositions" (1984: 562, n. 2). "It expresses first the *result of an organizing action*, with a meaning close to that of words such as structure; it also designates a way of being, a habitual state (especially of the body) and, in particular, a *predisposition, tendency, propensity* or *inclination*" (Bourdieu 1984: 562, n. 2).[4] As such it is not to be equated with the effects of straightforward propaganda (that is, a vertical relation between a conscious manipulator and the receiving masses); rather, it permeates, and is sustained by, people's practices and thinking. Like the primary socializing agents of the bourgeois family, the culture industry tells people what to think of themselves, what they should aspire to, and what a good or successful life would look like. Anticipating Althusser and Foucault, Adorno is not just arguing that the culture industry is manipulative; his more fundamental point is that it partakes in the creation of individuals. Subjects come into being through subjection and identification, that is, by internalizing imperatives arising from the surrounding culture — from film, radio, magazines, and television, but also from institutionally embodied structures of symbolic production such as corporate offices, schools, organized tourism, politics, and so forth. Adorno's examples range from the employee's appearance (shining white teeth) to taking up a hobby and workers calling one another "Bob and "Harry" in order to obliterate personal distance so as to ensure smooth co-operation in the workplace. Unlike Althusser and Foucault, however, Adorno importantly resists the reduction of the concept of subjectivity, or rather the concept of the autonomous subject, to the effect of ideology alone.[5]

This consideration can be said to have both a normative and descriptive component. Normatively, the resistance follows from the very idea of immanent critique that marked Critical Theory from the outset: if the analysis shows the so-called autonomous subject to be nothing but an ideological construct, then the emancipatory intent of the theory would collapse; there would be nothing to defend. Descriptively, the resistance towards a totalizing notion of co-optation along Foucauldian or Althusserian lines follows from empirical observation. In the late essay "Free Time," for example, Adorno (1998b: 174–5) refers to a study conducted in 1966 which aimed to determine how the German population reacted to the wedding of Princess Beatrix of Holland and the diplomat, Claus von Amsberg. By contrast to the standard view of Adorno as a die-hard cultural pessimist, he concludes that

> many of those interviewed ... suddenly behaved completely realis-
> tically and criticized the political and social importance of the
> same event that in its much-publicized uniqueness they had gazed
> at in breathless wonder on their television screens.... . Apparently
> the integration of consciousness and free time has not yet wholly
> succeeded.
>
> (1998b: 175)

While passages such as these may yield the impression that Adorno was sanguine about the conditions of autonomous judgment-formation in late capitalist societies, it is important to note that they do not occur very often and that, when they occur, it is usually in conjunction with more totalizing claims. However, their sheer existence demonstrates that Adorno, despite the invocation of a Hegelian notion of total mediation, does not wholeheartedly endorse the view that the integration effected by the culture industry (in its widest designation) is without cracks or fissures. While infrequent, there is room for some exercise of autonomy.

As previously mentioned, for Adorno, the only real potential for autonomy — or rather some form of semi-autonomy — arises with the figure of the intellectual, for whom theory becomes a tool by which to maintain one's reflective distance from culture. The theorist suspends faith in culture as it stands and speaks in the name of a counterfactual audience: "Walter Benjamin's thought on critics whose task it is to uphold the interest of the public against the public itself can be applied to cultural policy itself" (1991b: 112). Leaving aside, for the moment, the challenges facing this position, which will be analyzed in more depth in Chapter 8, what interests us is that the manufacturing of consent — the near ubiquity of ideology — is in deep tension with fundamental ideals of democracy, which presuppose that collective will-formation builds on, and is sustained by, autonomous individual will-formation. If Adorno is right, then liberal political theory, which holds rational agreement among free and equal agents to be the source of political legitimacy, is necessarily incapable of showing such legitimacy to be actualized. Rather than taking for granted that such agreements can and do occur, an Adornian analysis would concentrate on the impediments to the formation of autonomous political judgment. Only in tandem with an analysis of culture (in its commodified state) can political theory realize its project of grounding the legitimacy of institutions.

A weakness with Adorno's position is that it, apart from the references to the intellectual, generally lacks resources for conceptualizing resistance and spontaneity on the level of cultural consumption. As we have seen, he all too often reverts to a rather crude vision of manipulation modeled on his perception of fascist political propaganda. Honneth (1991: 79–80) powerfully argues that his work suffers from a lack of mediation between, on the one hand, the macro-level of structural analysis relating to socio-economic conditions, and, on the other, the micro-level of individualized styles of interpretation and modes of perception. Along the same lines, Bernstein (2001: 130, n. 74) claims that Adorno lacks a social psychology that can indicate why and how agents come to identify with the imperatives that structure their own domination. Unlike Honneth, however, Bernstein believes that such an account can be provided, suggesting that Judith Butler's writings on power might be a candidate. Central to Butler's argument (1997) is the paradox that autonomous subjectivity can only come into being through identification with power. Drawing on Freud's 1923 essay "The Ego and the Id," she more specifically argues that the ego-ideal — which conditions and limits the ego's capacity for rational action — is the sedimented result of a history of passionate attachments and identifications with objects of libidinal cathexis. Since resistance presupposes a strong and well-integrated ego-ideal, such identifications are unavoidable conditions for individual political and social action. While Butler's theory calls for an extended analysis, it is worth noticing that Adorno, in the essay "Freudian Theory and the Pattern of Fascist Propaganda," indeed outlines a theory of social psychology that shows up many parallels with that of Butler. As I argued in the previous chapter, however, it is doubtful whether this theory can be extended to non-totalitarian contexts.

## Needs and need-interpretations

Of great centrality to Adorno's account is the notion of false need-interpretations, or what he, following standard Marxist terminology, simply calls false needs. Since the culture industry is geared towards the maximization of profit, it is dependent, as advanced capitalism in general, on constantly generating new demands. Historically, the rise of the culture industry must be viewed as the result of a larger set of changes in Western societies — in short the shift, in the late nineteenth century, from a liberal to an organized phase of capitalism. Whereas the liberal phase still allowed for a great deal of autonomy among its possessing classes, the organized phase — as Adorno was witnessing it in the United States of the 1940s — is based on a logic of consumerism, i.e., a system whereby the conscious and unconscious inculcating of dispositions to spend and invest has become the central driving force of the economy. The Keynesian fiscal policies of the New Deal and the American as well as German societies of the 1950s and 1960s made large-scale mass production possible by enabling the participation of wide groups in mass consumption. The systemic imperatives were thus irresistible: without such participation, the centralization of capital and the emphasis on technological change that such centralization presupposed would be impossible.

Philosophically speaking, then, the very category of needs is mediated by society. As Adorno argues in the essay "Theses on Needs," any attempt to distinguish between surface and deep needs — between needs that involve interpretation, and needs that simply arise naturally — is misleading: even the most apparently fundamental need such as hunger is mediated by cultural expectations of what is tasty or healthy, as opposed to the distasteful or unhealthy. It is important to emphasize, however, that Adorno is by no means a complete "culturalist." He is not rejecting the role of nature in accounting for the constitution of needs. His point, rather, is that deep or natural needs are not untouched by the processes of symbolic exchange. While the process of historical mediation makes it impossible to detach nature and culture from each other, the "nature-factor" can never be eliminated: man, as it were, is nature all the way up and interpretation all the way down.

This careful qualification of the concept of needs stands in contrast to what has become known as postmodern accounts, in particular that of Jean

Baudrillard, with whom Adorno has often been compared. In Baudrillard's work on seduction from the late 1970s, needs are wholly generated within a spectacular logic of the commodity fetish, hence the moment of nature, whether understood as use-value, substance or simply essence, has no place within the system of late capitalism. For Baudrillard, who rejects the Marxian distinction between base and superstructure, capitalism is less an economic system than a system of symbolic exchange in which desire gets constituted by the emptiness of the free-floating signifiers: what we want is desirable precisely because it is hollow, devoid of any inside, the pure surface, or even image, of the exchangeable item disconnected from history, nature, and natural needs — the simulacra for which there is no original, or rather, from whose play "the original" is created.

While Adorno agrees with Baudrillard that the exchange value enjoys both economic and cultural priority over use-value, his critique of the culture industry is entirely predicated on the today rather old-fashioned concept of nature. As we have seen, though, "nature" designates a feature of the constitution of needs which, in the absence of dialectical mediation, is completely indeterminate. Since needs are shaped by our self-interpretation, and self-interpretations are mediated through and through by the system of exchange, there can be no sudden "revelation" of needs, and no social and political action that can once and for all bring the subject to a full awareness of itself as a natural being. Unlike Baudrillard, however, who in his more recent work has started to lament the loss of otherness, viewing the totalization of the society of the spectacle as a "crime" rather than as a cause for celebration and envisioning an apocalyptic event that would shatter the simulacra, Adorno can only recommend critique and negation, the unending process of enlightenment whereby heteronomous need-formations are brought to reflective attention. That which for Baudrillard will require a theological event of messianic significance is for Adorno a moment in modernity's indefinite process of obtaining self-reassurance.[6]

Adorno further argues that need-interpretations that are generated by the culture industry are false not because they *a priori* fail to match the "real, immediate and natural" needs we may have, for no such needs exist, but because they arise in a system whose ultimate end is that of profit, rather than the happiness and integrity of its members. Thus, the critique of false needs, unlike in the late Baudrillard, where it becomes indexed to an unpromising undialectical juxtaposition of culture and nature, must take place within the framework of a more general critique of late capitalism.

## Ideology

Considering how common it is to think of the early Frankfurt School as being primarily engaged in ideology critique, it may be surprising to find that the notion of ideology appears rather infrequently in Adorno, and that when it appears it is usually surrounded by a set of anxious qualifications regarding its meaning and viability as a focal-point with reference to which critique can occur.[7] In his "Contributions to the Theory of Ideology," Adorno tries to locate this notion within the framework of a larger analysis of late capitalism, starting with some important conceptual and historical remarks. Initially, to say of a system of beliefs that it is ideological means to suggest that it somehow rests upon, or expresses, an epistemic mistake. The classical Marxian analysis of the burgeoning bourgeoisie of the late eighteenth century would be an example of this type of ideology critique. According to Marx, the property-owning class characteristically represented its own particular interest as having general significance; it thereby conflated particular and general interest. Thus, the enlightenment celebration of freedom and individualism fitted well into the aspirations of entrepreneurs and stockbrokers but did little to address the concerns and interests of workers and proletarians. The point, of course, is not that workers are (or should be) disinterested in achieving freedom and individualism; it is, rather, that promoting these interests without taking the social conditions of their satisfaction into account means to suggest, falsely, that their satisfaction is generally available.[8] Ideological mistakes become a species of misrecognition.

On another level, therefore, as the example already suggests, the conflation of particularity and generality is more than an epistemic mistake. By masking the asymmetrical distribution of resources in a society whose reproduction is based on capitalist exchange, it also serves to uphold and apparently legitimize a relationship of domination or hegemony. Thus for a belief to qualify as ideological in the pejorative sense it must not only be false but serve the socially specific purpose of supporting those who unjustly exercise power over others. Now both true and false beliefs, as well as justified and unjustified ones, may be able to fulfill this purpose. If considered on its own terms and in isolation from the questions of justification and truth, a purely functional view, which takes ideology to consist in its capacity to stabilize relations of domination (*Herrschaft*), would be incapable of respecting the distinction between justifiable and unjustifiable relations of domination.[9] In order to avoid a position according to which no room would exist for a sense in which ideology is false (which would entail a pernicious relativism), it is necessary to combine the functional view with a normative conception of universalizable interest. For Adorno, following the Marxist tradition, it is mainly expressions of false consciousness that, in conjunction with their system-legitimizing capacity, deserve to be called ideological.

Adorno importantly notices a radical divergence between those, such as Weber, who restrict the concept of ideology to cover singular historical events, and those, such as Althusser and Pareto, who use it for totalizing purposes. Unlike both extremes, Adorno — and this is a genuinely dialec-

84

tical point — insists that ideology, though predominantly false in its *de facto* application to specific historical configurations, almost always contains a moment of truth. From the fact that in classical bourgeois societies freedom and individualism have been falsely represented as generally available, it does not follow that they should be rejected as focal-points of political aspiration. As Adorno (1973b: 151), inspired by Hegel's logic, suggests, a concept such as that of freedom reveals a dialectical contradiction as soon as it is applied to an individual in a specific social context. To say of someone that he or she is free forces us not only to recognize this person's transcendence of that characterization (the predicate's, as it were, necessary inadequacy in relation to the subject) but to face the idea of freedom itself, which presupposes the even more comprehensive idea of a free society: the concept thus contains a normative or anticipatory content that transcends the bad (unfree) context in which it is applied.[10]

> To this day, [the individual] will experience this "more" as his own negativity. The substance of the contradiction is that individuality is not yet — and that, therefore, it is bad wherever it is established. At the same time, that contradiction between the concept of freedom and its realization remains the insufficiency of the concept. The potential of freedom calls for criticizing what an inevitable formalization has made of the potential.
>
> (Adorno 1973b: 151)

Unfortunately, Adorno does not consider any objections to this argument. In particular, it falsely presupposes that the notion of freedom is uncontested, such that the utopian anticipation negatively contained in its ascription would be specifiable with a view to universal acceptance. While the contradiction between the concept of freedom and its abstract realization is often blatant, what its realization would require, however, must be a matter of political negotiation and reflection: it is not written *a priori* into the concept itself.

A more promising way to interpret Adorno consists in introducing the vocabulary of ordinary language philosophy. According to Cavell (1979), in order to make (full) sense speakers need to be responsible for the implications of their utterances, by which he means the commitments and obligations that they project in given speech acts and which can be read off from those acts as material inferences. Such projecting and observing of linguistic implications articulate who the speaker is and hence what she takes to be authoritative in her everyday practices. Thus, what "freedom" means becomes a function of how, and under which conditions, this predicate is used by individuals in specific cases. Through self-reflection, speakers may be able to clarify for themselves the range and meaning of given predicates. Cavell (1976: 31) calls the statements produced by such acts of self-reflection "categorial declaratives." Producing a categorial declarative typically involves a) citing *instances* of what is ordinarily said in a language ("We do say ... but we don't say —"; "We ask whether ... but we do not ask whether —"), and b) occasionally accompanying these instances by *explications* of what is performatively implied by their enunciation ("When we say ... we imply (suggest, say) —"; "We don't say ... unless we mean—").[11] For a given speaker, such investigations articulate what, to him or her, is authoritative, yet apart from the experiential involvement of singular individuals with reference to which they can invite others to agree, they do not claim objective validity.

Following Cavell's definition of a categorial declarative, we may think of an Adornian analysis of an existing concept as an attempt to explicate, by citing instances of its use, the performative implications that the concept may have for a specific speaker. The concept is thereby confronted with a social reality whose determination turns out to conflict with the concept's own implications. According to Adorno, such a conflict would typically be experienced as suffering. A good illustration of such an experiental analysis can be found in Richard Sennett's *The Corrosion of Character* (1998). In this book Sennett analyzes interviews he has done with workers in the new, "flexible" economy. The workers are asked to define their situation with reference to the concept of freedom. As the interviews progress, the interviewees, undergoing a process of self-reflection involving sustained thinking about their place in the often harsh and uncertain reality of the contemporary labor market, gradually find themselves forced to reconsider their initial (and ideological) definition of this concept. Indeed, rather than being, as neo-liberal ideology would have it, more free than in the older economy, they realize that greater flexibility actually entails the need for an intensified adaptation to the imperatives of the labor market. By shifting attention, for example, from the number of hours spent at work to "free and creative projects" undertaken, the employer undermines security and stimulates competition, thereby promoting greater loyalty and ultimately a stultified form of freedom. Thus by "testing" the concept of freedom against the worker's *experience*, a contradiction arises between what it unreflectively purports to entail and what it actually entails. As in Hegel's *Phenomenology of Spirit*, the concept is ideological if it experientially fails to provide the knowledge (or content) that its proponents claim that it provides. Dialectical experience, we could say, engenders a sense of loss or despair at having to acknowledge that the experience of the object no longer can be accounted for in terms of hitherto implicitly accepted determinations.[12] As Adorno sees it, the aim is not to follow Hegel in offering new and ultimately final universal determinations of objecthood that once and for all will evade contingency and establish absolute knowledge, but to hold on to that which inaugurated the need for a new conceptual determination, namely the notion of dialectical experience itself, which is the painful experience of particularity as being resistant to one's universal conception of objecthood.

According to Adorno, the most fundamental form of ideology, serving perhaps as a kind of meta-theory of ideology, is identity itself, the mindless and objectified repetition of sameness without any reflection or attempt at authorization.[13] Inscribed in the concept itself is the primal illusion of the identity between it and the thing itself in the absence of the subject's individual experience. To criticize ideology can thus be equated with offering an experientially based self-reflection with regard to a given concept. It then becomes a dialectical effort, hence the importance of the notion of experience for Adorno's negative dialectic.

## The crisis of experience

Experience (*Erfahrung*) is a significant concept, and as one commentator, Grenz (1974: 44), has argued, in being the main instrument of critical negation, it aspires to play the same role for Adorno as the proletariat does in Lukács, namely to create dialectical movement in an otherwise frozen and reified structure of social determinations. Roughly, Adorno's reflections on experience can be divided into two groups: first, those that, following the lead of Benjamin's essay "The Storyteller," focus on the impoverishment of experience in contemporary late capitalism; second, those that, following Hegel, seek to formulate a genuine moment of conceptually mediated and dialectical cognition which points beyond the present. Being dialectically related in that knowing the negative entails reference to its possible negation (and vice versa), the two types of reflections are mutually determinative. For the moment, however, I want to concentrate on the notion of experiential impoverishment, which for Adorno is intrinsically, though not exclusively, linked to the impact of the culture industry. In the *Dialectic of Enlightenment*, such a connection is forged by means of an imaginative employment of Kant's notion of schematism. The culture industry performs the same service for the individual's capacity to experience the world as the schematism does for the Kantian subject, which is *a priori* to provide homogeneity between concepts and representations of objects being subsumed under them. "Its [the culture industry's] prime service to the customer is to do his schematizing for him... . There is nothing left for the consumer to classify. Producers have done it for him" (Adorno 1979: 124).

Unfortunately, Adorno does not distinguish properly between schematizing and classifying. To classify is possible in so far as we possess concepts or categories by means of which the classification takes place. For instance, a student can be classified as eligible for a grant or not, depending on whether he or she satisfies certain criteria that have been agreed upon in advance. Let us, again following Cavell (1979:

9–12), call these "official criteria" and distinguish them from the more fundamental "linguistic (or conceptual) criteria." To say that the culture industry classifies in the first sense would in Adorno's case not be very illuminating. It would be like holding that the industry classifies one piece of music as jazz and another as rock, and that it does so according to certain pragmatically adopted marks. What Adorno seems to be claiming is not just that a certain (arbitrary) order is imposed on the world (such that objects are sorted on the basis of stipulated or "official" criteria) but that the linguistic criteria themselves, in accordance with which we identify objects as such and hence make classification (and identification) possible in the first place, are manufactured by an independent system from whose conscious control agents are alienated. Whereas the application of official criteria allows a class of objects to be carved up in a certain way, depending on our interests and purposes, the application of linguistic criteria tells us what an object *is*. It regulates the correct use of a concept. The former process is often trivial (though in many cases necessary); the latter is fundamental, suggesting that concept-formation itself (knowing what a thing *is*, as opposed to knowing that a thing can be categorized under this or that heading, depending on the official criteria we choose to apply) is systematically influenced by the paradigms and images provided by the culture industry. Rather than something the individual, by actively inheriting linguistic criteria from a living linguistic community, is expected to be responsible for, the constitution and sustenance of linguistic or conceptual criteria is colonized and controlled by a mechanism for which no one is responsible. Put bluntly, the postcard has not only become more important than the site itself but has actually replaced it: rather than something that individualizes the subject before the other, making her unique and irreplaceable, thus responsible in relation to the other, experience itself has become an exchangeable item, threatening to make the individual itself superfluous and unknown.

For Benjamin, the destruction of experience can be read off from the demise of the storyteller. Whereas the traditional storyteller's activity was predicated on the possibility of ordering events in meaningful, organic sequences which were capable of being universally communicated, the structure of experience in modern life is such that events are essentially isolated and desultory, making their recounting a fundamentally private undertaking. Culminating in the age of information, experience is reduced to facts and statistics, fungible items which have no intrinsic significance and in relation to which no one is encouraged to exercise independent judgment. In Adorno's generalization and radicalization of this view, the experiences shared by the audiences of the culture industry are created by an impersonal structure in which the individuals do not count for one another. Despite its universality, it fails to create a genuine symbolic community. All it does, rather, is to perpetuate sameness. Adorno's society is both unitary and fragmented.

## The paradoxes of cultural criticism

"Culture is only true when implicitly critical, and the mind which forgets this revenges itself in the critics it breeds" (Adorno 1997c: 22). In its constitutive lack of criticism, the culture industry represents the antithesis of true culture. Yet how, given the near total pervasiveness of commodification implied by the notion of the culture industry, can the heroic enlightenment vision of culture as inherently critical, expressed in this quote from the essay "Cultural Criticism and Society," be conceived, let alone actualized? In short, how is cultural criticism possible?

Adorno approaches this question by means of a series of qualifying statements. In general, the cultural critic is a contradictory figure. The critic is discontent with civilization, wanting it changed or replaced in the name of some unadulterated nature or a higher historical stage. However, there can be no position available to the critic that would not always already be "mediated down to its innermost make-up" (1997c: 19) by culture itself. Like Hegel's "unhappy consciousness," it is as if the cultural critic finds herself incapable of bridging the gap between the source of authority, itself hopelessly beyond grasp, and the facticity of her present cultural location: the more she wants to be outside culture, the more she remains caught up within it. Equally paradoxical, however, is the fact that her criticisms, rather than effectively denouncing culture, confer a spurious dignity and autonomy on it: "Where there is despair and measureless misery, [s]he sees only spiritual phenomena, the state of man's consciousness, the decline of norms. By insisting on this, criticism is tempted to forget the unutterable, instead of striving, however impotently, so that man may be spared" (1997c: 19).

By means of these two opening moves, Adorno starts to mark the distance between himself and the implicit opponent of this essay, namely the *conservative* cultural critic. In the eyes of the conservative critic, culture is autonomous. Consisting of values and motivational schemata that, while historically situated, get embodied in cultural expressions (works of art, philosophical systems, etc.), culture is for the conservative defined by its distance from the material conditions of life, that is, from the physical labor by means of which society is reproduced and regenerated. (Indeed, the German word *Kulturkritik*, which Adorno admits to finding offensive, connotes conservatism. In trying to appropriate the term for his own uses, Adorno is thus forced to subvert the dominant use of the term.)

Classical examples of such conservative criticisms of culture are Nietzsche's discourse of nihilism or the lament over the disintegration of values in writers such as Hermann Broch and Robert Musil. To them, the alleged catastrophe of late modernity is predominantly a function of the disappearance of symbolic authority. With the loss — after five hundred years of secularization, individualism, and egalitarianism — of a unified source of symbolic authority, European societies are supposedly plunged into anarchy and motivational crisis. For Adorno, by contrast, culture is wholly dependent upon its unacknowledged other of material being, and its appearance of being autonomous, rather than being taken at face value, must be viewed as the result of a violently enforced division between mental and physical labor. Thus, culture is always "guilty." To think of culture as autonomous is to contribute to the perpetuation of it as myth — a hypostatized, fetishized structure of eternal values.

It does not follow, however, that Adorno reverts to a Marxist theory of reflection. Although culture has largely proven itself to be impotent before the power of capital, it is never simply a fungible ideological *Anhang* to the dialectical play of forces and relations of production. On the contrary, just the sheer fact of culture's ability to protest against status quo is enough to do justice to its continued and *de facto* divorce from the sphere of physical labor. High culture, Adorno argues, exists in the mode of a broken promise: its claims cannot be brushed aside until its promise — a unification of mental and physical labor, of culture and nature — has been achieved.

So how is cultural criticism possible, then? It would seem that the premise of a reified social totality would invite some notion of transcendent critique: since there is no non-reified position *within* social totality, it seems to follow that the only way to avoid a performative self-contradiction between, on the one hand, radically criticizing totality, while on the other, belonging to the totality being criticized, is to anticipate or construct a position *outside* it. Only then would the epistemological conditions of criticism be reconcilable with Adorno's understanding of ideology as socially necessary appearance. According to Honneth (2000), the kind of critique one finds in Adorno is precisely of a transcendent kind.[14] Employing indirect means of communication — irony, hyperbole, fragmentary or non-systematic writing, and so on — a work such as the *Dialectic of Enlightenment* aspires to "a bird's eye view" of modern culture. A pertinent question, of course, is whether such a position really is available. And if available, how effective?

The competing claim would be that cultural criticism must proceed immanently: following the method of Hegel's *Phenomenology of Spirit*, culture must be criticized according to the standards and principles that it immanently or implicitly operates with. Thus according to Zuidervaart (1991: xix), "[immanent critique] continues in the critical theory of Adorno and his colleagues, where it provides 'a means of detecting the societal contradictions which offer the most determinate possibilities of emancipatory social change.' "[15] In Adorno's (1997c: 32) own definition, "immanent criticism of intellectual and artistic phenomena seeks to grasp, through the analysis of their form and meaning, the contradiction between their objective idea and that pretension."

Adorno approaches this terrain by contending that cultural criticism is caught up in an antinomy between transcendence and immanence: both positions — either calling culture as a whole into question from outside, or confronting it with the norms which it itself has produced — may justifiably lay claim to correctness; hence *contra* both Honneth and Zuidervaart, there can be no simple either–or. By analyzing the two positions separately, it emerges that, on the one hand, the procedure of transcendent criticism correctly appreciates the totality as reified; thus it attempts to establish its criteria with reference to the critic's own position (as opposed to the position being criticized). Its claim to transcendence, however, is also its weakness. To take up a critical position on culture from outside would be tantamount to wanting to "wipe away the whole as if with a sponge" (Adorno 1997c: 32). Having rejected culture in its entirety, the transcendent critic finds herself forced to revert to ideas of "naturalness" or "purity," both of which form central elements of bourgeois ideology. The choice of a standpoint outside the sway of existing society thus betrays an affinity to "barbarism": it is abstract and, in its neglect of particulars, at one with domination.

The immanent critic, on the other hand, takes account of the need to take cultural particulars seriously. Unlike the transcendent critic, the immanent critic does not view ideology *in itself* — the free-floating signifiers, as it were, of cultural production — as being untrue. What is untrue is "rather its pretension to correspond to reality" (ibid.). Yet while immanent criticism escapes the abstractions of transcendent criticism, it easily becomes myopic and narrow. Not only is its activities restricted to the efforts of the intellect, thus being merely reflective rather than open to social change, but in its concentration on particular objects it fails to relate this particularity to the knowledge of society as a totality and of the mind's involvement in it. Immanent criticism, then, by immersing itself in the object, risks disregarding culture's dependence on economic reality.

The antinomy of transcendent and immanent criticism seems irresolvable. Rather than uniting the two positions in a third that would represent the sublation of their differences, what Adorno approvingly calls dialectical criticism thus becomes a non-position: neither does it take up a stand outside culture by comparing it to a utopian absolute, nor does it immerse itself in the object such as to idealize it. The dialectical critic of culture must embody and accept the contradiction between transcendence and immanence: "[He or she] must both participate in culture and not participate. Only then does he do justice to his object and to himself" (1997c: 33).

Adorno has surprisingly little to say about how this paradox can be sustained. The Janus-faced image of simultaneous participation and non-participation may invite comparison with Derrida's deconstruction of the dichotomy between inside and outside in his early essay on Bataille's "impossible" attempt at offering a transcendent articulation of the Hegelian negative.[16] While the Hegelian *Aufhebung* is produced entirely from within discourse, from within the work of signification, Bataille's notion of sovereignty questions the universality of Hegel's discourse without being expressible within it. Because it has no transcendent voice, sovereignty thus respects the immanent totality of discourse. At the same time, however, it exceeds this totality and in a sense undermines it. A crucial difference between Adorno and Derrida, however, is that Adorno views the necessity of taking up the paradoxical stance of participation and non-participation as arising from a historical, as opposed to a trans-cendental, demand. For Adorno, dialectical criticism responds to a specific social and historical configuration. If this configuration were to change, then the critic would also have to change. Yet how this double imperative applies to the critic in contemporary society is not clear.

The essay on cultural criticism makes more sense when read in conjunc-tion with Adorno's thinking about metaphysics. What are the conditions, he asks in his writings on metaphysics, for coherently experiencing trans-cendence, or that which exceeds the total structure of appearance? Will Adorno have to commit himself to the view that such an experience (and the obligation that goes with it) presupposes the coming into being of an entirely different social space? Or will he accept that it could be viewed as a moment, however repressed, within our actual practices? It is crucial to Adorno's thinking that such forms of experience can never be imme-diate, for if so, they would be indeterminate and ultimately void. Benjamin's incommensurability between the proper of the proper name and the universal determination of the predication must therefore be soft-ened and dialectically inscribed as mutually irreducible, yet internally related dimensions of language itself. According to Adorno, language contains an expressive element which mimetically reveals the particularity of the object, thus highlighting an elective affinity between the knower and the known, *and* a communicative element which reifies the meaning of the utterance by transforming it into an exchangeable item.[17] While a central thesis of the *Dialectic of Enlightenment* is that the process of rationaliza-tion has led the communicative element to dominate over the expressive, the actual tension between the two can never be entirely quenched in favor of reified language, of purely discursive thinking and literalness, for if that happened, cognition would become impossible: "If this moment [the expressive or mimetic element of critical knowledge] were extinguished altogether, it would be flatly incomprehensible that a subject can know an object" (Adorno 1973b: 45).

The concept of experience is hence antinomical: it is essentially composed of two dialectical and conflicting moments, one of which is universal (conceptual reification), the other of which is particular (mimetic appropriation). A metaphysical experience would let us experience this antinomy *qua* antinomy. In such an experience, which Adorno attempts in Proustian fashion to see realized "in the happiness ... promised by village names" (1973b: 373), the particularity of the object is promised in the concept itself, thus creating a melancholy sense of loss in the face of something very close yet unattainable:

> To the child it is self-evident that what delights him in his favorite village is found only there, there alone and nowhere else. He is mistaken; but his mistake creates the model of experience, of a concept that will end up as the concept of the thing itself, not a poor projection.
>
> (1973b: 373)

Adorno's conception of language is aporetic. It acknowledges that our response to the world is necessarily open-ended and unsatisfiable. Although language aims for it, there can be no absolute identification of the object; rather, the search for such an absolute identification is from an Adornian perspective itself an inhuman attempt to disengage linguistic practices from their historical and social embodiment, to speak outside the conditions under which words have meaning. However, acknowledging finitude and disappointment, as we do in noting the child's mistake in the quote above, must not be confused with believing that our words have necessarily failed. For Adorno, the task of philosophy is not to refute skepticism but to show the actual cost of repudiating ordinary language practices and their concomitant reliance on subjective qualifications and expression. Acknowledging finitude means to resist the skeptical temptation to suppress language's reliance on social practice, to resist the drive to reify meaning, while at the same time realizing that the possibility of responding to the social world as it is — as all it can ever be — is not *a priori* withdrawn from the logic of social practices and hence not from critique from a materialist standpoint. If Adorno's thinking calls for something like a transfiguration of our form of life, it will have to be from within — as a completion of, rather than simply a rebellion against, the project of enlightenment.[18]

On this reading, cultural criticism will be geared toward uncovering reification. It will proceed by employing a method of detecting inherent cultural contradictions and tensions, yet its animating and normative impulse will come from the metaphysical experience of the opposition between appearance and reality. While demanding, no dialectical critique in a world of totalized appearance would be coherent without some kind of appeal to transcendence.

## Adorno in the postmodern

There are numerous attempts to confront Adorno's position with post-modern culture, and we have already encountered those of Collins and Eco. Most of them take the form of arguing that Adorno's alleged insistence on the emancipatory power of high modernism, his sweeping and negative characteristics of popular culture, and his relentless desire to criticize identity-thinking in the name of an excluded other, provide little or no relevant starting-points for analyzing contemporary culture. Although Adorno offers a pioneering reading and critique of the artifacts of media culture, situating culture and communication within the capitalist economy and historical context of its day, thereby influencing the rise of British and American cultural studies, his approach is ultimately too reliant on the elite assumptions typical of German mandarin culture of the inter-war years to be of any genuine help today. At worst it may lead to a failure to acknowledge the conflicts and tensions, as well as the oppositional currents and claims, that in fact are being expressed in today's society. According to Kellner (2002: 106), for example, one sees today

> a society in conflict with competing groups struggling to control the direction of society, with progressive and regressive forces in contention, and with a variety of cultural artifacts offering diverse pleasures and oppositional form and content. In this situation, to have a dialectical and adversarial cultural criticism that intervenes in the struggles of the present moment, it is clear that we must move beyond Adorno while assimilating his intransigent oppositional stance and critical insights.

Tania Modleski, in *Studies in Entertainment*, makes a similar point, albeit from another direction. In her view, Adorno's work is now unhelpful not because it is uncritical but because its fixation on the high moderns fails to engage with the actual loss of utopian potential in high culture, and indeed also the institutional collapse of semi-autonomous high culture. Unlike Adorno, Modleski recommends that we instead look for that potential in what would traditionally be regarded as popular culture.

Even though, as we have seen, Adorno's apparently binary opposition between high and low culture is far more nuanced than both Kellner and Modleski presuppose, it seems almost a truism to suggest that his strong denouncement of mass culture fails to do justice to the politically subversive role that certain forms of rock music, film, or even television have played since the early 1960s. While his conception of popular culture is too monolithic and unitary, his canon of high works of art can equally be accused of being too limited to white, male European art. With regard to music in particular, his taste never strayed beyond the German–Austrian tradition;

desire for social justice, these groups resist corporate capitalism as a unified, total phenomenon, and they do so by perpetually searching for new spaces (such as the internet) in which to exercise autonomy. It is far from obvious that Adorno's thought contains resources for conceptualizing their activities. What is clear, however, is that the dynamics of such commitment calls for a serious rethinking of contemporary culture and the way in which the experience of specific forms of injustice demands an analysis of society as a whole. If the invention of new styles of political and social intervention can be effected by the establishment of new and experimental spaces in which imaginary significations can be projected, then these should be supported and not immediately rejected as mere examples of culture-industrial production.

# 5

# THE PERSISTENCE OF PHILOSOPHY

Adorno kick-starts *Negative Dialectics*, his main philosophical work, with a direct reference to Marx's 11th thesis on Feuerbach: "Philosophy, which once seemed obsolete, lives on because the moment to realize it was missed." Marx had asked philosophers to stop interpreting the world and start changing it: theory and practice were to be united in revolutionary activity; the overcoming of the contemplative attitude would signify a final reconciliation of subject and object, man and his social environment. While, in pre-revolutionary circumstances, unredeemed injustice and suffering called for philosophical critique, communism would entail the overcoming of philosophy, which now would have made itself superfluous. Writing after what he views not only as the miscarriage and mismanagement of actual revolutions but as the apparent historical impossibility of radical social change in the Western world, Adorno advocates a return to philosophy. The return is predicated upon a massive disappointment which radiates like a cold light from everything Adorno ever wrote. Philosophy takes on the form of a "melancholy science." It lives on by having failed to deliver its promise.

The failure to make the world conform to reason is not just a failure of practice: on the contrary, reason itself, which in its idealist configurations has been complicit with the historical development Western societies insofar as their progress has been governed by formal-identitarian principles, needs to be examined. Adorno's aim in *Negative Dialectics* is to rethink philosophy. He rethinks it both by exposing its categories to a historical metacritique and by dialectically reconfiguring them. The aim, however, is not to remain wedded to a contemplative attitude. On the contrary, the long detour through philosophy is meant to serve a practical and political purpose; indeed, negative dialectics *is* Adorno's political philosophy, though in a coded and highly mediated form — the only form which he sees as possible in a world that prohibits rational practice. In this chapter I examine this region of Adorno's thinking. I discuss his relationship to Hegelian dialectics, and more specifically his reflection on central notions such as freedom, experience, and the subject/object dyad. Of particular

98

importance is the notion of reconciliation, which many critics have taken as evidence of a certain latent idealism in Adorno. While I defend the claim that this notion plays a significant political role, I argue against the view that Adorno succumbs to a form of eschatological thinking. Ultimately, however, I suggest that his negative dialectics is riveted by an unresolved conflict between Adorno's two philosophical super-egos: Benjamin and Hegel.

## Negative dialectics

Adorno's relationship to Hegel and dialectical thinking has been the object of many scholarly debates on his work. Roughly, the divide has been between those, such as Martin Jay (1984b) and Jay Bernstein (1992), who happily assert the essential Hegelianism of Adorno and those, such as Lyotard (1974) and Nägele (1986), who either have felt that he was too Hegelian to be of any use in the anti-Hegelian climate of much recent Continental thought, or that philosophical influences on his work other than Hegel — particularly anti-Hegelian thinkers such as Benjamin, Nietzsche, or Kierkegaard — should be brought more to the fore than has hitherto been done. Matters have not been made easier by the spectacular resurgence of Hegel in contemporary Anglo-American scholarship. In the works of Robert Pippin (1989), Terry Pinkard (1996), and John McDowell (1994), a new and postmetaphysical Hegel has emerged, a Hegel vastly different in both scope and intention from the totalizing masterthinker Adorno criticizes. Thus being "too Hegelian," "not Hegelian enough," or perhaps embodying "a latent Hegelianism," as the dominant characterizations in debates on Adorno tend to pronounce, says very little unless it is made reasonably clear which Hegel one has in mind.

In the following I want to suggest that while his reading of Hegel ultimately is inseparable from his own progressive delineation of what the project of a negative dialectics amounts to, the debate between those who do and those who do not regard him as a Hegelian is sterile: Adorno is neither a Hegelian nor an anti-Hegelian. Indeed, his approach to Hegel's work is eminently bipolar, involving both passionate rejection and painstaking defense. As will become clear, however, both the Hegel he rejects and the Hegel he defends are, from the standpoint of current scholarship, extreme: the one a die-hard rationalist whose philosophy represents the culmination of Western idealist metaphysics; the other a self-divesting spokesman, by no means dissimilar to Adorno's portraits of Benjamin, of mimetic nonidentity. For Adorno, "standing Hegel on his head" means not only separating the one from the other, the "bad" Hegel from the "good," but to conduct an immanent critique of Hegel in the same spirit as that with which Hegel himself approached other thinkers' work. Unfolding the truth content of Hegel's philosophy requires "reading him against the

grain," i.e., confronting its claims and contradictions with its own aspirations and criteria, as well as with the limits and necessities imposed on it
by the social context within which it was conceived.

We have seen how Adorno's castigation of Hegel as being a philosopher
of integration and repetition is designed to highlight the admittedly
contentious homology between dialectical identification and industrialized
mass murder. Aimed more generally, however, Adorno's thesis implies that
the Hegelian dialectic can be viewed as a figuration of late capitalism itself,
whose logic privileges exchange-value over use-value, and which has
congealed into an apparently reconciled totality. According to this line of
thought, the Hegelian dialectic, since it construes the Absolute as the
totality of categorical mediations within a field of immanence, is a philosophy of totality. In the age of totalitarianism, this is precisely what we do
not want.

Adorno's interpretation of Hegel's self-moving Absolute as an "absolute
integration" should not be confused with the more familiar Marxist association of Hegel with German imperialism and fascism. Nor does he claim,
as does Karl Popper in *The Open Society and its Enemies* (1967), that
Hegel was hostile to the very value of freedom and self-reflection. Rather,
it is in viewing totality itself as rational that an ideologically enforced
complicity arises between Hegel's social thought and the man-made disas-
ters of the twentieth century: "Satanically, the world as grasped by the
Hegelian system has only now, a hundred and fifty years later, proved itself
to be a system in the literal sense, namely that of a radically societalized
society" (Adorno 1993b: 27).

Pure identity, stated in Hegelian terms, is tantamount to the successful
identification of identity and nonidentity, the negation of negation: "To
equate the negation of negation with positivity is the quintessence of identification; it is the formal principle in its purest form" (1973b: 158). On
Adorno's reading, this is violent because the movement of negation is
such that it always conceives particularity, difference, and nonidentity
as being abstract or immaterial, and real only insofar as it is mediated by
the integrating universal. Hegel's subject–object, his conceptual mediation and ultimate reconciliation between subject and object, is itself
subjective and arbitrary. As the late Schelling was the first to argue, it
fails to reach out towards and determine the object itself in its own
integrity. Thus, in the death camps, no particular determination of the
victims was allowed to be considered authoritative or morally relevant;
the only thing that decided one's status was the identification with the
general or universal predicate of being a Jew. Repetition, the endless recur-
rence of the *Immergleiche*, became the only acknowledged criterion of reality.

Whether Hegel actually ever supported such a subsumptive notion of
reason is, however, highly dubious. Indeed, Hegel's critique of the
Enlightenment, as expressed in his reading of Rousseau, by and large

agrees with Horkheimer and Adorno's diagnosis of it in the *Dialectic of Enlightenment* and elsewhere. In the section on the Enlightenment in the *Phenomenology of Spirit*, in which Hegel discusses various ways in which the ideal of self-determination became implemented in modern European culture, we find him criticizing Rousseau's notion of freedom by observing the French Revolution as its test case. On Hegel's interpretation, absolute freedom demands that one's own will should coincide with a universal or impersonal will, that is, with what Rousseau, in the *Social Contract*, calls the general will. As Hegel sees it, the problem with this conception is that while only society as a whole can embody the general will, for government to be possible someone in particular will have to claim that they have a privileged access to the general will and that they are able to represent it in their decisions. Since the king is no longer seen as being in a position to represent the universal, we find the Jacobins doing so instead. However, even the Jacobins, armed with the universal, cannot transcend their particular interests. All they can do, on Hegel's reading, is to eradicate those whom they consider not to conform to the general will — hence Robespierre and the terror. Hegel (1977: 362) writes: "But in absolute freedom there was no reciprocal action between a consciousness that is immersed in the complexities of existence, or that sets itself specific aims and thoughts, and a valid *external* world, whether of reality or thought; instead, the world was absolutely in the form of consciousness as a universal will, and equally self-consciousness was drawn together out of the whole expanse of existence or manifested aims and judgments, and concentrated into the simple self." All that the proponent of absolute freedom is capable of is to destroy the particular will that stands opposed to it; it is not able to produce what Hegel calls a positive work, that is, a social organization, since this would stand opposed to its claim to radical freedom. The upshot of Hegel's critique is that abstract universality equals particularity and that, as such, it inevitably slides into violence.

It seems that Adorno's complaint against Hegel should not be that the particular is subsumed under a universal according to formal rules of identification (which would be homologous with his reading of Auschwitz) — then this is what Hegel himself famously criticizes in Kant's and Fichte's subjective idealisms, denouncing it as abstract *Verstandesdenken* — but that the intransigent, material particular only receives determination within the teleological movement of the Hegelian system itself. The first step in Adorno's painstaking revision of Hegel's dialectic is therefore to reject its drive towards mediation, systematicity, and closure, and rather than looking for a third term which reconciles the opposition between the universal and the particular and drives the dialectic to a higher stage, to highlight the nonidentity or contradiction between them. A negative dialectics is focused on the moment of negation, demonstrating that what appears to be a seamless conceptual totality is in fact scarred by antagonisms. It does not, as in Hegel's *Logic*, unfold as a rationalist ontology, but as an anamnestic operation whereby totalities are broken up, identities criticized, continuities disrupted, and concepts dismantled. A negative dialectics aims at defending the particular against false identification and, ultimately, to release it and "rid it of coercion, including spiritualized coercion" (Adorno 1973b: 6). Like deconstruction, it can only be practiced by means of actual readings, yet the contradictions it detects are objective. In his constellative reading of Hegel, Adorno traces the desire to disrupt identity along explicitly Benjaminian lines, emphasizing in particular how Hegel's dialectical *Darstellung* seems to murmur and rustle in mimesis of the nonidentical:

> In its microstructure Hegel's thought and its literary forms are what Walter Benjamin later called "dialectics at a standstill," comparable to the experience the eye has when looking through a microscope at a drop of water that begins to teem with life; except that what that stubborn, spellbinding gaze falls on is not firmly delineated as an object but frayed, as it were, at the edges.
>
> (Adorno 1993b: 133)

Although it may seem somewhat unspecified and devoid of concreteness, the genuine political thrust of such a negative dialectic is relatively straightforward, namely to provide a model whereby rational resistance towards conceptual systems that, rather than identifying its object as it is in itself, subsumes it and transforms it into an exchangeable item, is made possible. A negative dialectic forms the basis for an ethics of resistance; it "indicates the untruth of identity, the fact that the concept does not exhaust the thing conceived" (Adorno 1973b: 5). Thus, whereas the predicate in a predicative statement pretends to exhaust the subject, the negative dialectician points to the lack of coincidence between the many determinations of the particular and the unified and general attribution made by the predicate. Likewise, with regard to idealist metaphysics, while the human subject is the universal that purports to discover itself completely in the object, the Adornian operation consists in revealing the transcendental difference between the object as it appears for us and the particular object as it is independently of our determinations. A third example would be society itself in its relationship to the individual. While society functions as the universal that triumphantly subsumes everyone under its generalized processes of integration, the restless, desiring, rational individual actually testifies to a contradiction between universal and particular. The same negative logic is at stake in the interplay between exchange-value and use-value, or in the difficult relationship between spirit and expression in the art work. It defines Adorno's critical project. The "good" Hegel, then, is the Hegel for whom (1993b: 30) "philosophy is ... essentially negative: critique."

Since there is no positive moment, no resolution, in which a new determination follows from the collapse of the initial determination into a
contradiction between what it claims to offer and what it in fact provides,
it is far from self-evident, however, that this should be called a dialectic.
The contradictions it piles up, as well as the experiential content which
arises from it, are closer in spirit to Kant's antinomies, for which no dialectical resolution is available, than to the progressive movement of
conceptual determinations which is the bread and butter of the Hegelian
dialectic. The main difficulty of Adorno's negative dialectics, as we will
see, is that, while aiming to contain a heterological element, it follows
Hegel in refusing to conceive of negativity as external to conceptuality
altogether.

In a second political moment, which is connected to the first, a negative
dialectics, following Hegel, criticizes all appeals to immediacy. Given that
every concept is mediated by the dialectical relations in which it stands to
other concepts, and that the totality of such mediations in late modernity
is deemed to be false and marked by antagonisms that fail to be recognized, philosophy can make no reference to foundations, origins, or
principles that are treated in abstraction from such relations. The thinker
being most directly the target of such a critique is clearly Heidegger, whose
thought Adorno incessantly rebukes for reverting to some notion or other
of the *Ursprung*. Whether in the so-called jargon of authenticity, in which
concepts are fetishized as quasi-sacred, self-evident, and original, or with
regard to the ontological difference itself, according to which the general
concept of Being is posited over and above the temporal finitude of beings,
Heidegger fails, Adorno contends, to acknowledge the concrete social and
historical conditions of his own thinking.

There is a pronounced tension between the claim about the universality
of mediation, on the one hand, and the emphasis on negativity, on the
other. In fact, this tension runs through much of Adorno's thinking,
including his reflection on needs and individuality. We have seen how he
theorizes needs as both culturally mediated and containing an element of
nature. About individuality, moreover, he (1993b: 45) characteristically
contends that "everything individual is socially preformed from the outset
and at the same time nothing is realized except in and through individuals." Likewise, in his discussion of the so-called preponderance of the
object, which forms a substantive constituent of the systematic Part Two
of *Negative Dialectics*, he argues that while objects are mediated by
subjective categories, they always exceed their mediation: "An object can
be conceived only by a subject but always remains something other than
the subject, whereas a subject by its very nature is from the outset an
object as well" (1973b: 183). In yet another passage, we read that "One
can no more speak of mediation without something immediate than,
conversely, one can find something immediate that is not mediated"

(1993b: 59). I will later return to the epistemological problem arising from this doctrine. For now I simply want to dwell on what looks like a conflict between a Hegelian vision of the dialectical exhaustion of immanence and a Benjaminian (undialectical) desire for radical otherness.

Now Adorno himself is likely to deny that this conflict is endangering his position. For him, it is rather an objective contradiction, arising from the irreconciled character of modern society. A true redemption of the object would not hypostatize it as some ultimate and underived other but would seek to bring about some kind of harmony between concept and object (or subject and object) which would rid the object of "coercion" while at the same time ensuring that it was given within the parameters of possible experience, that is, as immanent to the epistemic framework at the subject's disposal.

But where does this leave us with regard to the dialectics itself? In one passage, Adorno tells us that reconciliation would "open the road to the multiplicity of different things and strip dialectics of its power over them" (1973b: 6). On one possible interpretation, such a genuine reconciliation sounds like an anarchistic moment that would involve an escape from dialectics. Indeed, in this quote Adorno seems to suggest that a truth-event of this sort would transcend the conceptual register of any dialectics. Yet why isn't, on an alternative interpretation, the very notion of reconciliation, even when used by Adorno, itself an arch-Hegelian figure that cannot be conceptualized except as the unwanted "identity between identity and non-identity"? Isn't Adorno actually trying to out-Hegel Hegel by claiming that while the Hegelian system failed to mediate subject and object, reconciliation, whenever and wherever it occurs, is nevertheless a legitimate philosophical and political aim? Indeed, isn't Adorno's concept of reconciliation, whether it involves a "togetherness of diversity" or an "elective affinity" exactly what Hegel aspired to but presumably did not achieve?

This is the point at which a whole generation of postmodern or post-structuralist thinkers have launched their attack on Adorno. According to Lyotard (1974), Adorno is a thoroughly dialectical thinker who is committed to all the wrong causes: a notion of totality, a desire for reconciliation, an objectivist historical teleology, and a strengthening of the (in his view, essentially bourgeois) subject. By contrast, Lyotard — especially in his works of the 1980s — calls for a dismantling of totalizing narratives of historical progress, a critique of universalism, a strong defense of the plurality and incommensurability of cultures and language-games, and an overcoming of the subject. If we concentrate on the organizing concept of reconciliation, it cannot be denied that Adorno occasionally uses it in an affirmative mode, though not in order to anticipate the overcoming of every conceptual conflict and the achievement of a complete determination of the object in the Hegelian sense of absolute knowledge but rather to outline the possibility of a transgression of the representational together with a somatic realization of the object which excludes the intermediation of both concept and image. In his 1928 text on Schubert, for example, he establishes a connection between sudden, uncontrolled weeping and the "final reconciliation" allegedly promised in this music between man and nature. Fleetingly invoking utopia, the weeping is a negative, bodily response, the counterpart to the somatic notion of happiness. Indeed, deeply buried in the semantic layers of Adorno's materialism there is an almost Schopenhauerian longing not only for an unguarded encounter with the not-I, but a submersion into an unmasterable, Dionysian alterity, culminating in the complete indistinction between subject and object. Although predominantly associated with a regressive, narcissistic sexuality, in the *Dialectic of Enlightenment* Adorno (1979: 227) compares it to the Freudian death instinct and Caillois' *mimétisme*, viewing it as "the trend to lose oneself in the environment instead of playing an active role in it; the tendency to let oneself go and sink back into nature." It is hard to imagine a vision of reconciliation more foreign to the humanist account of subjective reappropriation that one finds in Hegel (and which Lyotard aims to criticize) than this dark romantic reunion with nature.

Ironically, while writing his initial critique of Adorno, Lyotard was himself positioned in close proximity to this thematics. Like other post-structuralists of the 1970s, most notably Deleuze, the Lyotard of *Discours, figure*, for example, posited the by now familiar counter-image of the neurotic self locked into its own compulsive repetitions — namely, the flux of a perpetual change of being in which neither subject nor object can be imagined, but only radical difference without negation, predication, or determination. The structural difference between the early Lyotard and Adorno is not so much that the former conceives of the supersession of a repressive relation between subject and object in terms of a schizophrenic regression to the Other and the latter in terms of a reconciliation modeled on the resurrection of nature; the essential difference, rather, is that Adorno — again not retreating from the paradoxical consequence of his position — wants to *affirm the subject in its moment of involuntary anni-hilation*. Whereas Lyotard envisions a total overcoming of the subject, Adorno seeks to strengthen it by exposing it, as if in a moment of illusion or semblance, to the primary processes from which it has arisen.

Indeed, as will be developed further in my discussion of the sublime, the moment of reconciliation is always inserted into a logics of illusion: recon-ciliation represents the negation of the false; it is, as it were, a utopian mirror that permits a glimpse into a condition in which the subject/object-dyad is radically transfigured, yet with reference to which the subject can only measure its distance from the state of reconciliation. As the analysis of fascism and the culture industry abundantly shows, while the ideal of reconciliation itself is bound to be regressive and therefore false, it ulti-mately comes to function as a negative concept — an experiential reminder of the irreconcilability of subject and object in a false social totality in which "reconciliation has become a satanic parody" (Adorno 1973–86: XII, 34).

According to Welsch (1990: 128–37), starting with the *Philosophy of the New Music*, Adorno gradually abandons his erstwhile emphasis on reconciliation, which he feared would remain ideological, in favor of "doing justice to the heterogeneous." One difficulty, however, with Welsch's "postmodern" account is that it from the outset forecloses the possibility of indicating historical tendencies capable of leading to a state of reconciliation. The irruptive moments of justice being done to the heterogeneous would of necessity be exceptional; hence they seem to invite the formation of political attitudes that are quietist and resigned. Indeed, Welsch's emphasis on heterogeneity seems to destabilize the notion of general, progressive history to such an extent that no concept of progress would be able to counter the universality of myth and fate.

Another problem with Welsch's position is that it, weary of the dialectic, too quickly disengages the notion of heterogeneity from the contradictions and oppositions within which it will unavoidably be inscribed. It could easily represent a return, familiar from much poststructuralist discourse, to a pure subjectivism in which one, instead of negating the false, seeks something ineffable which transcends it.

An advantage, though, is that, being coherent with democracy's need to renounce the vision of the social as consisting of organic unities, Welsch's suggestion would make it easier to reassert Adorno's lifelong quest for happiness and "eternal peace" (1974a: 157) within the parameters of a democratically constituted and open society. As opposed to the naturalization of power which, as Lefort (1988: 11) argues, is essential to organic social totalities, it would emphasize heterogeneity, and by implication plurality, difference and play — hence that power is unrepresentable, and that no one in particular can justifiably represent power without violating democracy's constitutive openness.

Adorno never fully resolved the paradox of wanting to non-identically identify the non-identical. Since identification, for him, inevitably involves a reduction to equivalence, the yearning for reconciliation will of necessity be aporetic and disappointing, encouraging an ultimately frustrating oscillation between a Hegelian desire to sublate and a Benjaminian desire to seek the nameless thing which transcends mediation. Although Adorno recognized this issue, indeed affirmed the paradox, encouraging his readers to "think at the same time dialectically and undialectically" and "to bring the intentionless within the realm of concepts" (1974a: 152), he never fully worked out its implications for his own thinking. So far, let it suffice to say that the paradox can only be softened if the non-identical is considered a moment within identity. If identitarian reason must presuppose a moment of non-identical givenness, then the task of a negative dialectic, rather than anticipating some sort of wholly reconfigured state, will be to criticize the identitarian suppression of the non-identical.

## The critique of ontology

Adorno's reading of Heidegger continues to bring up the thorny issue of how identitarian reason can be criticized without lapsing into some form of unwanted, arbitrary immediacy. It also makes up a highly political part of *Negative Dialectics*, anticipating by more than two decades many of the most consequential aspects of the Heidegger debate in the late 1980s. Of course, whereas this debate was especially relevant (and damaging) to the many Heideggerian versions of French poststructuralism, Adorno's Heidegger was predominantly — although his first text dealing with fundamental ontology appeared as early as 1931 — situated within the conservative climate of the postwar Federal Republic. While fully aware of the disastrous affiliation between the Freiburg thinker of Being and the Nazi regime, Adorno viewed Heidegger as the most advanced spokesman for a whole generation of conservative, even reactionary, German intellectuals, including Ernst Jünger, Carl Schmitt, and possibly also Arnold Gehlen and Helmut Schelsky.

Adorno's take on Heidegger, and indeed on the whole generation which he allegedly represents, is perhaps best known from the 1964 *Jargon of Authenticity*, which was originally planned as a separate part of *Negative Dialectics*. The *Jargon* was conceived as a scathing attack on German existentialism, arguing that its interest in poetic language boils down to an ideological desire to endow certain words and phrases — "being," "earth," and so on, borrowed from a rural metaphorics of preindustrial peasant proximity — with a privileged semantic and political authority. In a society dominated by the abstract exchange-relation, such a procedure of fetishization, he argues, produces pseudo-concreteness and false forms of immediacy. While, in a well-established democracy, the anti-enlightenment cult of origin may just be bad art, in the Germany of the 1930s it became official policy.

Although this book gained great popularity when it appeared, its lack of concern with the deeper philosophical worries that animate his antagonists' views together with its impatient, harsh tone and uncompromising restriction to a very particular line of Heideggerian thinking, makes it less rewarding to a contemporary audience. It has also, which is even more unfortunate, been instrumental in creating and maintaining an unfruitful and hostile opposition between Heideggerian and Adornian schools of philosophy, inviting French poststructuralists, committed to Heidegger's thinking, to deem Adorno irrelevant and contemporary Habermasians, on the other hand, to dismiss Heidegger altogether.

As Mörchen (1981) rightly emphasizes, no real encounter between Adorno and Heidegger can ever take place unless the many parallels that exist between their projects are acknowledged. While explaining its genesis in radically different ways, they both aim to criticize the predominance of formal-instrumental reason. They both seek to delimit the rational applicability of science and to resist the naturalization and reduction that is entailed by the predominance of natural sciences in ontological disputes. They both try to overcome the Cartesian emphasis on abstract methodology and foundationalism, aspiring instead to make philosophy concrete and dynamic. Finally, they are both deeply hostile to modern mass culture, and even though Adorno's investment in high modernism sets him apart from Heidegger's idiosyncratic romanticism, they both seek to counter what they view as degenerate cultural and political expressions with more authentic forms of art and writing.

In the light of these at least apparent similarities, Mörchen (1981: 480) asks whether there is a "general" or "over-all" objection to Heidegger in Adorno. What is it that really sets them apart? On Mörchen's account, the best candidate for such an objection consists in the latter's rejection of the thinking of Being (*Seinsdenken*) as such. While it is hard to disagree with Mörchen's general assertion, a lot more work is required in order to spell out *why* Adorno comes to reject it and what its ramifications might be. In trying to assess Adorno's critique, the problem that immediately arises, however, is that significant parts of it rest on highly dubious, if not downright incorrect, interpretations of Heidegger's texts. Of particular pertinence in this respect is Adorno's unfortunate tendency to equate Heidegger's juxtaposition of the ontological and the ontic with some form of Platonic distinction between essence and appearance. Given Heidegger's tremendous effort to liberate his thought from traditional metaphysics, it is chastening to observe how quickly Adorno associates his work with a preoccupation with essences.

The major charge that Adorno repeatedly makes is that Heidegger illegitimately transforms key notions of human existence (*Dasein*) and historicity into ontologized conceptions. From being notions that ought to belong to the domain of historical reality (or what Heidegger would call the ontic), they become notions of essence, of the attributes of history as such, and thus fail to be informed by empirical or contingent history. Like the idealism it seeks to overcome, fundamental ontology views essence, absolute principles, and abstracting procedures as more fundamental than the concrete subjects and objects of human history. As a result, not only does Heidegger, who extends the "claim of all *prima philosophia* to be a doctrine of the invariant ... to the variables" (1973b: 129), unduly ontologize the ontic, he also assigns an unjustified priority to the ontological, thereby assimilating living history to the petrified structure of self-sameness that Adorno sees as mythical.

Historical events are thus immunized against moral objections: in ontologized history there can be no space for genuine memory. Fundamental ontology advocates "submission to historical situations as though it were commanded by Being itself" (1973b: 130). Consequently, "Of the eternal idea in which entity was to share, or by which it was to be conditioned, nothing remains but the naked affirmation of what is anyway — the affirmation of power" (1973b: 131).

In response, it could be argued that Adorno's own conception of natural history, which is designed such as to view history as the relentless unfolding of abstract universality, itself amounts to a form of historical essentialism. However, for Adorno, even if history and dialectics *seems* to be at a standstill, the metaphysical priority is always on the side of contingent history — the history of concrete, singular bodies and entities. The mythical history of repetition, while objective in that it remains a social and historical *a priori*, thus ultimately remains illusory. It is contingent history which is real in the metaphysical sense. When Heidegger, by contrast, assigns priority to the ontological, then it is not because it is metaphysically prior in the Platonic sense of being more real but because Being, in the analysis offered in *Being and Time* and elsewhere, is considered to be the ultimate source of intelligibility. Since the meaning of Being is construed in terms of originary temporality, and since originary temporality is the transcendental condition of intelligibility in general, it follows that what Heidegger — as his reading of Kant in *Kant and the Problem of Metaphysics* abundantly demonstrates — actually aims at is to provide a transcendental account of experience, though in a temporalized sense. As opposed to what Adorno claims, Heidegger does not operate with an opposition between essence and appearance. The only — though significant — sense in which he might be interpreted as a Platonist is that Being, for him, becomes the *exclusive* source of intelligibility. As he makes clear in *The Origin of the Work of Art*, since politics must be predicated on the *Stiftung* provided by the event of Being's own disclosure, the constitutive plurality which marks a democratic polity should be rejected. Moreover, since the structure of Being is beyond possible deliberation by an autonomous subjectivity, the order it provides will necessarily be heteronomous and therefore potentially authoritarian. The Kantian modernist in Adorno therefore rebukes ontology for its "readiness to sanction a heteronomous order that need not be consciously justified" (1973b: 61).

Noting that Being, for Heidegger, is meant to transcend its conceptual determination in the sense that it does not refer to any determinable entity, Adorno records a similarity between their projects: they both aim at revealing the nonidentity in identity. However, Heidegger ultimately surrenders this dialectical ambition by holding that the linguistic category of "Being" bears a privileged and direct relation to its "object." Grammatical form, Adorno argues, is presented as apophantic content, thus "[transforming] the ontical task of 'is' into an ontological one, a way of Being to be" (1973b: 102). On Adorno's account, this means that

Heidegger falls behind the nominalistic critique of conceptual realism. Rather than respecting the difference, starting with Ockham and Bacon, between concept and object, *de dictum* and *de re*, Heidegger reverts to what amounts to an Aristotelian identification between language and being. It is not human practice but the structure or substantiality of Being itself that determines the meaning of "Being." In order to know what "Being" signifies it becomes necessary to have recourse to an immediate, primeval, and non-conceptual X; thus, the thinking of Being regresses into a pathos of sheer invocation, making the endeavor to think Being beyond conceptual mediation obscure and irrational.

Given his diatribes, in the *Dialectic of Enlightenment* and elsewhere, against positivism's (and indeed modernity's) "system of detached signs" (1979: 18), it may seem surprising and indeed inconsistent that Adorno invokes nominalism in his critique of Heidegger. However, the appeal to nominalism is not meant to suggest that only particulars have a real existence, but that there is always a non-identity between concept and object that calls for dialectical reflection. While the ontologist attempts to close the gap between language and world by endowing Being with a special sense of depth and authenticity, the dialectician accepts the gap and tries to inscribe it within an oppositional structure that can be developed further.

The problem with this critique is that Heidegger never reduces thinking to such simple gesturing. Behind the self-evidence with which we use the word "Being" in predication stands an enigma that can only be approached through an interrogation of the entity for which Being is an issue, namely Dasein in its everydayness. The "forgotten" question of the meaning of Being requires an anamnesis of the ordinary and the everyday. What prevents Adorno from discussing the analytic of Dasein with the scholarly care it deserves? Is its powerful objections to the Cartesian subject, its critique of truth as correspondence, and its anti-idealist temporalization of Being in general too closely related to Adorno's own concerns for him to be able to deal with it properly? Or is it that Heidegger's political engagement has for ever tainted it, regardless of its philosophical merits? Is the proximity of Heidegger's thinking to his own too uncomfortable for Adorno to bear? One can only speculate.[1]

What is clear, however, is that Adorno, for both political and philosophical reasons, wants to resist the later Heidegger's dismissal of the value of autonomy and his concomitant debunking of the project of gaining a specifically modernist form of self-reassurance. Thus we now need to turn to Adorno's discussion of freedom.

## Freedom

The three "models," each comprising a single chapter, that make up the final part of *Negative Dialectics* relate obliquely to Kant's three transcendental ideas — freedom, God, and immortality — with reference to which humans, according to the *Critique of Practical Reason*, are entitled to hope but not to obtain cognitive assurance. The first deals with freedom in Kant's practical philosophy, the second with Hegel's conception of World Spirit (*Weltgeist*), and the third with the question of death (and metaphysics) in the late capitalist society after Auschwitz. The many different levels at which Adorno's argument seems to be unfolding in the chapter on freedom, on which I now want to focus, makes it both bewildering and suggestive. It is, for one thing, a sustained meditation on the liberal (Kantian) tradition of political thought. Continuing the critique of liberal thought that had been initiated in the *Dialectic of Enlightenment*, the metacritique of practical reason, which was first presented in Adorno's 1964–5 lecture course *Zur Lehre von der Geschichte und von der Freiheit*, is by far the most overtly political section of Adorno's *Negative Dialectics*: the originary space of freedom *is* political, and individual freedom can only be fully realized in a free, rational society. However, it is also a social, psychological, and metaphysical investigation into the concept of freedom itself, offering an outline, though largely negative, of what real freedom would entail. Finally, Adorno embarks on a metacritique of Kant's own theory of transcendental freedom, arguing, as Lukács did before him, that it represents a form of reified or identitarian thinking.

Within contemporary Continental philosophy, the concept of freedom has recently been the object of a spectacular revival, having for decades been dismissed, whether in Althusserian Marxism or in Derridean deconstruction, as little more than a humanist illusion. In the work of thinkers such as Alain Badiou and Jean-Luc Nancy, the concept of freedom has crucially demanded articulation: in the first, according a logic of truth-events; in the second, by way of a reconceptualization of Heidegger's and Schelling's ontologies of freedom. On the one hand, it seems obvious that Adorno would have distanced himself from both of these positions: from Badiou's notion of freedom as fidelity towards a truth-conferring event because of its implied demand for submission and its invocation of immediacy with regard to the purity of the event; from Nancy's ontology because it postulates a source of authority—the anarchic, Heideggerian abyss (*Abgrund*) or *chorâ* — transcending the scope of autonomous subjective reflection. While, from an Adornian standpoint, Badiou falsely indexes revolutionary politics to an arbitrary act of decision that retroactively obligates the political subject, Nancy refers the subject to a transsubjective order of temporalized foundationalism, thereby failing to break with the predominance of myth. Having said that, however, Adorno would on the other hand sympathize with several of the concerns that motivate both Badiou's and Nancy's projects. All three of them are in full accord that theorizing the notion of freedom requires no reinstatement whatsoever of the classical humanist philosophy of the subject.[2] In order to think freedom coherently, there is no need for a metaphysics of the subject as a distinct substance or *hypokeimenon*. Moreover, they all share a deep-seated animosity towards the widespread ideological misuses of the notion of freedom, especially in contemporary liberal democracies. Real freedom, they would argue, is inseparable from a transformation of the social conditions within which current societies reproduce themselves. Ultimately, freedom is a political task; its realization can never be restricted to the solitary individual.

In the *Negative Dialectics*, Adorno relates the notion of freedom to the philosophy of German idealism. Its mandate, he maintains, stemming from the ideological interest of the burgeoning European bourgeoisie, consisted above all in transparently justifying the existence of freedom. Against the conventional moral attitudes of the old culture of the Holy Roman Empire, which were stifling and conformist, the representatives of the educated German citizenry searched for ways to position them-selves as self-directed and authentic. Suddenly appeals to the old order were replaced with a new desire to accept no normative content, whether theoretical or practical, as binding unless it had been rationally validated by the individual agent. As Whitebook (1995: 136) points out, at least four dimensions of this "short intermezzo of liberalism" (Adorno 1979: 87) must be taken into account: the creation of a civil society as a realm in which individuals can pursue their self-interest; the rise of the modern family, in which individuals were free to pursue their own sexual, romantic, and emotional happiness; the separation of the family from civil society; and, finally, the rise of a patriarchal society which, according to the Freudian theory of the Oedipal triangle, was an essential condition for the formation of autonomous individuality. While Adorno certainly highlights the ideological function the notion of freedom had for the rising property-owning bourgeoisie seeking to secure its posses-sive individualism against the interests of the state and the nobility, he dismisses the standard Marxist tendency to view it simply as a super-structural reflection. Not only was the ideal of self-determination embedded in a particular part of the social structure of the time, it also lays claim to universal significance: all men ought to take an interest in their own freedom. Having said that, however, there is an ambivalence in Adorno's account in that both the emergence and the downfall of the individual is, according to his argument, located historically with great specificity. It is therefore questionable whether Adorno's definition of autonomy can be assessed independently of the laissez-faire capitalist, indeed bourgeois, circumstances in which he considers it. In Whitebook's (1995: 137) formulation, "*Homo oeconomicus* and *Homo criticus* were not entirely unrelated."

As subjects are increasingly objectified by the economical, technical, and administrative pressures that they face within the social system as a

112

whole, the enthusiasm for freedom largely wanes, leaving only the false freedom of consumerism in its wake. Moreover, the super-ego, whose successful integration into the psyche is a necessary (though obviously not sufficient) condition of human freedom, is today predominantly external-ized and ultimately replaced by political or symbolic sources of authority over which the rational subject has little or no influence. Although its status as a historically mediated and yet universally significant category is beyond dispute, the value of freedom seems in most people's eyes to have become obsolete. Apart from the socially objective reasons why this occurred, Adorno enlists the failure to articulate a notion of freedom that escapes the twin evils of abstraction and subjectivism, both of which emerge from his reading of Kant.

In order to fully understand the metacritical analysis of Kant's thinking about transcendental freedom, it is important, however, to bear in mind another fundamental aporia that besets Adorno's dialectic of freedom. If autonomy is understood — and it may well be — as the capacity to stand back and disconnect oneself from the immediate impact and demands of one's surroundings, then, given the account of the enlightenment impulse as stemming, ultimately, from the instinct of self-preservation, where self-preservation takes place through the control of outer nature and the sacrifice of inner nature, the ego's autonomy must be extensionally equiva-lent with domination. Put differently, freedom then becomes a function of compulsion, or indeed its necessary complement. As we will see, Adorno reads Kant's doctrine of the causality of freedom as inadvertently demon-strating the equivalence of autonomy and domination; in the language of transcendental idealism, Kant thus reproduces what Adorno, following Freud, views as the fundamental scar on human subjectivity. The problem, evidently, is that Adorno thereby seems to paint himself into a corner: for how can his naturalist account of the ego allow for an account of freedom that would escape the logic of domination and violence?

Central to Kant's analysis is the antinomy between freedom and neces-sity, between the transcendental freedom of rational will, on the one hand, and nature, defined in terms of causal, law-like interconnectedness between events, on the other. In the *Critique of Pure Reason*, Kant claims to have shown that the categories of transcendental subjectivity, with particular emphasis on causality, legislate *a priori* for the objectivized domain of nature; thus, against the Humean onslaught on such categories, his work aspires to endow modern natural science with a strong claim to rationality and objective truth. The problem of freedom arises as a response to the necessitarian claim of universalist scientific (Newtonian) ontology, that is, the view, as Kant (1986: B473) states it, that "everything in the world takes place solely in accordance with laws of nature." Against this thesis stands, in the third antinomy, the antithesis: "Causality in accor-dance with laws of nature is not the only causality from which the appearances of the world can one and all be derived. To explain these appearances it is necessary to assume that there is also another causality, that of freedom" (1986: B473). Without freedom, the very notion of rational and moral accountability, and indeed also of human agency, would collapse, hence Kant desperately needs to show that the postulate of freedom is at least compatible with the naturalist's claim to necessitarian universalism.

The key, very roughly, to the resolution of the antinomy is the distinction Kant establishes in the transcendental analytic between phenomena and noumena, or between the order of things as they appear and the order of things as they are in themselves. Since only the former order is extensionally equated with nature under laws, we are entitled to view the existence of freedom as a possibility. However, since freedom, if it is to exist, will have to be related to a spontaneity that transcends the order of appearances, it cannot be known objectively: we can hope and believe that the will is free, indeed as moral agents we are inevitably committed to the existence of freedom, yet since it would exceed the domain of possible experience, no knowledge of it is possible. It remains a transcendental idea.

Adorno's dialectical reading of this argument has many twists and turns. In one sense, Kant's stark antinomy can be deciphered as a veiled description of the fate of freedom in modernity. Rather than being actual and thus effective in the empirical sense, freedom is marginalized and indeed excommunicated from the socio-historical world of empirical events. Lacking embodiment, materiality, and concretion, transcendental freedom does not seem realizable in sensible form. At best, it becomes the possession of isolated individuals, themselves pieces of nature and thus subject to external laws, in a fragmented social whole. Indeed, since nature is considered a mechanical system, reflecting the more general reduction of being (including social and historical being) to its identitarian coordinates, there is reason to distrust our self-presence as morally responsible agents in the world: materiality and freedom are radically, and through *a priori* legislation, disunited. Adorno warns in this regard against the temptation, widespread among the German romantics, to respond to the antinomy by considering beauty as freedom in appearance. In Schiller, he argues, this move leads to a false reconciliation of an antinomy which, rather than being resolvable in theory or aesthetic practice, needs to be acknowledged as a social fact.

Lukács, whose reading of Kant's third antinomy in *History and Class Consciousness* no doubt inspires Adorno, follows Schiller in demanding a genuine *Aufhebung* of the opposition between transcendental freedom and natural necessity. For Lukács, as well as Adorno, the Kantian system, by imprisoning the subject in self-imposed yet socially intransparent categorical structures, reproduces on an allegedly *a priori* level (or rather what appears to the alienated agent as *a priori*) the *a posteriori* or historical reifications of social reality. However, unlike Adorno, Lukács responds to the antinomy and its implied disunity of subject and object by introducing a social force, the industrial proletariat, capable of effecting a synthesis between them. Whereas Kant had construed the antinomy from a theoretical point of view, thus hypostatizing the division between subject and object, the notion of the proletariat brings to the fore a practical point of view: if, through a social revolution, the proletariat could reappropriate its own essence by abolishing the capitalist world of reification, then the third antinomy would be overcome historically and a genuine reconciliation would ensue.

While both Adorno and Lukács believed that freedom must be actualized politically, only the latter felt able to identify a historical subject in the grand Hegelian sense that was ready to do so. Both Adorno and Lukács wanted to conceptualize freedom as a mediated unity of difference, a *bei-sich-selbst-im-Anderssein*, yet only Lukács was willing to invest faith in the Marxist category of the proletariat. For Adorno, as we will see in more detail shortly, freedom, if viewed in real-historical terms, seems at best restricted to perform a determinate negation of the false totality; its only foreseeable rationale is to be exercised as resistance to bad practice.

But how? Returning to the discussion of Kant's concept of freedom, it is worth noticing that Adorno's interest in individual resistance does not lead him to reject Kant's notion of autonomy. Indeed, in at least one passage he directly endorses it: "The only true force against the principle of Auschwitz would be human autonomy, if I may use a Kantian term: that is, the force of reflection and of self-determination, the will to refuse participation" (quoted in Hohendahl 1995: 58). As previously mentioned, Adorno's favorite term for this ability to resist, to be self-authorized, is *Mündigkeit*, which famously appears in Kant's text "Answering the Question: What is Enlightenment?" in conjunction with the Horatian injunction *sapere aude!*[3] *Mündigkeit*, he argues, would be a necessary ingredient in any account of true democracy. Emphasizing the equivocation in the notion of *Mündigkeit* or autonomy as between standing apart and being self-authorized, in the *Negative Dialectics* and the *Lectures on Kant's Moral Philosophy* he points out how Kantian autonomy is dialectically predicated upon a repression of drives (*Triebe*) and the concomitant establishment of a strong and punitive super-ego.

The interpretive practice of never discussing Kant without bringing in Freud has a long history in Adorno. By couching moral behavior in terms such as duty, law, constraint, and respect, Kant shows an awareness of the dialectic of enlightenment — the price agents pay in order to be in a position whereby they, as Kant demands, are able to freely adopt maxims that all rational beings can accept. Following Hegel's critique of Kantian rigorism, however, Adorno views the coercive character of Kant's moral philosophy as false. The identifying principle operative in the demand for subjection to a universal principle, a moral law that is universally binding regardless of circumstances and empirical inclination, should be under-stood as "the internalized principle of society" (1973b: 241). Kant is incapable of envisioning "the concept of freedom otherwise than as repression" (1973b: 256). It follows that personal happiness (*Glück*) must be rejected as a morally acceptable incentive to action: the *Critique of Practical Reason* can only acknowledge as morally recommendable maxims that make no reference whatsoever to the satisfaction of desire. Kant's moral agent thus anticipates all the essential features of a repressed, neurotic patient who acts not out of a genuine sense of what is right, but because his or her own impulses are compulsively curbed by a blind demand to remain in conformity with the law.

Adorno makes a lot out of Kant's talk of a causality of freedom. In his view, Kant construes freedom as a special kind of causality and then, in a second step, models the causality of freedom upon the causality of nature. Just as, in order to answer Hume's skepticism, the causality of nature must be objective and necessary, and thus follow from rules (a causal relation, for Kant, always presupposes an objective and *a priori* rule linking antecedent and consequent), so also must the causality of freedom:

> The substance of its own freedom — of the identity which has annexed all nonidentity — is as one with the "must," with the law, with absolute dominion. This is the spark that kindles the pathos of Kant. He construes even freedom as a special case of causality. To him, it is the "constant laws" that matter.
>
> (Adorno 1973b: 250)

Since causality, in Kant, is a rule-governed relation, it follows, Adorno believes, that when causality is extended to the intelligible sphere, it will jeopardize the notion of freedom. The problem with this interpretation, however, is that Kant evidently does not align causality of freedom with causality of nature. Since Kant rejects compatibilism, it is not just a "special case" of the latter but rather a distinct form of causality involving the idea of an absolute spontaneity (the unconditioned with respect to causality), the capacity to initiate a series of causally related occurrences, without itself being the causal consequence of antecedent properties of the agent, including the antecedent state of the agent. Very roughly, Adorno fails to appreciate that, for Kant, spontaneity is the ability to act strictly as the result of the subject's own self-determination. What, according to Kant, distinguishes actions from events (having one's body move, say, as a result of the impingement of either external or internal material givens) is that actions are undertaken according to reasons; and free agency is the capacity to act on the basis of imperatives (or maxims) in general (not merely the categorical imperative) such that the action becomes intelligible as an action. It is therefore always possible to ask a rational agent *why* she did what she did, what the point of her action might be. In doing so there is always an implied reference to what a rational person would do, or rather, what it makes sense to do insofar as one is responsive to reasons and hence rational. Judgment as such, in other words, is *normative*; it involves appeals to what a reasoning being would say and how things *ought* to be in the light of deliberation. In *Religion within the Limits of Reason Alone*, Kant formulates the thesis underlying this view in terms of the incorporation of incentives into maxims that can be the object of rational consideration.[4] As he puts it, "freedom of the will [*Willkür*] is of a wholly unique nature in that an incentive can determine the will to an action *only so far as the individual has incorporated it into his maxim* (has made it the general rule in accordance with which he will conduct himself); only thus can an incentive, whatever it may be, co-exist with the absolute spontaneity of the will" (Kant 1960: 19). Adorno fails to acknowledge that the adoption of a rule or principle of action cannot itself be regarded as following from rules. Rather, it must be conceived as an act of spontaneity, and as such the law is not imposed from the outside but is an immediate expression of one's status as a rational agent.

There is obviously a lot more to be said about Kant's conception of rational agency. What concerns us here is that Adorno misses out on what, for Kant, it means to be, not subject to various motivational forces, but the subject of one's deeds. However, Adorno needs such an account in order to be consistent with his own adoption of a Kantian principle of autonomy. According to Eldridge's (2002: 19) retrieval of the Kantian position, "As beings who are open to the authority of reasons, we bear an aspiration to live freely, fully in the light of reasons we have articulated for ourselves, in awareness of the nature and proper functioning of our own powers, rather than imbibing them from things." Why should Adorno want to dismiss this as an interpretation of Kant? Indeed, it is an ideal he would have subscribed to himself. By associating behavior according to law with a reified form of subjectivity, he does not recognize how an indefinite range of incentives, including bodily desires, can be incorporated into maxims and thus be made the object of a free will determining itself. If Kant is a rigorist, it is not because he rejects desire-based action as inherently irrational but because he, viewing it as heteronomous, rules it out as morally unworthy.

Performing a determinate negation of his image of Kantian moral philosophy, Adorno goes searching for an account of freedom in precisely those domains that Kant would have dismissed as giving rise to heteronomy. Freedom, he argues, requires communication with a rather mysterious anarchic other of reason which he, in the *Negative Dialectics*, calls the addendum (*das Hinzutretende*). It is remarkable how emphatically Adorno insists, on the one hand, that a considerable level of coercion is necessary for self-resolved moral behavior to be possible, while, on the other hand, by locating genuine absence of constraint, and hence freedom, in the addendum, moves the discussion of freedom towards a consideration of drives and the unconscious. Even though he seems close to contradicting himself, it is easy to see the negative rationale for the adoption of this view. If the establishment of a self-identical ego is itself based on acts of coercion, then the negation of such coercion would seem to be found in a solidarity with that which has been repressed. As always, Adorno is far from recommending any kind of "return to nature." Rather than relinquishing autonomy, his aim, rather, is to consider it in relation to its otherness — in relation, that is, to the object "which either grants or denies autonomy to the subject" (1973b: 223).

In *Zur Lehre von der Geschichte und von der Freiheit*, Adorno turns to Shakespeare's *Hamlet* in order to elucidate the notion of the addendum. Finding himself in a post-medieval world devoid of moral certainties, Hamlet, the intellectual, appears as a victim of the new and early modern demand for autonomous reflection. As opposed to the active Fortinbras, who represents the medieval world of chivalry, Hamlet famously cannot bring himself to act. Rather than revealing himself to others, he remains stifled, passive, locked inside his own interior monologue, incapable of translating the father-ghost's demand for revenge into the decisive deed. In philosophical terms, Hamlet's problem is that unless an experience can provide motivation from outside the space of reasons, the sheer reflection itself retrogrades into an empty gesture, leading to skepticism and nihilism. In order to do what he so desperately wants and thinks is right but is unable to justify, he needs a shock experience, or what Adorno calls "a sudden impulse" that throws him into action. It is the wound — hence a somatic intervention — being inflicted at the end of the fifth act which brings about the necessary addendum for action to occur.

"The realization of Hamlet's political and moral project," Adorno (2001b: 326) writes, "requires regression, the return to an earlier, anarchic level." But what kind of regression? Why isn't this simply a lapse into the heteronomy he otherwise so adamantly criticizes? Adorno considers this objection and claims that the impulse, the addendum, rather than weakening the rational, identical self of moral and political deliberation, in fact strengthens it. The regression should not be viewed undialectically, as a straightforward suspension of the ego, but rather, along Hegelian lines, as a movement of self-identification in otherness. Referring to Freud, Adorno bolsters this argument by recalling how, in psychoanalytic theory, the free and reality-oriented ego itself, insofar as respect for reality is a function of the more general pleasure principle which governs the primary system, can be viewed as an extension of libidinal energy into the secondary system. The very possibility of therapy is predicated upon the fact that the ego and the id, rationality and desire, are less foreign to one another than suggested by the Kantian system of moral psychology. Of course, Adorno would resist both an undialectical invocation of libidinal transgression, as in Deleuze and Guattari, and a call for a dialectical mediation between ego and id, as in Marcuse. The point of the dialectic, rather, is to conduct what the *Dialectic of Enlightenment* refers to as a "remembrance of the nature in the subject."

Apart from the sheer difficulty involved in offering a coherent reading of this argument in itself, a serious problem, however, with relating the notion of addendum so closely to Freud's theory is that Freudian regression is a movement towards repressed infantile desire whose irresistible and repetitive urge for outlet, when met with resistance from the ego, produces a symptom-formation. Alternatively, what is it that distinguishes the addendum from the impulse which gives rise to a dream or a parapraxis? Or why, to put it bluntly, is Adornian regression liberating and Freudian regression just the occasion upon which a neurotic symptom is being created? While there is hardly any answer to this question in Adorno's own exposition, it might be added to his analysis that the moment in which Hamlet finds himself capable of acting is simultaneously the moment in which he overcomes his melancholy and starts to mourn by recathecting libido onto external objects. Perhaps the addendum can be understood as the moment of release that initiates mourning and transforms the state of debt into autonomous political action? Such action would here entail the liberation of the ego from its deadly fixation on the lost object (the father) and the achievement of an independent social positioning of the self in relation to others. Mourning would thus be equated with autonomy, and it would allow the individual to affirm the lost object's (i.e., the father's) independence and transience, which itself is required for autonomy to be possible: for without the acceptance of division and separation, hence mourning, there would be no individual.

Such a reading would be consistent with larger strands of Adorno's thinking, in particular his intention of conceiving the "correct" relation between subject and object as requiring an act of confession according to which the subject acknowledges its distance and otherness vis-à-vis the object. In Hegel's *Phenomenology*, such a confession takes place when the "hard heart" experiences the consequences of its separation from the community. In desperately seeking to authorize its normative relation to the world from the standpoint of a purely individual and isolated act of "authentically" projecting meaning onto the object, the "hard heart" learns that in order to discover meaning and acquire communal recognition it needs to release the object from its own holds.[5] In Freudian terms it needs to mourn — to accept transience and otherness. The weak Messianic moment in Adorno asserts itself precisely in this act of sudden acknowledgment of difference whereby the object is retained, as it were, in its absence — and as a promise.

Given the rather extraordinary revival, in contemporary continental philosophy, of the theme of Messianic, anticipatory politics, this might be a useful occasion upon which to delimit Adorno's thinking from that of Derrida in this respect. In *The Specters of Marx*, Derrida reads Hamlet's acquisition of responsibility not as evolving from a process of mourning but as based on a Schmittean decision that itself is reached in a state of uncertainty and exception. While Adorno seems to emphasize the moment of decision as well, it is important to recognize that unlike Derrida, for whom "the state of debt" is responded to in the absence of, or without constraint from, moral and juridical rules, Adorno's account of free decision is based on an ethical acknowledgment of violence and a concomitant desire to mourn.[6] By contrast, in Derrida's weak version of political Messianism, the moment of autonomous judging is destabilized by the constitutive "madness" of decision for which the source of authority is excessive in relation to the scope of autonomous reflection.

Behind Derrida's approach stands the whole discourse of Levinas, in which the self is supposed to become devastated, traumatized, unenthroned, and indeed to substitute the other for itself — all symptoms of extreme melancholy. According to Freud's classical paper "Mourning and Melancholia," whereas mourning is a reaction to loss whereby libidinal investment is recathected, thus liberating the ego from the deadly fixation on the lost object, melancholy conceals an aggressiveness toward the lost object, thus revealing the ambivalence of the depressed person with respect to the object of mourning.[7] The melancholic imbeds the lost object in herself so as not to lose it. However, since the love for the object has been effected on a narcissistic basis, which places the self in a relationship both of identification and aggression, it ends up devalorizing itself with the same passion as it formerly valorized the object. As is the case in Levinas's concept of persecution, of being persecuted by the other, the psychic malady of melancholy is therefore potentially infinite: it knows no work of mourning, no positive or symbolic law to be acknowledged; all it knows is an infinite self-divestiture and self-negation before the divine and violent Other with whom the ego identifies. It is precisely in the recognition of this infinite debt that the Messianic spirit — the promise of promises, originary *and* deferred — of Levinas comes to the fore.

By contrast, Adorno stakes his account of Messianic disruption and anticipatory politics on the availability of a much more Kantian notion of autonomy. At the end of the day, the autonomy on offer in Adorno must be keyed to the notion of determinate negation. The best candidate for autonomous deliberation (and hence freedom) is theory itself, where theory must be understood as negative dialectics. In a thoroughly anti-Nietzschean gesture, Adorno insists that freedom, rather than being creative on its own, arises as a response to given social configurations and conflicts. It unfolds as a mournful passion for critique.

# 6

# THE POLITICS OF AESTHETIC
# NEGATIVITY

> This is not the time for political works of art; rather, politics has
> migrated into the autonomous work of art, and it has penetrated
> most deeply into works that present themselves as politically dead,
> as in Kafka's parable about the children's guns, where the idea of
> nonviolence is fused with the dawning awareness of an emerging
> political paralysis.
>
> (Adorno 1991–2: II, 93–4)

The quote is taken from the last paragraph of the 1962 essay
"Commitment," which Adorno wrote as an extended polemic against
Brecht. It is brimful of implications: political art is a thing of the past; politics survives in the age of total administration, though only in a form
which resists and negates it; autonomous and "politically dead" art can
claim political relevance; a "migration" of political content has occurred,
draining the sphere of direct political intervention and collective action of
meaning, and assigning to art the role of a placeholder of the political. In
*Aesthetic Theory* (1997a: 243), Adorno's posthumous opus magnum, we
accordingly find the beholder of an advanced work of art being described
as a *zoon politikón*, capable of contributing towards a politics of pure
praxis.

In this chapter I examine how Adorno combines art's claim to radical
autonomy with its political and critical potential. I start by looking at how
his position relates to Benjamin's notion of art's claim to have a political
voice and then proceed by discussing the crucial notion of truth-content
(*Wahrheitsgehalt*). Ultimately, I argue that Adorno must be read as a theorist of the sublime and that the sublime represents art's challenge to
identitarian reason.

## The Adorno–Benjamin dispute: aura and de-aestheticization

The publication of Walter Benjamin's celebrated essay "The Work of Art
in the Age of Mechanical Reproduction" in 1936 plunged Adorno straight

into a hugely influential controversy over the relationship between art and politics.[1] At the time of responding to this essay, Adorno had already been an avid reader of Benjamin for more than ten years, and in the early 1930s he had even been teaching *The Origin of German Tragic Drama*, Benjamin's early masterpiece, at the University of Frankfurt. Moreover, Adorno had also been discussing some of Benjamin's most recent writings with him: "Paris, Capital of the Nineteenth Century" (also known as the Arcades Exposé) and "The Paris of the Second Empire in Baudelaire." The criticisms Adorno proposes must therefore be viewed as directed not simply towards the essay itself but towards the Benjamin that Adorno knew as the author of a number of other works, some of which — especially the *Trauerspiel* study — intimately informed his own thinking. When Adorno turns against Benjamin, he takes issue with what he considers to be his friend's self-misunderstandings and not with Benjamin's work *per se*. It is an immanent critique, addressing not just Benjamin but ultimately himself insofar as his own thinking was shaped by the work of this philosopher.

"The Work of Art" essay belongs to Benjamin's most Brechtian and explicitly Marxist phase. Its political context is fascism at its most triumphant, while its aim is to argue for the functional transformation of culture along Marxist lines. Disguised, at least in part, as a study of art's progressive loss of aura, the essay seeks more specifically to uncover the conditions for what Wolin (1994: 184) describes as "a materialist *Aufhebung* of affirmative bourgeois culture." In attempting to resist fascism's powerful aestheticization of the political, art has to shed its naive claim to autonomy and be politicized. Art, now serving the ends of communism, must act as an immediate counterforce to fascism:

> Mankind which in Homer's time was an object of contemplation for the Homeric gods, now is one for itself. Its self-alienation has reached such a degree that it can experience its own destruction as an aesthetic pleasure of the first order. This is the situation of politics which Fascism is rendering aesthetic. Communism responds by politicizing art.
>
> (Benjamin 1969: 242)

The notion that culture must transform itself in order to resist fascism is obviously compelling. (Indeed, Adorno himself, as we have seen, makes this into a cornerstone of his postwar cultural criticism.) Insofar as fascism, as manifested in works such as Marinetti's *Manifesto of Futurism* or Jünger's theory of total *Mobilmachung* in *The Worker*, is capable of fashioning its own violence into a work of art, mobilizing the forces of aesthetic production for progressive political ends becomes an important strategy for communication and counter-attack. In view of the build-up of the Nazi war machine, the idea of saving or protecting the domain of autonomous art seemed to Benjamin both irrelevant and reactionary. So-called autonomous art — epitomized by the *l'art pour l'art* movement of the second half of the nineteenth century — arose as a response to the commodification of art. Under the conditions of fascism, however, the problem of commodification became subordinate to the more immediate threat of unchecked violence and war. As Benjamin viewed the situation, since bourgeois culture had done little or nothing to prevent the rise of fascism, it was either in manifest demise or itself the material for a new and sinister fascist vision of self-glorification. The question which any reader of Benjamin remains faced with, and which Adorno will be focusing on, is whether the political employment of art can avoid the fascist instrumentalization of art. In order to create a genuine and radical alternative, there must be a clear and essential difference between fascist aestheticized politics and communist politicized art, a difference which Benjamin must have worked out in detail.[2]

Benjamin's position rests on a number of assumptions concerning the history of art as well as its conditions of reception. Of great centrality is the well-known claim that art, with the invention of techniques for its mechanical reproduction, has lost its erstwhile aura. Traditional, pre-modern art, Benjamin submits, had a unique existence: it did not allow reproducibility. The only possible reception of such work would take place in the quasi-sacred mode of the "here and now." Any attempt to reproduce it would destroy the aura. To experience such a work meant to be faced with an object which at one and the same time was ineffable or distant *and* present. In order to illustrate the historical notion of aura, Benjamin uses an example taken from the realm of nature:

> We define the aura of [natural objects] as the unique phenomenon of a distance, however close it may be. If, while resting on a summer afternoon, you follow with your eyes a mountain range on the horizon or a branch which casts its shadow over you, you experience the aura of those mountains, or of that branch.
>
> (1969: 222–3)

In *Aesthetic Theory*, Adorno reads Benjamin's notion of aura in terms of the notion of "atmosphere" and refers to it as an "objective meaning that surpasses subjective intention" (1997a: 275). For Adorno, the aura takes on the role of a residue of non-intentional meaning which, as we shall see, can be exploited (in advertising for example) as well as cultivated (in advanced art). On Benjamin's account, the aura pertaining to man-made artifacts is explicitly sustained by traditional, ritual practices. It was ritual which provided the requisite guarantee of the work's authenticity and hence authority. With the rise, however, of technical means of reproduction, art disinherits its previous dependence on ritual; it thus loses its aura (which cannot be reproduced but presupposes the "here and now"), and rather than being esteemed in terms of its "cult value," that is, its value as a unique and privileged entity, it takes on what Benjamin calls "exhibition value," by which he means a relation, or rather a point of intersection, between work and onlooker. In the age of film and photography, Benjamin (1969: 224) observes, "to ask for the 'authentic' print makes no sense." As a result of technical development, authenticity becomes an unsustainable category. The object, one might say, no longer purports to embody an intrinsic authority. Its claim now becomes communicative; it can function not as an object of veneration but as an instrument of communication, thus revealing hitherto unexplored potentials for political employment.

Benjamin's essay can be read as effecting a simple inversion of the conservative lament over the loss of symbolic authority in modern culture. While agreeing with the conservative in assigning a pre-eminent world-historical role to the "decline of the aura," Benjamin subverts the terms whereby this decline is assessed. Rather than simply viewing the decline of the aura as a bad and unwanted process, expressive of a cultural crisis, its disappearance should be taken as an opportunity to rethink the role of art completely. De-aestheticization, the progressive unravelling of the work's claim to be an autonomous aesthetic object, should be supported and encouraged, not resisted. However, the interest that Benjamin takes in the changing conditions of the production and reception of art indicates that he is up to more than just rehearsing a conservative genealogy while reconsidering its implicit system of values. With regard to film, he argues, since both its production and reception is *collective*, this medium challenges the predominantly *private* and *solitary* conditions for the production and reception of bourgeois autonomous art, making it eminently suitable for the transmission of political ideals in a mass society. Moreover, through the use of montage, the viewer is brought to awareness of the artificiality and conventionality of the medium by being exposed to *shock effects*. Film thus carries with it a moment of Brechtian *Verfremdung*: radically at odds with the ideal of passivity and submission to the authority of the work characteristic of bourgeois autonomous art, it forces the onlooker to take an active, reflective attitude to the seen.

Looking back at Benjamin's essay some seventy years later one cannot help being struck by the rich and powerful relationship it proposes between technical development, anti-aestheticism, and political mobilization. Benjamin transforms an essentially Marxian argument about technology and the impact its development has on the relationship of production into an argument about art, showing how the development of artistic forces of production in his own time has reached a point that radically calls the claim to artistic autonomy into question. Even more striking, the essay (leaving one to think of it as a kind of theoretical analogue to Duchamp's urinal) seems with an almost eerie precision to anticipate and even sum up a large number of the tectonic shifts that took place in the art world in the 1960s: the general renunciation of art's claim to autonomy or semi-autonomy, the widespread orientation towards seriality and technically reproducible media, the indifference towards the high/low distinction, and the replacement of what Michael Fried, in his classic 1967 essay "Art and Objecthood," calls absorption and independent acknowledgment of presentness with theatricality and communication.[3] The transition from the high-modernist claims of abstract expressionism and color-field painting to minimalism, post-minimalism, and various forms of pop art and conceptual art can, and has been, theorized with reference to this essay. When Adorno engages with Benjamin's claim to be able to appropriate the work of art for political purposes, he implicitly tests his thinking about art's relation to society against artistic practices that were left uncommented upon and not theorized in *Aesthetic Theory*.

Adorno presents his response to Benjamin's "The Work of Art" essay in a number of instalments, starting with a long and elaborate letter dated March 18, 1936, then continuing in the 1936 essay "On the Fetish Character in Music and the Regression of Listening" (which constitutes a kind of indirect attack on Benjamin's position), before he, more than three decades later, returns to it in *Aesthetic Theory*. It is obvious to any reader of this material that Adorno's animosity towards Brecht, whom he, quite rightly, views as the formative influence on Benjamin in the mid-1930s, tends to shape his assessment of "The Work of Art" essay. "Indeed, I feel," he writes (1999a: 132) in the March 1936 letter, "that our theoretical disagreement is not really a discord between us, and that my own task is to hold your arm steady until the Brechtian sun has finally sunk beneath its exotic waters."

Adorno always strongly resisted both Brechtian production and Sartrean *engagement*, both of which he took to reduce art, including its specific capacities for political judgment and intervention, to immediate political statements or enactments, thus eliminating the productive distance between art and society necessary for social critique to be possible: "Social struggles and the relations of classes are imprinted in the structure of artworks; by contrast, the political positions deliberately adopted by artworks are epiphenomena and usually impinge on the elaboration of works and thus, ultimately, on their social truth content. Political opinions count for little" (1997a: 232). Adorno is convinced that in a world of universal mediation there can be no art which can speak directly to an audience without being trapped in a logic of false immediacy. The rejection of Brechtian production relates to his more general suspicion of communication, leaving social realism without any room for effective critical engagement. It also forms the basis for his caustic critique of

Lukácsian realism, which he, in the 1958 essay "Extorted Reconciliation," accuses of drawing a problematic and historically untenable distinction between form and content, naively privileging the latter as the primary conveyor of representational capacity.[4] (Of course, Brecht and Lukács radically differed in their assessment of the Modern Movement: while Brecht often appeared as a staunch champion of avant-garde technical innovation, Lukács clung to a conception of socialist realism modeled on the nineteenth-century realism of Balzac and Tolstoy. In an article from 1938, published in the journal *Das Wort*, Brecht lashes out against Lukács for regressing to a formalist position whereby historically superseded products of a particular phase of class history are used to generate principles for assessing the political value of contemporary literary production.[5] In Adorno's view, where they concur is in their desire to invoke popular realism as a means to unmask the causal and ideological nexus whereby bourgeois society effaces its own contradictions.) By failing to consider the dialectical operations of form and construction, the garden varieties of realist doctrines, even when aspiring to let art articulate hope and intimations of the not-yet-existent by portraying the historical contradictions of advanced capitalism, inadvertently find themselves regressing to an affirmative position: rather than essence theorized as a negative totality, their object remains a function of social appearance; hence the art work's claim to embody objective social criticism disintegrates.

Adorno's attack against the invocation of immediate political effect in art has aroused considerable vehemence on the Left. However, as Jameson (1996: 188) rightly points out, there has hardly been "any kind of left consensus on the possibility, or even the desirability, of a properly political aesthetics; nor even on the immediate political effectivity of the most 'committed' works of art." Yet what Adorno in effect objects to in laying bare the Brechtian streak in Benjamin's essay is rather its apparent failure to distinguish itself from fascism's collapse of the very distinction between art and political propaganda. If fascism renders politics aesthetic by means of propagandist spectacularity and communism renders the aesthetic political by means of socialist-realist rhetoric, then what is the deep and ultimate difference between these two forms of cultural politics? In both cases, the art work is potentially reduced to a means for achieving a political end: in fascism, by staging the social body as an organic, self-enclosed work of art; in communism, by substituting a notion of communication and immediate social critique for the work's claim to autonomy.

In view of this impasse, Adorno's strategy is to reconsider the modernist differentiation between autonomous art and politics. Benjamin, he argues, proceeds undialectically when he, on the one hand, views technically reproduced art in general as politically progressive, while, on the other, rejects *all* autonomous art as being inherently "counterrevolutionary:"

... it seems to me that the heart of the autonomous work of art does not itself belong to the dimension of myth ... but is inherently dialectical, that is, compounds within itself the magical element with the sign of freedom... . Dialectical though your essay is, it is less than this in the case of the autonomous work of art itself; for it neglects a fundamental experience which daily becomes increasingly evident to me in my musical work, that precisely the uttermost consistency in the pursuit of the technical laws of autonomous art actually transforms this art itself, and, instead of turning it into a fetish or taboo, brings it much closer to a state of freedom, to something that can be consciously produced and made.

(Adorno 1999a: 128–9)

Technological development is not only relevant for the artistic revolutions brought about by methods of mechanical reproduction; there is also a dialectic of technique or rationalization pertaining to autonomous art itself. It follows that Benjamin's association of *l'art pour l'art* with the notion of a closed, organic, de-temporalized and ultimately mythical work must be rejected. Using Mallarmé as his example, Adorno argues that advanced art of the late nineteenth and twentieth centuries has been premised on the progressive rationalization of its principles of construction, leaving no room for an affirmative deployment of aura. In its reliance on a disenchanted and fragmentary method of articulation, modern art is cold. By sacrificing its traditional claim to totality and aesthetic illusion (while nevertheless remaining illusory in the German sense of *Schein*), it speaks negatively of the false world it has left behind. Such is Adorno's crucial departure not only from Benjamin's "The Work of Art" essay but from virtually every progressive aesthetic agenda of the twentieth century, including surrealism and the neo-avant-garde movements of the 1960s and 1970s: the moment of political resistance, protest or anticipatory reconfiguration, rather than being displayed or exercised in media or practices that are indifferent to, resistant towards, or skeptical of, the claim to autonomy, must be located at the heart of the autonomous work of art itself.

Turning to the other pole of Benjamin's allegedly flawed dialectical argument, Adorno maintains that the progressive consequences to accrue from the technical development of more popular art forms are quite limited. Just as Benjamin was too dismissive of the significance of advanced modernist art, associating modernism with the monumentalizing tendencies of nineteenth-century *l'art pour l'art*, so he overestimated the potential of film and photography, purportedly the most non-auratic forms of art, to become popular vehicles of revolutionary political expression. Rather than being non-auratic, these media are in effect capable of producing their own counterfeit versions of aura — that is, the exuberant, seductive, and fetishistic cult of stars and atmosphere that Adorno will view as complicit with the overall affirmative character of the culture industry. (This anti-Benjaminian argument is developed in great detail in the 1936 essay "On the Fetish Character in Music and the Regression of Listening," in which Adorno, for the first time, applies a Lukácsian notion of reification to culture as such, arguing that contemporary culture is thoroughly commodified, leaving audiences to focus their desires exclusively on exchange-value.) What Benjamin thought would pave the way for a new political and anti-aesthetic art led instead to the development of a system of cultural distribution which uses people's desire for entertainment as a means to generate profit. The idea that the powers of technique alone will bring about a higher degree of political consciousness among workers is thus the ironic version of the optimistic techno-political economism of Kautsky and the Second International: it disregards the regressive and socially manipulative potential of the new media technologies, and it over-estimates the inclination of the working masses to be receptive to the emancipatory elements that may be offered. There is no rationale whatsoever, Adorno (1999a: 131) submits, for making immediate appeals to "the actual consciousness of actual workers, who in fact enjoy no advantage over their bourgeois counterparts apart from their interest in the revolution, and otherwise bear all the marks of mutilation of the typical bourgeois character." Finally, the media of film and photography, which Benjamin, following Brecht, believed would encourage an active and experimental attitude to the work, foster passivity and hence authoritarian attitudes. Rather than leaving room for participation and self-reflection, film in particular, with its extraordinary powers of seduction, is an inherently non-participatory medium. (In the late essay "Transparencies on Film," Adorno goes on to qualify his view of film, arguing dialectically that its element of passivity may also be its distinguishing merit: Antonioni's *La Notte*, he claims, allows for an intimation of natural beauty which is made possible in part by the viewer's fixed and distant position vis-à-vis the images, creating a trancelike atmosphere.[6])

While in need of more unpacking in order to make full sense, Adorno's defense of so-called autonomous art against Benjamin's critique immediately runs up against difficulties. One issue which surfaces in the letter to Benjamin is how Adorno stands with regard to the concept of aura. On the one hand he agrees with Benjamin that the auratic element of the work of art is declining — not just because of its technical reproducibility but also because advanced art has subjected itself to a process of rationalization. On the other hand, risking contradiction, he attributes aura to the products of the culture industry. Mechanically produced art has, as it were, adopted the cultic qualities of pre-modern art while cynically exploiting them for purposes of easy seduction and manipulation.

The "cult of stars," for example, projects a counterfeit aura to its images; thus the culture industry "is defined by the fact that it does not strictly counterpose another principle to that of aura, but rather by the fact that it conserves the decaying aura as a foggy mist" (1991b: 88). Whereas Benjamin held that mechanical reproduction eliminated the aura, Adorno argues that by means of the systematic employment of cliché, sentimentality, and quasi-romanticism it can be mass produced; thus there is a "real" and a "false" aura. The fact, however, that many artists working with mechanically reproducible media, including most notably Bill Viola, have introduced genuinely auratic moments into their work seems to call into question Adorno's general association of mechanical reproduction with the merely quasi-auratic. Moreover, autonomous works of art — Benjamin and Adorno mention Derain and Rilke — may themselves display the same kind of false aura as that of the culture industry. Hence despite what Adorno seems to suggest in his writings on the culture industry, there is no uniquely intrinsic connection between mechanical reproducibility or cultural mass production and false aura. Derain and Rilke are of "dubious quality," according to Adorno, not because they mechanically produce aura but because in thinking that real aura is immediately available in the autonomous art of the modern age they fail to submit their art to its own autonomous formal laws. The dividing line between auratic and non-auratic art thus does not coincide with that between autonomous art and administered, industrial art. In fact, authentic art, he sometimes writes, is radically non-auratic: "Schönberg's music is emphatically *not* auratic" (1999a: 131).

However, in *Aesthetic Theory*, Adorno starts qualifying even this assertion:

> Even when artworks divest themselves of every atmospheric element ... it is conserved in them as a negated and shunned element. Precisely this auratic element has its model in nature, and the artwork is more deeply related to nature in this element than in any other factual similarity to nature. To perceive the aura in the way Benjamin demands in his illustration of the concept requires recognizing in nature what it is that essentially makes an artwork an artwork. This, however, is that objective meaning that surpasses subjective intention. An artwork opens its eyes under the gaze of the spectator when it emphatically articulates something objective, and this possibility of an objectivity that is not simply projected by the spectator is modeled on the expression of melancholy, or serenity, that can be found in nature when it is not seen as an object of action.
>
> (Adorno 1997a: 274–5)

In this passage, Adorno conjoins several key ideas that are crucial in order to understand the strange political thrust of *Aesthetic Theory*: while claiming that the art work articulates a form of aura that is modeled on the perception of nature, he follows Benjamin's construction of the melancholic subject as entailing a decentering of the self and its normal range of experience. If Benjamin failed to articulate a viable theory of politically minded art, his theory of allegorical images, calling for a painstaking dissolution of all forms of abstraction to the point of reaching a non-intentional intuition of the absolute, returns in Adorno's elaboration of the advanced and rational yet negatively auratic work. While I shall later argue that the preoccupation with the concept of aura in *Aesthetic Theory* leads to a re-evaluation of natural beauty after its suppression in idealist aesthetics, it is now necessary to contextualize and develop Adorno's notion of the political more concretely in relation to art.

## Art and praxis

While often neglected in the critical literature, Adorno makes some very ambitious claims concerning the relationship between the advanced work of art and its political implications. Not only is art, even when it negates practical life, a mode of praxis but it is the "model of a possible praxis in which something in the order of a collective subject is constituted" (Adorno 1997a: 242). There is a hidden (in the sense that it has to be teased out, decoded) connection between the impact of art in its most hermetic form and the overtly political question of how universal interest is to be articulated and translated into rational, non-violent praxis. The truth content, he writes, of such works "cannot be separated from the concept of humanity. Through every mediation, through all negativity, they are images of a transformed humanity and are unable to come to rest in themselves by any abstraction from this transformation" (1997a: 241). The way in which the truth content of art works "points beyond their aesthetic complexion ... assures it its social significance" (1997a: 248). Insofar as artistic truth is transformative, however, art's self-exteriorization is "practical insofar as it determines the person who experiences art and steps out of himself as a *zoon politikón*" (1997a: 243). Indeed, Adorno even speaks of art as expressive of a "We:" "The *We* encapsuled in the objectivation of works is no radically other than the external *We*, however frequently it is the residue of a real *We* in the past" (1997a: 238).

These passages are not entirely consistent with each other. There is reference to at least two different conceptions of art's relation to collectivity: namely, art figuring as a site wherein the features of a collective We are anticipated *and* remembered. They are, however, consistent in their denial that such a We can ever be conceived other than as a counterfactual community. Unlike Hegel, for whom artistic truth and expressions of collective will-formation are also united in aesthetic semblance, art does not side with, or articulate the interests of, existing communities.

As Hegel's chapter on art-religion (*Kunstreligion*) in the *Phenomenology of Spirit* makes clear, Greek classical art was not restricted to a specialized, self-sufficient domain but something that permeated the entire life of the community in its ethical, political, and religious manifestations. By articulating the ideal, the unity between the finite and the infinite, art brought to expression the totality of Greek society. For Hegel, the Greek experience of freedom, expressed in art, sprang immediately out of the substantiality of the institutions within which the Greek citizen lived in a unity with his or her fellow men and gods.

In an even more overtly political gesture (more explicit than anything in Adorno and perhaps even Hegel), Heidegger, in the 1936 text *The Origin of the Work of Art*, considers great art, the Greek temple in particular, as capable of founding the horizon of social meaning. For him, the art work does for a historical people what transcendental subjectivity in Kant does for us all: it reveals a transcendental truth, the source of all significance.

Adorno's account is critical of both Hegel and Heidegger. While Hegel allows classical art to model a correct relation between individuality and universality but indexes it falsely to a society that *de facto* was in contradiction with itself (the Greek polis was no doubt a rigidly divided society), Heidegger, by situating the origin of the social order in an inscrutable artistic truth-event, ends up suppressing the political altogether.

In what sense is Adorno's "collective We" absent? Given the assessment of contemporary society as radically false and the consequent principle that the true can only be reached by negation of the existent, this collective — which only art is able to configure — can only be anticipated or remembered (for Benjamin and Adorno, there can be no anticipation without the redemptive remembrance of past injustice) as the for ever deferred state of non-violence. Art's true addressee cannot be the community comprised of its empirical or factual audiences but must be the community considered as objectively in need of another and more ideal form of communal existence. Art raises a counterfactual claim to non-violence that can only be received by an audience that in light of its objective situation anticipates a reconfigured social and political life. Art speaks to and for all those who have no voice and who silently suffers from the identitarian mechanisms of integration that define not only modernity but human history in general:

> But because for art, utopia — the yet-to-exist — is draped
> in black, it remains in all its mediations recollection; recollection
> of the possible in opposition to the actual that suppresses it; it is
> the imaginary reparation of the catastrophe of world history; it is

freedom, which under the spell of necessity did not — and may not ever — come to pass.

(Adorno 1997a: 135)

Yet what is the status of the political universal under scrutiny? Although Adorno, writing prior to the rise of multiculturalism and identity politics, does not elaborate on this issue in much detail, it seems clear that he refers to a single collective subject of universal significance. The problem with this is that it contradicts his otherwise more general suspicion of notions of large-scale, unitary collectivities. Is the collective subject in Adorno a counterfactual version of Lukács' proletariat, albeit without labor as the unifying characteristic? If so, then Adorno by extension seems to fall back upon a rather too Hegelian conception of the one true universal, ignoring the anti-identitarian demand for rupture and difference. Moreover, if keyed to art's anticipatory capacity, the notion of a collective subject of universal significance invites precisely the kind of narrow construction of the advanced art work that I was questioning at the end of Chapter 4. It seems that insofar as each art work makes a singular claim, the universal it antici-pates is never to be abstracted from the specific claim by which it was brought forth.

Much recent work in the French poststructuralist tradition, in particular that of Jean-Luc Nancy, has called the very notion of *a* universal commu-nity radically into question, opting instead for more Nietzschean conceptions of singularity or intensity as the constitutive feature of communal living. According to Nancy (1991: 35), the "inoperative commu-nity" has shed both the nostalgia for sacred founding and for an overarching universal: 'There is neither an entity nor a sacred hypostasis of community — there is the "unleashing of passions," the sharing of singular beings, and the communication of finitude.' Yet does this mean that the problem of universality has disappeared? In fact, the sentence just quoted, while rejecting universality, cannot help making an implicit appeal to it. The "unleashing of passions" and the "sharing of singular beings" are no doubt meant to be of universal significance.

Rather than speaking in the name of some sort of pre-given structure or universal, I would suggest that the advanced Adornian art work should be construed as *making a claim to community*. Like Kant's notion of a universal voice in the *Critique of Judgment*, it places an item of universal significance (the claim) before us and invites you and me to consider it. Unlike discursive reason, the arrogance of art, its impatient and uncom-promising claim to truth, and ultimately its authority, does not rest on a capacity to provide proof but rather on its willingness to reveal and take responsibility for the conditions upon which it makes the actual claim to universality. From an autonomous standpoint, the work makes itself repre-sentative and thus aims to speak for others while at the same time

133

accepting — since its claims are not based on an appeal to the *a priori* — that others may contest it.

In the final chapter I will return to this notion of the universal voice in the context of my discussion of the relation between Adorno's politics and liberal political theory. For now let it suffice to say that Adorno's reference to the *zoon politikón* can be interpreted in terms of the answerability of each consenting individual in relation to society and its normative arrangements. Taking his lead from Rousseau's explanatory myth of the social contract, Cavell (1979: 25–8) views each member of the polis, each consenting individual, as answerable not only to, but also for, the valid normative arrangements of a given society. For Cavell, therefore, citizenship becomes extensionally equivalent with autonomy, the independent ability to work out the normative content for which one is rationally willing to take responsibility, and in so doing to uncover the extent to which one's singular voice, aiming to speak for others while accepting that others speak for it, is representative of others.

Art thus partakes in politics; it has a political voice. In order to rethink the conditions of consent, however, the negative Adornian art work has withdrawn from the actual community by resisting every urge to affirm. Yet mere withdrawal is not tantamount to the complete undoing of consent but involves rather a radical dispute about its content. Hence the Adornian art work speaks in the name of a normative order which fundamentally challenges present arrangements.

## Autonomy and truth content

It has repeatedly been intimated that for the art work to be able to make such a (non-discursive) claim to universal validity, it must satisfy at least two conditions: it must do so from a position of relative autonomy, and it must have the ability to purport to speak truthfully. We therefore need to look more closely at how these two features of the advanced work, autonomy and truth content, both of which are crucially important to Adorno's account, can be established.

Adorno's position has regularly been dismissed on the basis that aesthetic autonomy is an unattainable, if not downright naive, ideal. Under no social conditions, least of all a capitalist system of exchange, can art lay claim to complete self-authorization, independently of all constraints. On the contrary, under capitalism an art work must actualize itself on the market in accordance with its exchange value: thus it cannot escape commodification. Rather than, as Kant argued, being an object simply of disinterested pleasure, the unfolding of a purposiveness without purpose, both the production and the reception of art are determined by the demands of purposive rationality which turn the work into a means rather than an end in itself.

If construed as an objection to Adorno, what this argument fails to take into account is the extent to which art, in his opinion, is always also a social fact, hence also a commodity: "Art's double character — its autonomy and *fait social* — is expressed ever and again in the palpable dependencies and conflicts between [art and society]" (1997a: 229). Independence from society became a distinct artistic aspiration with the rise of bourgeois consciousness in the eighteenth century, and since art's claim to autonomy must be viewed as socially mediated, it cannot be analyzed without taking the specific social structure on which it is predicated into account. Not only is art a commodity, however, it is what Adorno (1997a: 236), in a remarkable dialectical movement, deems an "*absolute* commodity" — a social product that has totally and without remainder erased its own use value and become identical only with itself. As a result of this dialectic, the art work becomes a pure fetish; enacting a kind of vicious parody of the emptiness of late-modern exchange relations, it purports to have no function or purpose, no "being-for-society," an entity that is wholly self-enclosed and self-referential, in short the autonomous monad that Adorno seeks to describe it as. Yet the manner in which art negotiates its status as a commodity is not the only aspect of this dialectic. Advanced art finds itself in the precarious position of having to avoid selling out to the culture industry, which would jeopardize its seriousness, while, at the same time, resisting the temptation of *l'art pour l'art*, which would condemn it to "integration as one harmless domain among others" (1997a: 237).

While commercial co-optation reduces art to entertainment, autonomy carries with it the danger of neutralization: "... once artworks are entombed in the pantheon of cultural commodities, they themselves — their truth content — are also damaged. In the administered world neutralization is universal" (1997a: 228–9). As an example, Adorno (1997a: 229) instantiates "radically abstract art," which soon after its heyday in the 1950s became both decorative (to be hung in corporate boardrooms) and too securely institutionalized for its own survival as radical and challenging art.[7] One might add that many of the artists that during the last three decades most prominently continued the Adornian legacy have run into the same impasse. Their iconoclastic unfoldings of the negative sublime have become, by curators in Europe as well as the United States, so energetically and quickly called upon as the embodiment of seriousness that in the early 1980s the gesture of negativism, being unwittingly transformed into an administered resistance to human suffering, started to wear itself out.

Yet while such processes of *Entkunstung* remain a constant threat to autonomous art, the differentiation of art and art criticism into what Habermas, following Weber, has called a separate sphere of validity, concentrating on aesthetic value rather than discursive truth, has been a necessary condition for the establishment of art's claim to autonomy in the first place. In order to achieve freedom, art, which previously enjoyed a cult function, serving integrative needs of closely-knit, pre-modern societies, had to shed its complicity with empirical interest. It is at this stage, though, that Adorno introduces his dialectic of semblance (*Schein*), arguing that art's constitutive distance from labor inevitably taints it with an air of being luxurious and ultimately superfluous, leaving it with a culpability that it can only shed by revolting against the beautiful illusion it has become in its differentiated state. The only practice which in modern societies is cognitive in the emphatic sense of being capable of breaking through the universal spell of the exchange principle *appears* as non-cognitive — as nothing but art and therefore a piece of semblance. By sacrificing aesthetic beauty, its appearance of being art only, art atones for its culpability and acknowledges the non-identity that generally prevails between labor and nature, mind and matter, reason and its other, thus transgressing its own differentiated logics (as conveyor of beautiful semblance) and expressing what Adorno calls truth content. As elsewhere in Adorno's work, truth appears as the negation of semblance. It is "the semblance of the illusionless' (*Schein des Scheinlosen*) (1997a: 132).

According to Adorno, such a process of sacrificial self-divesture is best thought of as the negation of aesthetic synthesis effected by each art work's painful opposition between mimetic-expressive and constructive/technical-rational elements. If concentrating, like Rilke, exclusively on the former, it collapses into affirmative illusion; if concentrating, like the later Schönberg, for whom the twelve-tone principle, according to Adorno, degenerated into a compositional *technique*, exclusively on the latter, it comes to side with the identitarian reason it seeks to oppose.

> The refusal by art works to compromise becomes a critique even of the idea of their inner coherence, their drossless perfection and integration. Inner coherence shatters on what is superior to it, the truth of the content, which no longer finds satisfaction in expression — for expression recompenses helpless individuality with a deceptive importance — or in construction, for coherence is more than a mere analogy of the administered world. The utmost integration is utmost semblance and this causes the former's reversal: Ever since Beethoven's last works those artists who pushed integration to an extreme have mobilized disintegration.
>
> (Adorno 1997a: 45)

What Adorno calls the spiritual dimension of a work of art is its capacity to negate empirical reality. It negates it not by leaving it behind, but by allowing empirical reality to appear as unreconciled and scarred—that is, *as what empirical reality really is.* Unlike the synthesis effected by discursive-identitarian reason, however, the aesthetic synthesis openly and without mercy displays the violence and opposition that, in an unreconciled social configuration, marks the relationship between the universal and the particular. The cruelty and dissonance which is experienced in advanced works of art — the expression of pain and sorrow in the late Schubert, for example — is a function of their extraordinary tension between the coldness of their autonomously chosen principles of construction and the sensuous materiality of their mimetic appropriation. Such art works pronounce truth directly and non-discursively yet without ultimately evading their illusory condition.

We have seen how art formally can be said to have a political voice but not yet how this voice gains concrete content. If related to the notion of truth content, it should now be possible to encapsulate Adorno's claim for a political art by suggesting that the modeling of genuine sociality which he attributes to advanced art is a function of its commitment to reconciliation between universal and particular.[8] By placing before its audience the violence characterizing the non-identity between universality and particularity, it negatively prefigures a different and less violent sociality, allowing (though in conjunction with rationality) repressed nature to return to the ego:

> ... in aesthetic images precisely that is collective that withdraws from the I: Society inheres in the truth content. The appearing, whereby the artwork far surpasses the mere subject, is the eruption of the subject's collective essence. The trace of memory in mimesis, which every artwork seeks, is simultaneously always the anticipation of a condition beyond the diremption of the individual and the collective.
>
> (Adorno 1997a: 131)

In Bernstein's (1992: 273) useful elaboration, art works

> are an illusory *polis*, or an analogon of religious community. In thinking our fate now no such illusory support is possible; the "we" that would sustain political judgement and praxis has disappeared from direct view; "we" do not know, directly or indirectly, who "we" are. Our "we" has gone underground, appears only through the theoretical tracing of the fate that has rendered us strangers to one another.

If we return, finally, to the debate with Benjamin, it would seem that Benjamin's prognosis that advanced art would respond socially and politically by shedding its abstract claim to autonomy and undergo a process of de-aestheticization was right on target. Most contemporary art is predominantly non-auratic; and by being almost exclusively realized in reproducible media such as film, installation, and video, it does not lay claim to privileged optical experience or aesthetic presence. Nor does it pretend to be inscribed in a historically necessary development of its internal principles of construction. However, the questions which Adorno raises to Benjamin have not gone away. In order to rise above mere documentation, propaganda, and illustration, art needs to embody a claim to resistance that can be exercised in a space within which it is free to follow its own logic. While there has never been an autonomous art in the abstract sense, the Adornian requirement today would be that art continues to address the interest of those whose voices are stifled and repressed, and that it does so as art.

## The politics of the sublime

The category of the sublime, and the way it reverberates with epistemological and political concerns, has been at the forefront in a number of recent aesthetic debates. It was central to Lyotard's discourse of the 1980s, in which it was employed as a paradoxical figuration of the impossibility (or unpresentability) of ideas of totality, finality, and closure. In Lyotard, the sublime represented a postmodern rebellion, albeit within the framework of a generalized modernism, against form, order, and teleology. Drawing on Barnett Newman's writings (and behind him, Kant) on America as the post- or non-historical space of the sublime event, he showed how the postmodern sublime can be invoked in order to license a break with linear historical narratives, and hence how it serves to underwrite a conception of radical aesthetic and political experimentalism. The sublime is that which shatters all attempts to totalize, harmonize, and present the absolute.[9] In an even more recent manifestation of the resurgence of the category of the sublime, Bataille's concept of the formless (*l'informe*) has inspired the materialist anti-formalism of American critics such as Rosalind Krauss and Hal Foster. In their accounts, the notion of the sublime can be used in order to contest the modernist priority of the optical over the subliminal and unconscious.[10]

Adorno's approach to the sublime differs substantially from those of both Lyotard and Bataille.[11] While closer to Lyotard than to Bataille, whose undialectical celebration of transgression would strike Adorno as politically naive and pernicious, the general lack of consideration given to questions of form and principles of construction in much of the most recent debate stands in sharp contrast to the dialectic of form which dominates the discussion in much of the *Aesthetic Theory*. Moreover, as one might expect, Adorno is deeply ambivalent with regard to the notion of the sublime, and rather than adopting it in a straightforward affirmative fashion, shows the concept of the sublime to have its own dialectic. On the one hand, we find him claiming (1997a: 196–7) that "The sublime, which Kant reserved exclusively for nature, later became the historical constituent of art itself. The sublime draws the demarcation line between art and what was later called arts and crafts." On the other hand, the sublime is a corrupt category in that it traditionally (especially in the late eighteenth and nineteenth centuries) was associated with the celebration of domination implicit in the worshipping of power and sheer magnitude. There is something pathetic and hollow, or even downright silly, and in some cases frightening, about the manner in which some art (Adorno points to Richard Strauss, yet also, of course, to the fascist aesthetic of heroic classicism) marshals the sublime for the purpose of instilling a sense of submission or dumbfounded admiration in its recipients. In Hegel's *Aesthetics*, for example, the sublime is explicitly linked to architecture and by implication to a theistic or totalitarian politics whereby the absolute (the source of the ruler's authority) remains entirely non-presentable and inscrutable. Thus architecture becomes a mysterious display of sheer power.[12]

A large part of the challenge for Adorno is to reconceptualize the sublime in such a way that it retains its authority while shedding its complicity with power and domination. The sublime must be able to announce itself in the fragmented, destabilized, and scarred expression of ephemeral particulars — that is, in the artistic expressions (Beckett, Celan, Webern) on which Adorno stakes his hopes. As in Lyotard, Adorno's notion of the sublime is related to Kant's influential account in the *Critique of Judgment*, according to which it presents the onlooker with something that seems to violate the conditions for categorically determined intuition. Despite its traditional emphasis on magnitude, the Kantian sublime confronts the experiencing (transcendental) ego with its own limits, though not, as Adorno would like, with the concomitant rethinking or even redrawing of them.

Albrecht Wellmer (1997) has argued that while the category of the sublime is indispensable to any understanding of modernist art, Adorno's interpretation of it ends up linking the art work to a grand Hegelian quest for reconciliation. According to Wellmer (1997: 117–18), Adorno locates the modern sublime in "the tension, grown to unmeasurable proportions, between the reality of the modern world and a utopia veiled in black, between a state of complete negativity and a state of reconciliation." As a result, he argues, Adorno commits himself to the existence of an eschatological abyss between the present and possible (reconfigured) future, and, by implication, to an overly pessimistic view of the present. What he should have done was to realign the artwork to language and more specifically to the way in which, following Habermas, unconditional validity claims are raised in every speech act. In the performative attitude of communicating subjects, unconditional validity claims are set forth within a concrete natural and historical setting, thus making reference to the ideal an integral part of everyday speech. According to this view, the possibility of social and political resistance is contained within the structure of the speech act: every utterance implicitly anticipates an unconstrained community — however counterfactual — of communicating agents oriented exclusively towards validity. Rather than serving a logic of reconciliation, the sublime art work — or the experience of such a work — should be seen as expanding the space of communicative praxis:

> Art is part of the world of meaning, a part through which this world opens itself to its borders and abysses, remembrance of nature in the subject; by transforming the terror of what is unintelligible into aesthetic delight, it widens, at the same time, the space of communicatively shared meaning.
>
> (Wellmer 1997: 131)

While indebted to Habermas' formal pragmatics, Wellmer's account amounts to a categorial extension of hermeneutic criticism for whom meaning is always universally communicable. The appeal to communicability and to the pragmatic continuity between artistic and discursive truth-claims fails to register, however, the extent to which modern art has been willing to put communicable meaning at risk. Indeed, if modern art does not transcend the level of hermeneutic meaning and instead appropriates and transforms experience into transparently communicable items of meaning, then the promotion of non-identity, crucial to Adorno's project of uncovering aesthetic truth-content, must fail. If being indexed to the dialectical event of communicative reason's self-appropriation, art's experiential impact becomes bound to the purity of Wellmer and Habermas' vision of communicative reason.

Another difficulty with Wellmer's reading of Adorno is that the close relation, in this account, between the sublime and aesthetic delight (or beauty) makes it difficult to distinguish clearly between advanced art and products of the culture industry. In the name of a justified suspicion towards a too rigid opposition between "high" and "low," a downplaying of this distinction is certainly, as I argued in Chapter 4, both justified and historically right. Yet Wellmer goes too far in the opposite direction. By leaving little or no room for experiences that are not commensurable with the immediate satisfaction of desire, the modernist moment of painful sublimity, prefiguring a more adequate relation to one's needs and desires than the culture industry can provide, may seem to drop out altogether.

Finally, Wellmer fails to explain how Adorno's sublime can be interpreted as anticipating a positive reconciliation. In the idealist tradition, the art work's beautiful form (as opposed to sublime formlessness) is held capable of figuring a reconciliation between spirit and nature, freedom and necessity, morality and cognition. However, Adorno opposes such an idealist aesthetics, claiming that the thought of reconciliation can only be kept alive through negation. This is related to the fact that Adorno, as we have seen, became more and more suspicious of direct invocations of reconciliation, arguing that they ineluctably tend to be affirmative. Indeed, in *Aesthetic Theory* the sublime is primarily supposed to disunite and fracture false unifications and continuities:

The ascendancy of the sublime is one with art's compulsion that fundamental contradictions not be covered up but fought through in themselves; reconciliation for them is not the result of conflict but exclusively that the conflict becomes eloquent. Thus, however, the sublime becomes latent.

(Adorno 1997a: 197)

For Adorno, the consciousness of aesthetic modernity represents a critique of the triumphalism of sublation, dissolving the Hegelian confidence in a universal reconciliation of violated nature in the sorrow of departure and the pain of collapse. Thus Schubert's music, following out of the "release of the particular" from the compulsion to reconcile, is more modern than that of Beethoven; and it is also more sorrowful.[13]

## Natural beauty

Central to Adorno's conception of the sublime is his thesis, to which I now want to turn, that the modernist art work imitates natural beauty. While commending Kant's claims about the superiority of natural beauty over artificial beauty, Adorno promotes a parallel, though more radical idea, namely that natural beauty confronts the subject with its unacknowledged other. Adorno's thesis is that advanced art imitates neither nature nor individual instances of natural beauty but natural beauty as such. In *Aesthetic Theory*, this means that the art work, though "through and through *thesei*, something human, is the plenipotentiary of *physei*, of what is not merely for the subject ..." (1997a: 63). Art thus attempts to voice and give expression to the expressionless, to things: "Art works say that something exists in itself, without predicating anything about it" (Adorno 1997a: 77).

Adorno describes the experience of natural beauty as involving a form of shudder. As an "act of being touched by the other" (1997a: 331), shudder is the "remembrance" (*Erinnerung*) of a condition prior to the formation of the unitary subject in which nature was not yet subdued and dominated. As such it calls to mind both fear and, in its promise of psychological regression beyond the present configuration of the ego, temptation. For modern, civilized man, though, both the sense of danger and the attraction are obviously without any object: for him, the shudder arises from the confrontation with a *semblance* of alterity. Indeed, natural beauty can only appear as long as nature is being dominated. That is how its ambiguous and distant beauty is made possible. Natural beauty is thus "an image" (*ein Bild*). It shares with images our essential absence from the object of the image. Moreover, as image it is fleeting: any attempt to get hold of it or define it would cause its disappearance. As in Hegel, the aesthetic image can only speak truthfully through the mediation of *Schein*.

141

Hardly anywhere does Adorno's commitment to a modernist ideal of self-reflection and self-authorization come out more explicitly than in his historization of the category of the beauty of nature. Art redeems the incommensurability of numinous transcendence but only by domesticating it within the commensurable boundaries of artistic spirit. But is it possible to conceive of a commensurable incommensurability? Indeed, it seems that the transcendence achieved, if any, seems close to rehearsing, rather than resisting, the Hegelian movement of immanent self-reflection: the art work pays service to transcendence, but only *in strict immanence*.

In an effort to escape the horns of Adorno's dilemma — between an anti-modernist appeal to transcendence and a hyper-modern emphasis on reflexivity and mediation — we need to consider how the notion of mimesis is meant to syncopate with the experience of natural beauty. As the nonconceptual affinity of a subjective creation with its objective and unposited other, the self in a mimetic relation, rather than appropriating the object in its own image, enacts the assimilation of itself to the object as the passive actuality of a being-subject-*to*. In the mimetic mode of access the object is not met with as a self-identical presence and then subsumed under a generic term, but the object presents itself in its own nudity as an existence that embodies its own irreducible sense. The mimetic capacity actualizes itself primarily through affectability, that is, in the ability to let the object — *this* local object: the rose, the tree, the jagged edge of a cloud—resonate with or touch the subject. What, then, affects the spectator is the transitivity of presentation itself — the silent miracle of sensed existence as its own sense before any explicit symbolic signification.[14]

If the mimetic capacity is keyed to the term "aura," then it appears that the closeness of the "being-touched" should be viewed as combined with an ineliminable distance experienced in the apprehension of a sense that is beyond immediate will, want, and interest.[15] The fragmentary and heterogeneous sense of the object, the sudden irruption of its (inhuman) touch, thus presents its call from a *utopia* beyond the violent contingency of dominated (and hence manifest) nature. It is therefore unreal: its *there is* is not a finished presence, and its specific form of absence is not simply the negative other of a teleological movement towards its dialectical suspension in the universal. However, like nature's "flashes" (1997a: 72) of beauty of which Adorno speaks, presentation itself, the *praesentia* of being-present as distinguished from the presentness of presence, does have a positive existence. In its passing, it touches the subject as sensible existence — yet it has no proper place (or propriety) — except in art:

> The pure expression of art works, freed from every thing-like interference, even from everything so-called natural, converges with nature just as in Webern's most authentic works the pure tone, to which they are reduced by the strength of subjective sensi-

bility, reverses dialectically into a natural sound: that of an eloquent nature, certainly, its language, not the portrayal of a part of nature.

(Adorno 1997a: 78)

Successful works of art — sublime works of art — thus unwork themselves; they end where art may once again begin — with *aisthesis*, a multiple tracing out of the singularity of existence or the thing itself. The mute yet sounding language of nature precedes all appropriation and exceeds it; and when enacting its enigmatic touch it accomplishes what Adorno characterizes as a mimesis which consists solely in the art works' "resemblance to themselves" (1997a: 104). In their self-resemblance, works of art express nothing but their own beingness, their *haecceitas*. Like the Etruscan vases in the Villa Giulia of which Adorno (1997a: 112) writes that they seem to say something like "*Here I am* or *This is what I am*," they push art beyond the spiritual necessity of its presentation and are genuine exemplars of art after "the end of art." For Adorno, such an indifference is the new as such: an intriguing anonymity anxiously located along the edgy surfaces of *aisthesis*, a truth that touches and cannot but touch.

# 7

# THE TRANSFORMATION OF CRITICAL THEORY

I have so far restricted my discussion to Adorno considered as a first-generation Critical Theorist. What I have not done is to consider the fate of Adorno's thinking in the context of the transformations that have taken place in the tradition of Critical Theory over the last thirty years or so — transformations that, admittedly, have led many to reject Adorno's work as being either irrelevant or flawed. More specifically, what I have in mind is the criticisms launched by Jürgen Habermas and other proponents of the so-called communicative turn within Critical Theory. Unless I indicate why I find some of these objections (which by and large have changed the identity of Critical Theory and indeed influenced a whole generation of social and political thinkers) are misguided, my claim that Adorno's work deserves another chance will remain both vacuous and self-serving. I begin this chapter by looking at Habermas' account of the *Dialectic of Enlightenment*. I then go on to argue that this account fails to do justice to a number of important aspects of Adorno's project — to the notion of mimesis, but also to questions of language, sociality, and metaphysics, as well as his approach to the legacy of the Enlightenment. Of particular interest for me will be the implicit claim that Adorno, by failing to make a turn towards intersubjectivity, has repressed politics.

It would be misleading to regard Habermas as having performed some sort of abstract negation of his mentor's project. Despite obvious dissimilarities — such as Habermas' investment in the Kantian tradition of liberalism, his complete rejection of dialectical thinking in favor of formal-pragmatic reconstruction, and his lack of interest in problems of art and aesthetics — a number of the concerns that animate Habermas' project are indebted to Adorno. They are both engaged in trying to offer a theory of modernity that combines a diagnostic assessment of the present with an account of rationality constructed with an anticipatory intent. They both view contemporary Western societies as suffering from a one-sided process of rationalization, particularly in the way in which the markets and the bureaucracies, largely operating in a norm-free space of purely legal constraints, impose a too narrow scope for the exercise of non-instrumental

144

forms of rationality. They both agree that philosophy and the social sciences ought to cooperate in order to generate discourses of radical social critique. Finally, they both subscribe, in one way or the other, to the values of the Enlightenment — to self-reflexive critique, rational self-reassurance, the exercise of autonomy, and the defense of some version of cultural modernity.

Despite all of these general similarities, I want to show, however, that central features of their respective positions are mutually exclusive: that there is less of a *middle ground* between Adorno and Habermas than one may initially be tempted to believe.

## Habermas' account of Adorno

The basis for Habermas' assessment of Adorno is in large part drawn from the readings of the *Dialectic of Enlightenment* that he offers in *The Theory of Communicative Action* and *The Philosophical Discourse of Modernity*, both of which were published in the 1980s; thus the explicit source by reference to which the assessment is made is rather limited. Neither *Negative Dialectics* nor *Aesthetic Theory* is taken into extended consideration, and the same is true of the art-critical and the sociological writings. The extent to which his interpretation becomes representative of Adorno's work as a whole therefore in part becomes a function of the representability of the *Dialectic of Enlightenment* itself. If the *Dialectic of Enlightenment* can be shown to be less central to Adorno's project than Habermas, at least implicitly, makes it out to be, then Habermas' own take on it has less value as leading to an overall critique of Adorno than it would otherwise have had if wider regions of Adorno's thinking were considered. Before I start looking at the specific points that Habermas draws attention to, I want to suggest that the *Dialectic of Enlightenment* is indeed a peculiar and in certain ways devious text within Adorno's writings. Two dimensions stand out as particularly striking in this regard: its negative philosophy of history and its Nietzschean (naturalistic-reductive) approach to language, rationality, and concept-formation. Although they occasionally make themselves felt in other writings as well, there is no text by Adorno in which they play such a large role as in the *Dialectic of Enlightenment*. In Habermas' assessment, both dimensions, while taken to be representative, are crucially invoked in order to build his case against Adorno.

Habermas grapples directly with what Robert Pippin (1997: 331) has called "the great problem of all post-Cartesian or modern philosophy," namely how the modern orientation, in the wake of the downfall of the medieval synthesis and the collapse of Christian religion as a resource of legitimacy, can gain a comprehensive self-reassurance.[1] Obvious examples of such a demand for self-reassurance would be the early modern political interest in legitimate authority, raised by thinkers such as Hobbes and Locke, or the cultural interest in the value of certain institutions, say pedagogical and religious ones, raised by thinkers such as Kant and Rousseau, or the claims for aesthetic judgment as being logically independent of the pre-modern or classicist appeal to the eternal validity of artistic form. In all of these contexts, self-reassurance becomes a matter of self-determination or autonomy: the idea that no order is valid or legitimate apart from the possible assent of informed, rational individuals who are free and equal. However, the perhaps most radical and far-reaching implications of the demand for self-reassurance were reached in the natural sciences, the development and gradual independence of which would have been unthinkable apart from this quest. From Descartes' methodical doubt, which demanded that all knowledge-claims should be grounded in a universally available apodictic evidence, to Kant's transcendental deduction of the conditions under which finite human beings may claim to have objective knowledge of the world, the problem of the self-reassurance of modern science was addressed head-on with an uncompromising wish to liberate the sciences from every dogmatically held belief. Where Habermas' narrative in *The Philosophical Discourse of Modernity* takes off is with the sense of a crisis in modernity's defining project of obtaining self-reassurance—a sense which may first be said to take shape among members of the post-Kantian generation, in particular Hegel and Schelling, but also the German Romantics. Kant's brilliant undertaking of trying to expose the hitherto unacknowledged dogmatism of his philosophical predecessors, in particular Wolff, Leibniz, and the British empiricists, was itself, the post-Kantian generation argued, dogmatic. For example, it dogmatically presupposed the validity of certain categorical determinations of thought, as well as a strict distinction between concepts and intuitions.

In Habermas' opinion, the nineteenth-century philosophical discourse of modernity responded to the general sense of crisis in the project of self-reassurance in essentially two different ways. Hegel and his followers attempted to construct comprehensive narratives which could offer accounts of how and why we — the members of a given culture, *we moderns* — have come to adopt certain principles or justificatory criteria as binding. This way of responding to the crisis is still logically committed to the very idea of self-determination; it only construes it in more radical terms than previously. The second basic response — which Habermas calls the Nietzschean one, but which is indebted to Hölderlin and the late Schelling — recommends that we debunk the enlightenment appeal to autonomous reasoning entirely, that we regard it as a historically obsolete project, and that we adopt something else (mythology, will to power, life, imagination, transgression, in short *the other of reason* in all its possible forms).

In the chapter on Adorno in *The Philosophical Discourse of Modernity*, Habermas contends that it is plausible, if not unavoidable, to view

Adorno's project as aligned with the Nietzschean quest for a radically different alternative to the modernist ideal of obtaining comprehensive self-reassurance when that is interpreted as the pursuit of autonomy. Whereas Nietzsche, he suggests, denies from the outset the very possibility (and desirability) of reconstructing reason in terms other than the sheer non-cognitive will to power, thus reducing all normative and theoretical claims to validity to the expressive power of judgments of taste for which no rational validity claims can be made, Adorno similarly reduces reason to the level of non-cognitive domination and instrumental control.[2] Correspondingly, whereas Nietzsche rejects the ideal of autonomy (and the very notion of acting and thinking according to principles that are chosen on rational grounds) as being nihilistic and incapable of generating new values, Adorno refuses to accept a vision of freedom as consisting in a potentially reflective responsiveness to putative norms of reason, first, because it ideologically misrepresents the actual submission of the individual to the systemic forces of his or her society, and, second, because autonomy itself is just one more expression of the universal struggle for self-preservation that is explanatory of reason's complete fusion with power. Finally, according to Habermas, it is fair to classify Adorno's reaction to the crisis in the project of gaining self-reassurance as Nietzschean in so far as it seeks to appeal to an alternative to autonomy, namely that of "mimetic rationality," which is supposed to offer a conception whereby the subject no longer violently appropriates the object of knowledge in terms of its own, self-chosen norms and principles but receives those norms and principles from a perspective or source that metaphysically transcends the full conceptual grasp of a purportedly autonomous subjectivity. Put differently, Adorno adopts a line of thinking, or rather ideal, by which the subject no longer can be held accountable for the norms and principles according to which it thinks and acts, the consequence of which is that his own theory gets suspended in mid-air, unable to account rationally for its own claims to validity.

This is a complex argument. As I read it, it can be broken down into four steps:

1 The first concerns language. In Habermas' reading, since reason, for Adorno, is essentially, or at least *de facto*, instrumental, it follows that language itself, rather than being a vehicle of truth and representation, must be conceptualized as an instrument of domination.

2 It follows from the claim that reason *is* instrumental that the distinction between validity (or truth) and power collapses. With this Nietzschean move, however, Adorno undermines or implicitly rejects the conditions under which his own propositions (or any) can claim validity. His arguments, in other words, involve a performative contradiction: Adorno absurdly claims objective validity for the proposition

147

that objective validity is an impossible aspiration. Habermas' point is structurally similar to the classical rebuttals of radical (Protagorean) forms of skepticism that we find in Plato, namely that the skeptic finds himself faced with a dilemma: if the scope of his attack on rationality really were global, then it could not be rationally stated; if it is rationally stated, then the skepticism cannot be global. In Habermas' words, "If [Horkheimer and Adorno] do not want to renounce the effect of a final unmasking and still want to *continue with critique*, they will have to leave at least one rational criterion intact for their explanation of the corruption of *all* criteria. In the face of this paradox, self-referential critique loses its orientation" (1987b: 126–7). Now Habermas thinks that there is a way out of the aporia he claims to have detected in Adorno. If reason is viewed differently, namely as the raising of *rational claims to validity*, where rational argument is linked to the specific types of validity-claims made in the respective languages of science, morality, and art criticism, modernity does not have to be viewed as sliding into a self-destructive "dialectic of enlightenment." It can equally well be regarded in terms of the intensified unfolding of communicative rationality in each of the three spheres of "cultural modernity" (science, morality, art criticism). In Habermas' view, Adorno, however, because he holds a one-sided, reductive view of reason, tends to see in the achievements of cultural modernity nothing but the disenchanted quest for technical utility, meta-ethical skepticism, and entertainment.

3   In the light of the second point, since philosophical or critical reflection at best becomes a self-negating practice, Adorno, in attempting to establish an alternative model of reason, eventually invokes an intuitive competence operating beyond the range of conceptual thought. What Adorno calls *mimesis* is according to Habermas (1984: 382) a pre-conceptual, pre-reflective impact of the world from outside the realm of thought — something "about which he can speak only as he would about a piece of uncomprehended nature." Indeed, by emphasizing its ineffability, Habermas (1984: 383) compares the appeal to *mimesis* to elements of Judeo-Christian mysticism. Thus the introduction of *mimesis* opens a gap in Adorno's thought between that whereof we can speak, but only ideologically, since identitarian thinking merely classifies its object (as opposed to identifying it in its *differentia specifica*), and that whereof we cannot speak, but only mimetically relate to, which would be the world as it is in itself, apart from the distortions of instrumental reason.[3] On this reading, only modernist art practices (as developed by Adorno in the *Aesthetic Theory*) are able to give expression to nature as it is in itself, and philosophy "intentionally retrogresses to gesticulation" (Habermas 1984: 385), thereby renouncing its cognitive claims.

4    Certainly, it is hard not to sympathize with Habermas' view that if this (very roughly) is Adorno's position, then Critical Theory, if interpreted as an intellectual reflection on modernity and its philosophical and historical presuppositions, gets thrown into jeopardy. The lesson he thinks should be learnt is that Adorno philosophizes according to an outmoded and incoherent paradigm of thinking, namely the philosophy of consciousness, which needs to be replaced by a philosophy of language and intersubjectivity. Although Habermas lumps a number of discrepant positions (ranging from Descartes, Kant, Hegel, and Husserl to contemporary theories in the philosophies of mind and language) together under the heading "philosophy of consciousness," he seems to be claiming that for a conception to belong to such a paradigm, it has to satisfy at least four basic conditions: a) that consciousness, or at least the self-relation of the individual knowing subject, should (and can) serve as a foundation or underived ground for epistemology; b) that linguistic meaning is either identical with or the product of mental acts or representations; c) that the only attitude a subject can have to the world is an objectivating one (it can represent states of affairs or intervene in the world as the totality of states of affairs); and d) that representations and actions are actualizations of a basic strive for self-preservation.[4] On Habermas' reading, Adorno's alleged vacillation between the notion of identitarian thinking, on the one hand, as pervasive, and a radical, almost utopian, non-conceptual conception of mimetic impulses, on the other, ought to be understood as evidence of his incapacity to liberate himself from a philosophy of consciousness: he simply could not conceive of an alternative to identitarian thinking other than an anti-humanist vocabulary of a pure and unrecognizable singularity beyond the dialectical range of linguistic reflection and negation.

## Intersubjectivity and mimesis

Habermas' reconstruction calls for critical scrutiny. The first issue I would like to dwell on is whether Adorno can rightly be said to be a philosopher of consciousness in the sense indicated above. Since this claim is fundamental to Habermas' criticism and his belief that philosophy needs to move from a philosophy of consciousness to a philosophy of language and intersubjectivity, much hinges on whether it can actually be defended and, if so, on its actual implications. To be sure, no reader of Adorno can fail to be struck by his widespread use of the vocabulary of subject and object, a vocabulary which he largely inherits from German idealism. It is important, however, not to confuse the employment of these terms with the adoption of a representationalist paradigm. While Descartes' use of the subject–object distinction aimed at reinforcing his sense that the crucial question in philosophy is how skepticism can be overcome and the epistemic subject be assured that its representations correspond with an objective, mind-independent reality, Hegel's adoption of it, to which Adorno largely is indebted, invokes the distinction between subject and object not in order to suggest that philosophy's primary business is to prove the correctness of human representation but to generate a dialectic in which the subject's conception of what counts as objective (or valid) knowledge is constantly being challenged and tested. The result, in the *Phenomenology of Spirit*, of this dialectic is a progressive replacement of such conceptions, culminating with the realization that reason itself is of a social nature and embodied in practices of mutual recognition within a community of theoretical and practical agents. The initial account of an isolated, reflective subject faced with its own conception of objectivity is thus shown to be inadequate: for objective (transsubjective) validity to be possible, there must be shared or intersubjective standards to which the individual can appeal.[5]

One way of reading Hegel's subject–object dialectics is therefore to claim that while the imagery of an isolated, monological subject is an abstraction typical of enlightenment reason, the most effective way to criticize it is to proceed immanently by questioning it on its own terms. Like Hegel, this is precisely, I would argue, what Adorno does in his work. Adorno is not denying that the representationalist, Cartesian construal of the subject is misguided. Indeed, not only does he repeatedly stress that society precedes the subject, but there are concrete passages, such as the following which is lifted from a polemic against Husserl, in which he directly dismisses such a view:

> "My" ego is in truth already an abstraction and anything but the original experience that Husserl claims it is… . "Intersubjectivity" is posited along in it, only not as an arbitrary pure possibility, but rather as the real condition for being I, without which the limitation to "my" ego cannot be understood.
>
> (Adorno 1982: 230)

One can hardly imagine a more explicit affirmation of the primacy of intersubjectivity than this. Adorno views intersubjectivity as the condition of possibility for the constitution of subjectivity; thus, without language games of mutual recognition, there would be no "I" or "ego." The immediacy of consciousness is an illusion.

Thus, the central *explicans* for the possibility of a subject to relate objectively to the world is not given *a priori*, as a capacity to confer significance on or synthesizing a given content; rather, participation in society, in the normativity sustained by social practices, in socially enforced structures of material inference, explains how conditions of knowledge in general become possible. The subject internalizes and learns to master these practices through its process of maturation into a full member of society, where the criterion of full membership essentially entails the ability to employ its natural language. Conditions of knowledge are therefore empirically existent (accounted for in terms of shared practices and orientations, rather than a priori rules or categories), yet, like the transcendental categories in Kant, they provide a normatively structured relationship between mind and world.

The Husserl to which Adorno directs his critical attention is much closer to Habermas' vision of a philosopher of consciousness than Adorno ever was; indeed, it is precisely Husserl's inclination to want to posit the mind — the transcendental subject — as a meaning-generating, monological origin which Adorno criticizes so vehemently in this early work. So how can Adorno be accused of philosophizing according to the same paradigm?

The answer has already been indicated. Like Hegel, Adorno views modern agents as caught up in a deep form of alienation that discourages the unfolding of the social practices needed to sustain meaning. In a society in which human relationships are largely dominated by the objectivating logic of exchange, the communal practices by which rational linkages between concepts are made possible get reified. Such a reification is most appropriately seen as a process of abstraction: the individual speaker's complicated dependence on the community, the numerous ways in which one needs to inherit and exemplify one's own participation in communal practices for meaning and normativity to be possible, become hypostatized and eventually represented as an abstract structure, detached from its interconnection with the lived engagement of concrete individuals striving to make sense in specific situations. Indeed, the transcendental subject, whether in Kant, Fichte or Husserl, is for Adorno precisely such a representation: hence its truth (for us here and now) and falsity.

Adorno's claim against Habermas would be that the concept of intersubjectivity must be treated dialectically. While Habermas does distinguish between a performative attitude whereby people relate to each other as accountable subjects and an instrumental-strategic attitude whereby they monologically objectivize each other, he fails to recognize the intricate ways in which these two attitudes are mutually entangled in a dialectic that, under current conditions, has no obvious resolution. More specifically, by drawing a wedge between intersubjective practices of mutual recognition and instrumentalism, where the former is characteristic of the reproduction and production of the "lifeworld" and the latter of the externalized "system," Habermas remains committed to an idealist vision of intersubjectivism which fails to do justice to the notion, central to Adorno, that reason itself is distorted.

Adorno's hypothesis is not that intersubjectivity or mutuality is impossible because agents, as in the paradigm of the philosophy of consciousness, are metaphysically isolated, but that it is an achievement. As a result of our structurally enforced tendency to instrumentalize and objectify the other, such that we can control him or her and not be forced to reveal our dependence on this person's recognition, we live our lives in isolation, and no change of "attitude" or "mode of interaction" can alter it. As I want to argue more in depth in the next chapter, the political thrust of Adorno's writing consists in its desire to reconnect with the other and make genuine claims to communal recognition — despite the instrumental integration from above.

What about Habermas' reading of Adorno's employment of the notion mimesis? Is it true that Adorno, in order to make up for the alleged "normative deficit" which follows from the Nietzschean naturalization of reason, starts to appeal to some form of immediacy — a constraint on thought that comes, as it were, from outside the space of reasons? As I argued in Chapter 5, there is an element of Benjaminian desire for the unconditioned in Adorno. There are times when he seems, as Habermas claims he does, to call for something "about which he can speak only as he would about a piece of uncomprehended nature." However, this element must be balanced against the many passages, including much of the criticism of Heidegger (which Habermas strangely neglects), in which Adorno insists that whatever can be presented to the subject, even in the mimetic encounter, must in some way be mediated by its conceptual and rational outlook: "There is no peeping out. What would lie in the beyond makes its appearance only in the materials and categories within" (Adorno 1973b: 140). In another and equally Kantian passage, he claims that "Mediation of the object means that it must not be statically, dogmatically hypostatized but can be known only as it entwines with subjectivity" (ibid.: 186)[6].

According to Habermas, by taking *mimesis* to be a non-conceptual susceptibility to impacts from the world, Adorno commits himself to a form of transcendental realism, the claim that for a thought to be true it must correctly represent things as they are in themselves. In Adorno's assessment, however, such a view is found not in his own work but in Heidegger who precisely posits Being as foundational and immediate. Having done that, Heidegger is forced to welcome the consequence that the subject gets reduced to pure receptivity — the famous *Gelassenheit* which comes on stage after *die Kehre* — a conclusion which for both cognitive, moral, and political reasons is unacceptable to Adorno.

> The illusion of taking direct hold of the Many would be a mimetic regression, as much a recoil into mythology, into the horror of the diffuse, as the thinking of the One, the imitation of blind nature by repressing it, ends at the opposite pole in mythical dominion. The self-reflection of enlightenment is not its revocation.
>
> (ibid.: 158)

But this means that Habermas cannot that easily disconnect Adorno from the legacy of philosophical modernism. He cannot without further qualification side Adorno with the counter-enlightenment thinkers (Nietzsche, Heidegger, and so on) for whom the principle of modernity, namely that free, critical, self-reflective thinking will be the touchstone of validity in general, is dismissed in favor of some sort of metaphysical or romantic dogmatism. Although Adorno challenges the humanist ideal of self-authentication by seeking to thematize the preponderance of the object and its difference from subjective reason, he does so not by going beyond dialectics and conceptuality, but by providing a negative dialectics of self-divestiture that can immanently demonstrate the impossibility of full, unrestricted mastery of the object: "The object's preponderance is solely attainable for subjective reflection, and for reflection on the subject" (1973b: 185). Habermas fails to distinguish between a dialectical critique of the enlightenment *from within*, which is Adorno's position, and a counter-enlightenment rejection *from without*, which would be Nietzsche and Heidegger's position.

Yet is there not some truth in Habermas' claim that on the basis of Adorno's reduction of reason to instrumental rationality (as well as his related version of naturalism whereby reason is simply a function of the species' drive for self-preservation), it becomes impossible to arrive coherently at any account of ethical, moral, political, and cognitive normativity that would permit him to make his critical diagnosis of Western rationality? Indeed, is there not a "normative deficit" in Adorno's thinking that not only creates difficulty for his critique of reason but also prevents the formulation of a genuine ethics or politics? Can there be an ethics of non-identity or resistance if reason is identical with domination? These are pertinent questions, and Habermas deserves credit for having raised them with such force. Indeed, one can easily point to passages that not only seem to confirm Habermas' logical point about a performative self-contradiction but that look downright nihilistic in a disturbingly affirmative way. In Adorno and Horkheimer's chapter on "Juliette or Enlightenment and Morality" in the *Dialectic of Enlightenment*, for example, de Sade and Nietzsche are invoked as having heroically "trumpeted far and wide the impossibility of deriving from reason any fundamental argument against murder" (1979: 118). Although shocking, this is an assertion that needs to be read with some care. Adorno and Horkheimer's target is hardly reason in just any sense imaginable but reason in its distorted, rationalized form. If reason is simply an instrument for organizing and regimenting experience, then it follows that no end, and therefore no prohibition, can be sacred: whatever serves to increase the subject's capacity for domination, including murder, is rational and, since no competing rational demands of a moral nature are on the table, therefore permissible. When it comes to this specific passage, it is the representative of rationalized morality, and not Adorno and Horkheimer, who sides with nihilism.

Yet despite this restriction of the scope of Habermas' charge, the gist of it, namely that Adorno lacks an adequate account of the normative foundation of his critical claims, still needs to be addressed. In approaching it I want to suggest that it is imperative that one distinguishes between two issues that Habermas tends to run together when he discusses the problem of normativity in Adorno. One is the naturalization of reason. As we have seen, it is true that, like the American pragmatists or Wittgenstein, Adorno seeks to extrapolate his conception of reason from man's natural abilities in general: there is nothing extramundane about human reason; reason is fully "de-transcendentalized." Another issue, however, is what the sources of normativity may be. Clearly, one can accept, as Adorno does, the continuity between man's natural outlook and his rational capacities without having to admit that it follows that there can be no sources from which normative judgments can obtain their binding power. It is only when one reads Adorno as claiming that reason is for ever instrumental, and hence that no critique of reason with a view to uncovering a more extensive range of rational behavior can make sense, that one is forced into an anti-normativist position. However, Adorno's thinking, as we have seen throughout in this book, is premised on the claim that what we are able to view as reasonable may not be all there is to reason: reason can criticize itself and thus uncover dimensions that, while necessary for any orientation in the world, are repressed both by philosophy and by Western culture at large. On Habermas' own account, the fundamental source of normativity resides in the pragmatic presuppositions of speech that speakers implicitly commit themselves to in trying to arrive at mutual understanding. For Adorno, however, the fundamental source of normativity (and truth) consists in the claim every particular has of being nonidentical to its concept: it is the integrity of the object, its vulnerable uniqueness, which ultimately forms the source of ethical, moral, political, and even epistemic normativity. Although questions can be raised — as I do in the next chapter — about the coherence of this view, it is simply wrong to hold that Adorno's thinking inevitably succumbs to a form of ethical and moral non-cognitivism. Unlike Habermas, what Adorno does not do, however, is to attempt to provide a transcendental or quasi-foundationalist account of the sources of normativity. To do so would not only miss out on the fundamental historicity of normative commitments; it would also ignore the importance of the everyday normative commitments that Adorno, in *Minima Moralia* and elsewhere, seeks to bring to light. As we have seen, Adorno's strategy is to read off these commitments negatively from experiences of injury and suffering in everyday life, and the claims he actually makes are designed not to establish *a priori* validity but to invite others to consider them with a view to possible acceptance.

## Deliberative democracy and its limits

Habermas' criticisms of Adorno bring up far-reaching issues about human rationality and its implications for a critical theory of society. Before closing this chapter, I would like briefly to examine Habermas' claim to have provided Critical Theory with a proper political theory. According to Habermas and his followers, as a result of his oblivion to the logics of communicative rationality, Adorno, while certainly no anti-democratic intellectual, failed to develop a political theory. Indeed, not only did he fail to outline a democratic politics but he shunned the political altogether. While I hope to have shown that this is hardly the case, Habermas' own alternative to Adorno in this respect consists in developing a model of democratic legitimacy based on a communication-theoretic account of deliberative rationality. Since Habermas' negative critique of Adorno presupposes that such an account can be provided, it might be useful to sketch some Adornian objections to it before I examine in more detail in the final chapter what an Adornian model of democratic politics might look like.

In an article entitled "Three Normative Models of Democracy," Habermas contrasts his own proceduralist position with both classical liberalism and republicanism.[7] While the liberal envisions democratic politics as the attempt to achieve compromises of interest among essentially private, economically defined agents, where the state is supposed to be value-neutral and protect individuals' subjective rights, the republican views it in terms of participatory and virtue-based activities of mutually recognizing citizens within a community united by shared values and identities. For the republican, the state is not simply there to guarantee the subjective rights of private persons but to ensure that citizens are universally equipped with the conditions necessary for exercising their fundamental right to participate in the shared praxis of deliberating about the common good.

Habermas' principal objection to classical liberalism is directed towards its market-based construal of society as composed of instrumentally competitive agents. Roughly, this model neglects the social dimension of mutually co-operating citizens who respond rationally to each other's reasons; thus the only understanding of political legitimacy available to it is the essentially unsatisfactory notion of compromise within a situation aimed to ensure a *modus vivendi*. Indeed, liberalism in its most strict and minimalist form concerns itself exclusively with the rule of law, the defense of rights, and the protection of individual liberty, yet makes no necessary or intrinsic reference to democratic political ideals of equality, identity between governing and governed, and popular sovereignty. Ultimately, it risks suppressing the political altogether.

If liberalism drains political life of its ethical and communal meaning, then republicanism ethically overburdens politics. Although Habermas praises republicanism for its radically democratic interest in the idea that society should organize itself through communicative deliberation, he argues that on this view political discourse is misleadingly aligned with ethical discourse. Since ethical discourses presuppose a shared horizon of values, they inevitably do not do justice to the fact of value pluralism. In a complex, multicultural society, it would be naive to presuppose that every conflict can be resolved within a shared and tacit framework of values. Thus, for a genuine political system to function, discourses in which questions of justice whose scope transcends the particular collective and whose content is informed by universalistic moral reasoning will have to be institutionalized in addition to ethical discourse.

According to Benhabib (1994: 30), Habermas' view can be presented as an attempt to reconcile rationality with legitimacy. Thus,

> legitimacy and rationality can be attained with regard to collective decision-making processes in a polity if and only if the institutions of this polity and their interlocking relationship are so arranged that what is considered in the common interest of all results from processes of collective deliberation conducted rationally and fairly among free and equal individuals.

Legitimate institutions in a democracy are such that they embody an impartial standpoint which is equally in the interest of all affected. The only appropriate way of obtaining such a standpoint, however, is to consider the common interest as arising from public processes of deliberation — in the public sphere, in parliament and so on — which are constrained by the procedures of Habermas' discourse model. Essentially, the discourse model demands equality and symmetry between the participants affected by the norm in question, as well as the right to question the assigned topics of conversation.

There can be little doubt that Adorno would follow Habermas in rejecting both classical liberalism and republicanism. On the one hand, his opposition to commodification and the current dominance of strategic-instrumental rationality would make him deeply skeptical of the interest-based conception of democracy which one finds in liberalism. On the other hand, while hardly hostile to the virtues of political participation, Adorno would have reservations about the republican replacement of the economic model with a model oriented towards communal ethicality. Like Habermas, he would be worried about its potential parochialism, and he would dismiss its conviction that the ethical resources for a politics of direct communal self-determination are still intact and available. Although Adorno would consider a politics devoid of ethical reference as deeply nihilistic and ultimately anti-political, his claim is that for an ethically informed politics to survive, it is necessary to invent and explore forms of resistance and autonomous judging that fall outside the republican's faith in the availability of robust, communally sanctioned, ethical value-schemes. Republicanism simply does not do justice to the fact of rationalization and the risk of a concomitant slide into moral and ethical nihilism.

How would Adorno respond to Habermas' own model? I think an answer to this question, however provisional and speculative, would revolve around at least three major concerns. The first would be the significance Habermas assigns to the notion of consensus. While it can hardly be denied that a democratic account of institutional legitimacy needs this notion, it is equally important to keep in mind that a living democratic politics requires the acceptance of heterogeneity, conflict, and antagonism. According to Mouffe (2000: 48), the Habermasian model suffers from an inability to take into account that relations of inclusion–exclusion will necessarily be inscribed in the political constitution of "the people," and that no consensus can ever be more than provisional, a claim that some members of society make on behalf of all. The ideal speech situation with its vision of unrestricted inclusion therefore represents an untenable idealization on the basis of which no democratic principle of legitimacy can justifiably be derived.

The emphasis on agonistic confrontation — not between enemies but between adversaries that pursue different interests — as constitutive of politics has recently attained a new significance.[8] Consider for example the move to the right made by many traditional parties, including Blair's Labour and Schröder's SPD, on the left. By creating a "consensus at the center" and by euphemistically redefining themselves as "center-left," these parties effectively undermine the older left's preoccupation with equality and contribute to the establishment of an increasingly one-dimensional world of politics in which few virtues and interests beyond those of the market and its sacred logics are registered.

Another Adornian complaint against Habermas' view is that the nature of what can be accepted as a serious political claim or argument is severely restricted. According to Habermas, a serious political claim purports to be universally acceptable to all rational agents affected by the implementation of the norm in question. Such a claim is meant to convince others on purely cognitive grounds, that is in light of the reasons the speaker is prepared to adduce for its acceptance. Indeed, since being able to relate rationally and reflectively to claims to validity in the light of their reasons is the only way for speakers to prove that they are autonomous and accountable, it follows that accountability here necessarily entails rational argumentation. Accountability cannot be demonstrated in any other way. Clearly, Adorno would reject such a view. As we have seen, on his account there is a much wider variety of accountable behavior. Most obviously, in advanced art works (whose claim to be of political relevance Habermas can only accept insofar as it is "translated" into rational discourse by art criticism) Adorno, while certainly restrictive about the kinds of cultural expression that qualify as serious, sees a powerful arena of praxis and political engagement capable in some instances of bringing social conflicts more effectively and adequately into view than any "rational argumentation."

It might finally be useful for our thinking about Adorno's political stance vis-à-vis second- and third-generation Critical Theory to question Habermas' proneness, in his theory of political discourse, to want to draw a wedge between ethical, pragmatic, and justice-oriented discourses. Whereas ethical discourse, on the one hand, is supposed to be interpretive and self-reflective, aimed at uncovering and articulating shared values and identities within a local community, instrumental, moral, and legal considerations, on the other, can claim universal validity. Although this distinction represents a response to the familiar liberal preoccupation with social plurality, its price is that political initiatives that seek to transcend the parochialism of communal self-interpretation become drained of ethical motivation. If who I am and where I come from — my attachments and commitments, my history and my experiences (perhaps of ethical hurt and injustice), and indeed my sense of belonging to a collective that is united in specific forms of struggle and conflicts — if all that can only be politically relevant for myself and those with whom I share my ethical orientation, then politics in the universalist sense loses its interest, its power to motivate, and ultimately its meaning. If, for example, one looks at the long fight for the universal implementation of equality and (social and legal) justice in South Africa, then it is clear that there was always an existential and political continuity between micro-level ethical experience and macro-level discourses of justice. Just as ethical experience, one's personal and collective confrontation with systemic mistreatment, had moral and legal implications, laying the basis for a principled political stance, so was political experience, in the sense of debating issues of legislation and representation from a moral or legal standpoint, intimately informed by one's identity and position within a specific group's history of involvement with, or victimization by, the apartheid system. To isolate the ethical from the political represents a distortion of what politics can be.

These remarks on Habermas' account of politics may need a lot more elaboration. My main aim in introducing work which Adorno never saw and to which his own writing is not in any straightforward sense designed to respond was to deepen our understanding of Adorno and his position vis-à-vis the later development of Habermas' Critical Theory. The next chapter will continue the task of extrapolating Adorno's thinking into more immediate political contexts than he himself did.

# 8

# ADORNO IN CONTEMPORARY POLITICAL THEORY

Throughout this book we have regularly been exposed to the fact that while Adorno resisted the explicit formulation of a political theory, his social, philosophical and cultural understanding did involve an intense political assessment and engagement, albeit on a highly rarefied, theoretical level. In this chapter I draw on the political analyses we have seen so far in order to construct a more systematic account of what an Adornian politics might look like. It is true, of course, that such an enterprise necessarily will have to be of a provisional and hypothetical nature. Because it involves the employment of terms and arguments that are foreign to Adorno's work, it violates the dialectical demand for immanent critique. It also extrapolates material from contexts that, as we have seen, do not relate easily to politics, and it certainly stands in an uneasy relationship to his (politically motivated) resistance towards the political. However, I do believe that its rewards can be shown to be higher than its costs. Not only is Adorno's politics, as I view it, powerful in itself; it also stands up interestingly to more familiar positions in political philosophy. In particular, I shall argue that it contributes to a radical and perfectionist transformation of liberal democratic theory.

In the final part of the chapter I discuss the relevance of Adorno's work for feminism and deep ecology. I argue that although his contribution to both of these fields of intellectual engagement cannot under any construal be understood as straightforward, there are interesting and productive ways to make his work bear on them.

## Adorno and liberal political theory

We have seen that while Adorno's social theory draws on, and idiosyncratically blends, a number of motives from thinkers as diverse as Marx, Nietzsche, Weber, Freud, Benjamin, and Lukács, his politics is a lot less tangible, revolving around the intuition that advanced art is the only remaining medium of resistance in the age of totally administered societies. From what we know so far, it is not yet clear how Adorno's work may, in

159

ADORNO AND THE POLITICAL

addition to its complex affiliations with aesthetic modernism and Marxism, be relevant to contemporary political theory.

In particular it needs to be elaborated in more depth what its relation might be to the liberal political tradition and the debates surrounding the status of democracy. In Chapter 1, I suggested that Adorno seems to have displayed an ambiguous attitude towards liberalism, viewing it as histori-cally bygone and irretrievable, yet also as a conception of the political that commands respect due to its defining interest in protecting individual freedom and autonomy. There is little or no evidence, though, to the effect that he actually was some kind of anti-perfectionist liberalist *malgré lui*. While associating classical liberalism with a liberal state, bourgeois family-structures, and active individuals with considerable ego-strength — all of which is claimed to have been obliterated with the historical lapse into administered monopoly capitalism — the Marxist in Adorno would always, when looking at the classical, early phase of liberalism, counter these ideals with the facts of wage labor and class division. That is not to say, however, that he would be entirely dismissive of comprehensive theo-ries of so-called formal democracy. The two assumptions on which Marxist rejections of formal democracy are usually based — first, that socialism's more substantive and economically considered form of democ-racy would eliminate the need for formal justice, and, second, that a complete reconciliation of particular and general interest is desirable — are in fact disowned by Adorno. Indeed, a major worry he has with the Hegelian–Marxist polis is that its ideals of harmony and reconciliation tend to eliminate concern with opposition, non-identity, and freedom. No living democracy can do without the acceptance of conflict and plurality; thus the liberal presupposition that every society is composed of essentially finite and flawed individuals who need to negotiate rationally and peace-fully with each other in order to uncover the normative arrangements that may be of general interest cannot be completely foreign to an Adornian account of politics.

Adorno is, however, not consistent with regard to the question of formal justice. In one passage, he claims that if we simply rejected as ideology the legal requirement that unequal individuals must be treated equally and that parity should be the rule, then "we would be creating excuses for recidivism into ancient justice" (1973b: 146). The alternative to formal justice would be "the naked privilege of monopolies and cliques" (1973b: 146). Elsewhere, however, he seems skeptical of formal justice. In *Minima Moralia*'s aphorism number 66, for example, which is one of the few entries in which he directly confronts liberal political theory, we find him offering a critique of its central argument in favor of tolerance, namely that all individuals, despite race, sex, religion, and so on are of equal standing and worth. The invocation of the abstract value of equality, Adorno maintains, while intended to support tolerance, actually sustains totalitarianism, the systematic eradication of difference. "The familiar argument of tolerance," he writes

> that all people and all races are equal, is a boomerang... . That all men are alike is exactly what society would like to hear. It considers actual or imagined differences as stigmas indicating that not enough has yet been done; that something has still been left outside its machinery, not quite determined by its totality. The technique of the concentration camp is to make the prisoners like their guards, the murdered, murderers. The racial difference is raised to an absolute so that it can be abolished absolutely, if only in the sense that nothing that is different survives. An emancipated society, on the other hand, would not be a unitary state, but the realization of universality in the reconciliation of differences. Politics that are still seriously concerned with such a society ought not, therefore, propound the abstract equality of men even as an idea. Instead, they should point to the bad equality today, the identity of those with interests in film and in weapons, and conceive the better state as one in which people could be different without fear. To assure the black that he is exactly like the white man, while he obviously is not, is secretly to wrong him still further.
>
> (1974a: 102–3)

In his valorization of social difference, Adorno sounds like the standard multiculturalist of the 1980s and 1990s, defending identities against the discriminatory measures of the law and of politics. If anything, he certainly displays a liberal mind-set, emphasizing the defense and reconciliation of existing plurality and difference as the overriding goal of the well-functioning state (or universal). Several things go wrong in this little dialectical *tableau*, however. For one thing, the reference to "blacks" seems to imply that there is a given and invariant, yet socially relevant, difference between races, thus leaving out the fact that the differences that generate inequality are in most instances socially created. Which differences between black and white members of the population does Adorno want to see defended and institutionalized? If the answer is "cultural differences," then it becomes imperative to distinguish between those that are the result of social domination and those that are not, or at least can be freely accepted. It should be obvious that the most blatant cultural differences between black and white people in the United States (which is the country Adorno has in mind) are generated by huge asymmetries in economic and political resources. Indeed, if what Adorno intends to point to is the protection of different identities, he fails to take into account, following Edward Said and others, how identities are formed not just autonomously but in complex processes of projection that involve domination.[1] What it means to be a member of a less privileged ethnic or racial group is largely a function of what the dominant group takes to be determinative, hence accepting such differences in identity is often tantamount to supporting relations which in the end are predicated upon asymmetrical distributions of money and power.

For another thing, Adorno mysteriously confuses the demand for equality or equal treatment with totalitarianism, thereby grotesquely associating the liberal value of equality with the Nazi extermination of difference. The demand for equal rights amounts to a claim, first, to be equal before the law (which, after the introduction of the Nuremberg laws, the Jews and the rest of the German population were not); second, to be equally responsible for the laws (the Jews, as opposed to the non-Jewish Germans, had all their rights to political participation withdrawn); and, finally to be of equal worth or moral standing. In a political situation marked by radical practices of social exclusion, any possible fight against the dominant group would necessarily have to involve the making of a claim to formal equality. While not a sufficient condition of tolerance, formal equality is certainly required to insure the free interplay of different individuals and social groups.

Adorno's scathing attack on the sphere of legality echoes Marx's ideological critique of Hegel according to which, in bourgeois society, the law is always extrinsic to the real interests of the dominated class. Adorno extends and even intensifies this critique in some of the most problematic passages in the *Negative Dialectics*, claiming that

> law is the primal phenomenon of irrational rationality. In law the formal principle of equivalence becomes the norm; everyone is treated alike. An equality in which differences perish secretly serves to promote inequality; it becomes the myth that survives amidst an only seemingly demythologized mankind.
>
> (1973b: 309)

A difference between this quote and the previous one is that Adorno here seems to dismiss positive law in general. However, the premise — that a legal norm is valid for all legal subjects and is supposed to be applied similarly in similar circumstances (which arguably, by the way, is something well worth defending) — does not support the conclusion, namely that the system of positive law actually undermines and destroys individual identities. That certain groups or members of any society are capable of using the law to their advantage, or that some forms of legal practice serve to promote existing mechanisms of social oppression, is a common and in many cases valid criticism of the legal sphere. In this sense the law is never universal; it always serves to exclude those with scarce resources with which to legally represent themselves. To maintain, however that the law is necessarily partial and arbitrary because it operates according to a formal principle of equivalence is to throw the baby out with the bathwater.

Under the apartheid regime in South Africa, for example, the struggle for justice against racial discrimination often took the form of demanding legal or formal equality. To achieve such equality was tantamount to social recognition of an ethnic group that had been excluded during the whole history of European colonization. Indeed, Adorno can be criticized for failing to differentiate properly between different levels of recognition. According to Honneth (1994), it is crucial to distinguish between love, universal moral respect, and legal recognition. At all three levels agents recognize each other: on the first, as particular human beings defined by their needs; on the second, as rational creatures capable of setting their own ends; on the third, as legal subjects endowed with rights. To reduce the social recognition provided by the fundamental ideal of equality before the law to the two other levels — which might be a way of describing a Marxist priority of fraternity as opposed to freedom and formal equality — would all too easily create conditions in which injustice would prevail. Whereas justice and freedom must operate according to a logic of universality and equality, fraternity is local and draws distinctions between insider and outsider, friend and enemy, privileged and unprivileged. The Hegelian in Adorno would rightly be critical, however, of a too sharp and undialectical differentiation between these levels. There are times, for example, when a judge will be expected to show mercy. According to Adorno, though, the legal order is so "objectively alien and extraneous to the subject" (1973b: 310) that no comprehensive reconciliation of legality and morality is possible. Moral conscience will always be in potential conflict with the demands of the legal norm, yet no outline for an alternative form of mediation is provided. The only aim left to the negative dialectician is to demonstrate that there is a tension between the levels.

A more promising approach to the relationship between Adorno and liberal political theory would be focusing on the existential and intellectual burden which a liberal order ideally places on individual citizens who seek to act rationally as social and political critics of their own society. Is there a position that could mediate between Adorno's concerns and those of liberalism? In Stanley Cavell's perfectionist reconstruction of the myth of the social contract, the task is not to found the republic but to provide ongoing challenges to the normative political content for which citizens (implicitly or explicitly) take responsibility. A dimension of particular interest to Cavell arises when agents, in seeking to articulate such content, find themselves radically isolated from their fellow human beings. At stake, then, seems to be what Adorno engaged in throughout his career, namely some form of totalizing social or political critique.

Adorno is not a thinker whose name appears often in Cavell's writings. There are, however, some scattered references in his unpublished Spinoza lecture, "Praise as Consent: Arresting Voices," from 1998, in which Cavell speaks of Adorno (together with Benjamin) as being in the business of "charging [intellectual systems] with leaving out precisely the remainders and details of existence in which the life of a culture is revealed." Adorno, he continues, is "fighting specific philosophical conceptualizations ... which keep at bay the reality they sense." In the, for Cavell, closely related works of Benjamin, he finds an awareness that the cost of participating in democracy may be that, in the face of the injustices that I may come to acknowledge my voice as lent to, I find myself inexpressive and stifled.[2] The right response is then to be averse to conformity and to resist complicity with views that the individual cannot authenticate in an autonomous fashion.

Cavell further argues that the pursuit of autonomy and self-authorization involves reference to a community of mutually responsible individuals who consider each other as free and equal. A political community is a community in which each and every citizen ideally strives to articulate the universals that are supposed to be valid for all, hence each consenting individual is not only answerable to, but also for, the society and its normative arrangements.

Being rational is thus to accept full responsibility for one's own choices. By contrast, the everyday conformist rejects responsibility for the laws conferred on every citizen by the idea of the social contract. Rather than defining the extent to which he can conceive of himself as author of the social order, such an agent, by failing to estrange himself from prevailing opinion (as well as from himself), lets the community speak for him, yet without interrogating its right to do so. Conformity can thus be viewed as a form of unconsciousness; having repressed or forgotten their responsibility, conformists fail to define and express their (political) selves — hence, on Cavell's view, they fall short of obtaining a political existence.

Since it demands the reasoned agreement of all, the social contract can only be in full existence insofar as each individual is choosing to exercise freedom. In imperfect human societies (that is, in societies as we know them) the bonds between citizens are secured by obedience to agreements that are partial and secret. Rather than acting openly on behalf of the polis, citizens do not freely declare the basis of their consent; instead, they remain private, without a real voice, deprived of genuine citizenship. What informs social criticism, therefore, is a desire for impartiality, for asking whether one's obedience has come into being on the basis of incentives internal or external to the law. In Cavell's reading of the political romanticist, the withdrawal from the community becomes a concomitant re-connection with it: the more isolated the critic is from his community, the more openly and freely can he call upon his neighbors. Acquiring citizenship within Cavell's perfectionist framework becomes a question of finding one's own voice — of freely and individually assuming or declaring a position from which to speak.

Cavell is close to a classical, Aristotelian view of politics. Citizens realize their true nature within the framework of a rational state; hence freedom is nothing but the successful participation in such a community — or pure politics. What each single member of the polis can recognize as having assented to is not given *a priori* but constantly up for individual rethinking, discussion, and negotiation. However, Cavell significantly extends the polis — the sphere of mutual responsibility and citizenship — to include acts of negation and assertion that many theorists, both liberal and Aristotelian, would regard as of possible relevance only within the private sphere.[3] The most radical of such acts may even leave the agent unrecognizable.

Since I speak for others (while recognizing that others speak for me), my self represents an alternative self for all. Perfectionism thus includes the movement of the self from conformity to a higher level of self-reliance and thus also to a higher level of representability.[4]

Adorno would hardly be pleased with Cavell's conjoining of autonomous self-reliance with Heidegger's notion of authenticity.[5] Nor would he have much patience with Cavell's inclination to treat the political as independent and categorically distinct from the economy. Cavell's work cries out, it seems, for an historical account of why citizens fail to exercise their autonomy. The processes of rationalization inherent in late capitalism, in particular the dominance of the principle of exchange, receive little or no discussion. Finally, Adorno would be dismissive of contract theory in general, associating it, no doubt, with classical possessive individualism of the Hobbesian or Lockean variants, rather than with the Rousseauian position espoused by Cavell.

Speaking in favor of a Cavellian reading of Adorno's contribution to liberal political theory is the extraordinary responsibility, in a liberal order, which Adorno assigns to the individual. While Cavell's favored perfectionist figures include Emerson and Thoreau, writers who turn their back to society as it stands in order better to rearticulate its promises, Adorno appeals to the modernist art work and the uncompromising intellectual in order to keep the remembrance of politics alive. In both authors, conformism and prejudice constitute the supreme threats to democracy. Perhaps the deepest concern that animate both of them, however, is their denial of any account of universality that presupposes an impersonal and pre-given matrix or structure that unites the community and enables the philosopher to speak representatively. In their anti-foundationalist view, philosophy is instead bound to start and end with the separate self, and to shun the reference to the self means to forfeit the possibility of achieving authority. But this, though, suggests that the self, in order to find itself, must aspire to exemplarity — to be a parable of each life. Its expressions may be refused, or they may even be unintelligible, yet no route to mutuality exists other than the patient, if unassured, out-calls of separate individuals.

The potentially most damaging objection to this view as a basis for thinking about the nature of democracy is that it is elitist. We have already seen how vigorously Adorno was criticized for being elitist by the student activists. According to John Rawls (1971: 325–32), who provides a sophisticated elaboration of this charge, perfectionism as a political doctrine is inherently elitist and must therefore be ruled out as incompatible with democratic principles of justice.

If we concentrate on Adorno, then it seems that his elitism is always strategic.[6] He never promotes the pursuit of excellence for its own sake, but only as a means to achieve the degree of autonomy required for the constitution of a political voice. The problem, though, which I discussed briefly at the end of the first chapter, is that Adorno has a too narrow account of what the conditions are for an expression to count as autonomous. While he is not an elitist in the sense that he wants society to direct its principles of justice in such a way that they privilege the pursuit of excellence over other activities, he turns political engagement into something so rarefied that only a privileged elite might ever be in a position to partake in it. To be sure, such political positions are in principle open to everybody. However, when what they require is participation in pursuits such as modernist art practices or dialectical critique, then it follows that politics stands in danger of being drained of spaces in which to act. His work demonstrates to the full how fine the line may be between radical political aspiration and melancholic retreatism.

## Feminist interventions

On a first reading, Adorno's work appears to have little to offer with regard to issues related to feminism or feminist politics. Indeed, his valorization of the bourgeois family structure as well his celebration of high modernist male genius suggest, on the contrary, that his affiliations went in a patriarchal direction. However, as recent research has made clear, his writings do in fact display not only an awareness of feminist issues but actually a developed, though non-systematic, view of sexual difference and the conditions that enable women's exclusion.[7] In aphorism 59 of *Minima Moralia*, for example, Adorno defends a constructivist view of femininity, arguing that all talk of women's "nature" — that femininity is a given essence beyond possible critique and reflection — is reactionary: "The feminine character, and the ideal of femininity on which it is modeled, are products of masculine society. The image of undistorted nature arises only in distortion, as its opposite." In recent feminist theory, most prominently in Judith Butler, such anti-essentialism has become commonplace. However, in a long and somewhat rambling reflection that appears as one of the appendices to the *Dialectic of Enlightenment* Adorno (1979: 248) goes further than Butler and situates his critique of essentialism within the context of his Freudian–Weberian account of civilization, suggesting that women's *de facto* association with nature has called forth the same hatred as man, in the process of liberating himself from fate, has felt towards untrammeled nature: "She became the embodiment of the biological function, the image of nature, the subjugation of which constituted that civilization's title to fame." The witchcraft trials, for example, were thus means "at once to celebrate and to confirm the triumphs of male society over prehistoric matriarchal and mimetic stages of development" (1979: 248). Behind the bourgeois cult of feminine beauty, moreover, Adorno (1979: 249) hears "the ribald laughter, the withering scorn, the barbaric obscenity with which strength greets weakness in an attempt to deaden the fear that it has itself fallen prey to impotence, death, and nature." Femininity is a historically created category — an effect of domination.

The clear and present danger with this line of thought is that, by making the subjugation of women a function of nothing less than the process of civilization itself, it unwittingly serves to enforce, rather than criticize, the naturalization of gender-specific oppression. In crude terms, if the process of civilization is to blame for the inequality between the sexes, then no political course of action seems available that would promise alleviation of women's plight in a patriarchal order: this order would be as uncircumventable as civilization itself is. (This, of course, would structurally be the same objection as critics have leveled at Adorno's work in general: that the explanation of the ills of modernity is indexed to a level so fundamental that it jeopardizes all prospects for political change.) From a feminist standpoint, Adorno's position seems unhelpful in terms of contributing to political change in the relation between the sexes.

Another difficulty is that, despite his insistence that femininity is a signifier without necessary and sufficient content, Adorno tends to posit nature as the other of history, thereby reinscribing the stereotypical and patriarchal dichotomy between (instrumentally) active masculinity and passive femininity in his account of the process of civilization itself. According to Wilke and Schlipphacke (1997), the reading of *The Odyssey* in the *Dialectic of Enlightenment* demonstrates the extent to which male subjectivity, represented by Odysseus, is seen as constituted by the polarization of instrumental rationality and nature, where the latter is associated exclusively with female figures (the Sirens, Circe): "The female subject serves mainly an instrumentalized function on the male's way to self-actualization. Beyond that, the female subjects in this text are all associated with forbidden, though socially and politically impotent, forms of sensuality and are thus reconstructed out of stereotypical patterns of female images in patriarchal culture" (Wilke and Schlipphacke 1997: 299).

As Hewitt (1992) points out, the fact that the feminine represents a challenge to the masculinist regime of domination and instrumental reason could be viewed not simply, following Wilke and Schlipphacke, as an ideological reproduction of hegemonic patriarchal binarisms, but as an acknowledgment, rather, of women's capacity for effecting disruptions of paternalist systems of power. "Women are instrumentalized as the representatives of the possibility of exclusion understood as an *escape* from the all-inclusive system of power. In other words, the initial — and damning — exclusion of women from the philosophical project is reworked as a potential exemption from the totality of power as ontologized domination and of reason as a system of closure" (Hewitt 1992: 147). Although Hewitt's point is perceptive, it is far from obvious that Adorno ultimately provides an account of sexual difference that is able to challenge what Hewitt refers to as "the totality of power as ontologized domination and of reason as a system of closure." Beyond this, Adorno's attempt to reconstruct a different system of signification, linking mythological female figures by means of the notion of magical mimesis to a prehistorical, nature-like promise of happiness, ties feminine experience to a perspective that fails to achieve any real specificity within the dominant masculine discourse.

The debate concerning women's status as conceived within the framework of the *Dialectic of Enlightenment* is entirely predicated upon this work's controversial philosophy of history and in particular the anthropological dualisms around which it is structured. In his entries in *Minima Moralia* on marriage, however, Adorno takes another approach. The reason why women find themselves oppressed in their marriages is mainly to do with the role this institution plays in the modern market system, rather than with the age-old attribution of otherness to women consistent with the dialectic of enlightenment. As he argues in *Minima Moralia*'s aphorism 11, although marriage can ideally be viewed as a sanctuary from the coldness of instrumentalized human relations in the market-place — a space in which others are (and should be) genuinely treated as ends in themselves, rather than as a means to achieving extrinsic purposes — the parting of the couple, when financial and legal considerations enter the picture, demonstrates that what actually governs the relation between the spouses is the bad universality of exchange. As I read the entry, the point is not that marriage can be viewed exclusively in economic terms, but that there is a dialectic or inevitable tension that needs to be negotiated, and which perhaps can never be fully resolved in a bourgeois society, between the promise of intimacy and happiness, on the one hand, and the impact of economic necessity, on the other. Considered strictly as an economic institution, however, marriage has its place within a patriarchal order that sexually, socially and professionally compels women into subjection.

In any event, the near universal availability of contraception and women's increasing economic independence, especially after the 1960s, have radically changed the nature of marriage: few women are as inferior and dependent in their relationships today as they arguably were in the traditional bourgeois marriage towards which Adorno directs his criticisms. Yet is Adorno recommending its apparent successor, the "liquid love" (Bauman 2000) of short-term, "until-further-notice" engagement structured on the basis of narcissism and hedonism in a post-industrial consumer society, as constituting progress?

In his late article "Sexual Taboos and Law Today," Adorno views the sexual revolution of the 1960s as the erotic analogue of the culture industry: instead of offering genuine liberation from centuries of oppressive sexual regimes, it in effect creates false freedom and enjoyment. As soon as they stray beyond the boundaries of the old-fashioned marriage, the seemingly liberated libidinal energies get co-opted and administered by the commodified relations of the market-place, turning men and women into prostitutes and consumers who essentially buy and sell each other for whatever they are worth. However, Adorno (1998b: 81) adopts a liberal position regarding pornography: "It is both foolish and an infringement upon personal liberty to withhold pornography from adults who enjoy it." In doing so, he seems not only to disregard the subjection of women as mere objects of the male gaze inherent in most pornography but to contradict his previous lament over commodification. The same is true, I would argue, of his more unpleasant reluctance to condemn prostitution.[8]

In many ways Adorno seems caught up in the cultural contradictions of the 1960s. While decidedly skeptical of Marcuse's explicit invocation, in *Eros and Civilization* (which Adorno, in a letter to Marcuse, accused of being too "direct and immediate" and managed to have rejected by Horkheimer as part of the Institute's series of social-scientific studies[9]), of polymorphous-perverse sexuality in what was then seen as a battle against the genital structuring of the bourgeois sexual order, Adorno (1974a: 61) nevertheless brings himself to write that "He alone who could situate utopia in blind somatic pleasure, which, satisfying the ultimate intention, is intentionless, has a stable and valid idea of truth." According to Safranski (1998: 413), the reason why Adorno reacted so strongly against Marcuse's sexual politics was that the latter "had too openly revealed a production secret of critical theory — the idea of a successful culture based on a sexuality liberated into eroticism." Yet if Adorno had a share in this secret, it is equally true that the objections to Marcuse from an Adornian standpoint are compelling. Adorno would never accept Marcuse's minimizing of the significance of the Oedipus complex. Although costly to the extreme, the patriarchal decentering and taming of infantile, narcissistic omnipotence is an unavoidable condition of mature ego-strength. Moreover, the concept of primary narcissism, which for

Marcuse promises not only Nirvana, bliss, and *jouissance*, but also de-differentiation, and oblivion, has for Adorno no political value.[10] Ultimately, the only genuine claim to somatic happiness there can be must be made by the advanced art work. By resisting the desire to make good on this claim, the art work maintains it.

But is there, for Adorno, a specific mode or inflection in which the feminine voice, in its difference, can be considered in terms of its capacity for resistance, as opposed to simply being a function of the paternal and identitarian order of Western civilization? One text to consider would be the reading of Ibsen's *Hedda Gabler* in entry 58 of *Minima Moralia*. Central to this piece is Adorno's sense that Hedda finds herself in a position of having to put the social order as such on notice — her complaint is not simply with her marriage (although that is certainly a major part of it) but with the negative social totality within which she lives, against which she has no reasons that seem worthy of being taken seriously by her immediate surroundings. It makes no sense to ask her to participate in what Rawls (1971: 533) calls the conversation of justice, asking "why certain institutions are unjust or how others have injured them." According to Rawls (1971: 533), "Those who express resentment must be prepared to show why certain institutions are unjust or how others have injured them." If they are unable to do so, we can consider that our conduct is above reproach and bring the conversation to a close. However, in this case, since specific wrong is not claimable — all that her husband sees is a woman acting childishly — the failure of conventional morality (represented by the rigid Aunt Julle) means that Hedda's complaint must be shown, rather than stated or argued.

What must be shown is an event — call it sublime (Adorno thinks of it as viciously beautiful) — whereby the claimant, in her unknownness and resistance towards discursive intelligibility, transgresses the social totality within which she has been involved, thereby promising a radical political renewal. In Ibsen's play the event of transgression is apparent in Hedda's indirect, ironic denials, such as her icy mockery of Aunt Julle, culminating in her tragic and yet, to the other characters, incomprehensible suicide. There is a *jouissance* in Hedda — a siding with evil beauty against a degenerate morality — which, on Adorno's reading, takes the form of a declaration of independence so radical that, while subverting the logic of standard political discourse, it obtains a political significance of its own:

> So beauty finds itself in the wrong against right, while yet being right against it. In beauty the frail future offers its sacrifice to the Moloch of the present: because, in the latter's realm, there can be no good, it makes itself bad, in order in its defeat to convict the judge. Beauty's protestation against good is the bourgeois, secular-ized form of the delusion of the tragic hero. In the immanence of

170

society, consciousness of its negative essence is blocked, and only abstract negation acts as a substitute for truth.

(Adorno 1974a: 95)

One might see in Hedda Adorno's version of Hegel's Antigone: a feminine figure which, in the name of a law that cannot be communicated and therefore gets transposed into the apparently non-cognitive, aesthetic register, transgresses the patriarchal order in its totality, thereby risking utter misrecognition.[11] Whether or not such a tragic-heroic reading can escape the charge that it retains a traditional opposition between passive and active while subverting its standard association with women and men respectively is not entirely clear. Adorno's thinking about feminist issues is unstable, revealing a mélange of both reactionary and progressive attitudes.

## The ecological challenge

Since Adorno never seems to have taken any explicit interest in ecology, it may seem futile to want to relate his thinking to the cluster of concerns that are associated with this term. However, the fact that his work has increasingly been taken up by a number of environmental activists and intellectuals suggests that the relation may actually be well worth exploring. In strictly political terms, the Green movement, including its parties and organizations, has had a major global impact, culminating in the 2000 Kyoto agreement over the reduction of greenhouse emissions. The Green movement, however, has long been divided between a reformist and a "deep" ecological position. While the reformists have called for a more extensive protection of natural environments, as well as limitations of water and air pollution, and so on, though without questioning the priority of instrumental reason as such, the deep ecologists have been more radical, demanding a revolutionary politics based on a new cosmology and a new environmental ethic concerning the relationship between man and nature.[12] Adorno's work has hardly informed the reformist position. It is the deep ecologists who have shown interest in him and sometimes perceived in him an ally.

Yet does Adorno's work lend itself to such an appropriation? In some respects it clearly does. The most obvious one concerns the critique of modernity, and indeed of human history in general, as being permeated by instrumental reason, where instrumental reason (in modernity) takes the form of techno-scientific mastery and domination of nature. By viewing man's desire for self-preservation as the only source of authority with regard to questions of value in an otherwise disenchanted universe, the representatives of enlightened modernity devalorize every natural item to become just a fungible means in man's progressive renunciation and suppression of his natural being. Echoing Heidegger's notion of enframing, nature becomes a resource to be exploited by humans; thus nothing — no animal, no environment, no eco-system — counts as intrinsically valuable or worthy of protection: "Representation is exchanged for the fungible — universal interchangeability. An atom is smashed not in representation but as a specimen of matter, and the rabbit does not represent but, as a mere example, is virtually ignored by the zeal of the laboratory" (Adorno 1979: 10). According to many deep ecologists, Adorno's analysis shows how questionable the ideology of humanist anthropocentrism is: for rather than legitimately raising man out of nature on account of his reason and subjectivity, humanism appears as the ideological screen behind which man has waged war against nature in the name of progress and liberation. Unlike the reformists, many deep ecologists therefore reject humanism. However, if humanism is debunked, then so will also modernity, insofar as it is predicated on man's instrumentalist egoism, have to be called into question. In the eyes of most deep ecologists, Western modernity, with its vast techno-scientific machinery, is deeply corrupt and in need of replacement; hence the revolutionary undertone of so much of their writings.

Now the Marxist tradition has notoriously failed to take ecological issues into account. In Marx's view, it is human labor that bestows value and dignity on nature, and nature itself, especially in the *Capital*, is simply understood as the material to be transformed by labor, a mere means for further ends.[13] Although the early Marx's hopes, in the *Economic-Philosophical Manuscripts*, for a reconciliation between man and nature may seem to modify this assessment, Marx never considers such a reconciliation in terms other than the overcoming of alienated labor.[14] Adorno's rejection of the Marxist humanism of labor, as well as his replacement of the concept of labor with the category of instrumental reason, represents a challenge to Marxism. From an Adornian angle, the Marxian vision of labor as determining the metaphysical essence of man in his relation to nature becomes an expression of the same drive toward manipulative mastery that is so vehemently denounced in the *Dialectic of Enlightenment*.

It is important to keep in mind, though, that although Adorno is critical of Western, subject-centered reason as well as the idealist construals of subjectivity that he analyzes in *Negative Dialectics* and elsewhere, he does by no means seek to reject the notion of the subject, or subjectivity, as such. On the contrary, Adorno, as we have seen, insists on the need to strengthen the subject by, first, aiming to provide conditions for autonomous thinking and judging to take place, and, second, by searching for ways to acknowledge the subject's dependence on social and natural influences and sources of authority. For Adorno, since "the history of civilization is the history of the introversion of sacrifice" (1979: 55), any anti-humanism that calls for a demoting of the subject in general will

172

involve a potentially dangerous regression behind the enlightenment ideals that he undoubtedly wants to defend, however self-vitiating the process of civilization may appear to be. While sharing many of the counter-enlightenment intuitions about the relativity of the unitary subject, he sees no viable alternative to it. Perhaps the closest one gets to an opening towards considerations of a more reconciliatory nature is the well-known passage in *Dialectic of Enlightenment* where Adorno and Horkheimer speak of the need to conduct a "remembrance of nature in the subject" (1979: 40). While much can be said about the implications of this isolated phrase for Adorno's work as a whole, it certainly does not suggest that the violence which the unitary subject does to the particular, the suppressed, and the nonidentical should translate into a wholesale dismissal of the subject and a lapse back into an archaic matrix.[15] Indeed, Adorno seems to have had an almost instinctive fear of all forms of radical anti-modernist and anti-humanist thought, predominantly associating it with fascism. Indeed, the fact that the fascist parties of the 1930s, especially in Nazi Germany, represented the first organized political force to have formulated and implemented a policy of anti-anthropocentric ecological awareness seems to confirm Adorno's fear, although the simple inference from fascism's badness and its interest in ecology to ecology's badness, which sometimes is made, is no doubt invalid.[16] In order to demonstrate that deep ecology is ideologically unsound, it must not just be shown that it was taken up by the fascists but that, in doing so, they responded to aspects of ecology that themselves are complicit with, or bear affinity to, the fundamental convictions and tenets of fascist ideology. Obviously, the deep ecologists tend to be profoundly anti-authoritarian, often defending a kind of anarchist principle of "live and let live" rather than, as in fascism, wanting rigorous social stratification and obedience to centralized leadership. Their critique of humanism, however, may be said to be shared by fascist ideology; and the same is true of their Darwinian celebration of "life" as such at the potential expense of individuals.

This brings us to a second issue on which Adorno parts ways with deep ecology. In much of the history of ecological thinking, there has been a tendency towards privileging wholes and universals over parts and particulars. The German Romantics, for example, some of whom (the later Schelling in particular) can be listed among the first deep ecologists of Western culture, appropriated Spinozist and neo-Platonic ideas of unity not only for purposes of restoring, against Kant and Fichte's subjective idealisms, an at least partial continuity between mind and nature, subject and object, but also for retrieving a sense of nature as an independent, organic totality. For the later Schelling of the system of identity, nature is a living whole, and there is a single living force acting throughout it. In the work of Bergson, another source of inspiration for contemporary deep ecologists, the focus is on the "creative evolution" of the various species,

173

in comparison with which the individual is less ontologically real. While considerably less refined than the Spinozist, Romantic, and Bergsonist positions, the various "New Age" versions of this notion, such as the appeal to "gaya" and related conceptions, fall into a similar pattern. From an Adornian perspective, all of these views, however laudable they may be in reminding us of man's dependence on nature, subsume the vulnerable particular under the universal, thereby licensing violence in the name of "the natural" or "the necessary." If, for Adorno, myth involves the ordering of events in accordance with a scheme of inevitable repetition, drained of ethical and normative consideration, then the reification of nature as a totality, prevalent in deep ecology, represents a return to myth, rather than a way out of it. Deep ecology effectively proposes that we replace the congealed, second nature of reified industrial and post-industrial society with another and equally objectified structure, namely nature itself, now considered as a source of unquestioned authority. Adorno's call for the breakup of all projected totalities and identities implies no doubt a rejection of this particular dimension of deep ecology.

We have seen that Adorno's analysis of modernity has influenced proponents of deep ecology. But what about his normative and ethical vision? Does his defense of the subject and his critique of totality prevent his work from being useful to the articulation of a more positive and political vision of deep ecological engagement? According to Weber Nicholsen (2003), the most promising region of Adorno's thought in this respect may be the conjunction he exhibits of the neighboring concepts of aura, natural beauty and, in particular, mimesis. Roughly, what these concepts offer is a tool for radically rethinking man's relationship to nature, though without the anti-humanist and totalizing baggage that haunts standard accounts of deep ecology. Clearly, the risk of this being just another *ersatz* project, aimed at restoring harmony and returning to immediacy but without the social and economical conditions for a lessening of domination being satisfied, could hardly be greater. From an Adornian point of view, the vision of nature as providing some sort of sanctuary from an instrumentalized social reality would at best be compensatory. At worst it would represent an ideological screening of the mastery of nature that is required in order to consider it as an unthreatening, "friendly" Other. Even if one concedes these points, however, there are, I would argue, some distinct ways in which, in particular, the notion of mimesis could be developed so as to assist the articulation of some issues central to deep ecology.

One of them would be related to the question of intrinsic value which, while crucial to the political legitimization of deep ecology, has proved notoriously difficult to grapple with. Roughly, the debate has focused on whether or not value can exist apart from human interest and concern. While proponents of value realism hold that value can be accounted for independently of human interest, such that an animal or a forest deserves

174

our respect and care even if interest-based considerations tell us otherwise, critics of value realism insist that it makes no sense to speak of value in separation from a valuer. Since rational humans are beings that are held accountable for their judgments, it is only with reference to them that it becomes possible to say of some item that it *ought* to be esteemed. It seems evident, though, that Adorno would reject such a position. As Finlayson (2002) points out, Adorno strongly challenges the view that man, as it were, is the measure of all things, and that value is a function of rational choices and dispositions. An item, Finlayson argues, can call on our affection and demand our care apart from our rational desire to let it count as such. However, in contrast to the naive metaphysical realist, Adorno's account of intrinsic value would not be based on an appeal to values existing independently of human beings. Rather, if applied to the issue of intrinsic value, what the notion of mimesis suggests is that a thing, and by extension a body, can, when placed in a relationship of proximity to human beings possessed of a capacity for affection, itself *generate* an ethical demand. Just as, for Adorno, mimesis involves the ability to be touched by something to the point of partaking in, or completing, that other's expression of itself, so mimesis, when viewed in relation to the debate about intrinsic value, becomes the privileged mode in which agents are able to read off, or be affected by, an exterior claim that can only be received within a passive mode of allowing the integrity of the sensuous particular to matter. Thus, while value is something we perceive and which affects us from the outside, since mimesis presents itself as a relationship of communication and potential "reconciliation" between subject and object, the openness towards the non-identical other entailed by mimetic behavior becomes a constitutive moment in the creation of such value. Such an account permits us to insist that, though threatened by identitarian reason which progressively replaces our experience of natural and vulnerable being with an impersonal, "externalist" appeal to laws and putatively universal norms, the foundation of morally sensitive behavior towards nature stems from a receptiveness to an ethical demand that first and foremost is figured in our relationship to things. It is as if the open field, the rugged mountain, and the tranquil lake, each in their own way, call on us to nurture, protect, and respect them: those are examples of *das Unverfügbare* — that which resists our deep-seated urge to master and instrumentalize.

Perhaps, when applied to debates in ecology, the most intellectually satisfactory way with the notion of mimesis is to think of it in terms of what Wittgenstein would call a "reminder." However, mimesis figures in Adorno's extraordinary account of the beauty of nature as well. In contrast with the attempts to found an ethical theory with reference to mimesis, the beauty of nature provides only a reminder, suggestive of a reconfigured relationship between man and nature; it does not bring forth tools for the formulation of a comprehensive explanation of how moral behavior is possible. Moreover, the beauty of nature is an aesthetic, rather than a moral, category. In the absence of an easy passageway to the domain of the obligatory or commanding, nature's beauty will have to remain a cipher, relieved as it is of any constitutive role in a normative theory; thus the danger of morally overburdening the notion of mimesis is lessened.

I have already discussed how the beauty of nature actualizes itself for Adorno in terms of the register of the sublime. A striking dimension of this notion is how it encourages us to admit that all possible encounters with nature are historically mediated, while, at the same time, envisioning a dimension of reality that, though ultimately illusory (in the sense of *Schein*), prefigures the redemption of the object in its full integrity. In order to appreciate a piece of nature as beautiful, Adorno maintains, we must first have brought ourselves to a position of being able to master it. It is only at a (cultural, affective, technological) distance from nature that it can appear as beautiful. Rather than being a possible object of contemplation, uncontrolled nature is predominantly a source of fear, or, as the famous reading of the Sirens in *The Dialectic of Enlightenment* testify to, an object of unsublimated and hence potentially dangerous desire. However, Adorno also wants to avoid the romantic sentimentalism that traditionally has pertained to the notion of the beauty of nature and which today has become the preserve of the organized tourist industry. If offered in the guise of immediacy, natural beauty is ideological, suggesting that immediacy is available in a world of universal mediation. The alterity — or, as Adorno (1997a: 73) puts it, the "trace of the nonidentical in things under the spell of universal identity" — which presents itself in the encounter with natural beauty is always inscribed in a dialectic of illusion: the mountain or the ocean does not itself transcend the dominated order of appearing of nature; rather, it remains an allegory of what Adorno calls the precedence of the object in subjective experience.

While drawing on Kant's analytic of the beautiful in the *Critique of Judgment*, Luc Ferry (1995) appears to make a related claim, arguing that all that is needed in order to legitimize and provide intellectual support for (moderate) ecological activism is to point to the beauty of nature (together with its purposiveness) and how its encounter seems to create in us a sense of respect for nature in general. Ferry contrasts his own position with what he regards as the excessive demands of deep ecology for a new cosmology in which biocentric egalitarianism, the doctrine that no species, capacities or interests should be morally privileged, comes to play a fundamental role. The danger, he argues, with such a view consists in its lack of regard for the humanist heritage and its notion of the autonomous subject as an exclusive bearer of rights. The crucial difference, though, between Ferry and Adorno reveals itself as soon as their conceptions of natural beauty

176

are compared in their specificity. Although Kant interpreted natural beauty as aesthetically primordial, by adopting a Kantian approach, Ferry implicitly considers such beauty in terms of the famous "proportionate attunement," expounded in the *Critique of Judgment*, between the understanding and the transcendental imagination; thus his account of natural beauty remains idealistic. In the free play between the two cognitive faculties, the object does not play a philosophically constitutive role other than providing an occasion for such play. It is the play itself which generates the feeling of pleasure which, in turn, makes us ascribe to the object the predicate of beauty. While this has led critics to argue that, in Kant's account, anything can be beautiful, or even, since Kant links the grounds of judgments of taste with the conditions of cognition, that every object must be judged beautiful, it certainly suggests that the third Critique has little to offer with regard to what Adorno calls the preponderance of the object. For Adorno, there can be no beauty of nature without a materialistic moment of transcendence. As opposed to Adorno, Ferry remains totally committed to the humanist philosophy of the subject; thus natural beauty can only be tolerated insofar as it does not question the dominance of the subject. Adorno's dialectic is more complex:

> Natural beauty vanished from aesthetics as a result of the burgeoning domination of the concept of freedom and human dignity, which was inaugurated by Kant and then rigorously transplanted into aesthetics by Schiller and Hegel; in accord with this concept nothing in the world is worthy of attention except that for which the autonomous subject has itself to thank.
>
> (1997a: 62)

Although Adorno, as we have seen, certainly does not want to dispel the notion of freedom altogether, there is a strong tendency, especially in the later works, to want to confront the ego-principle with an alterity which is theorized alternately as nature, the unconscious, or mimesis. No robust normative basis for a deep ecology can be extracted from such thinking. Its function and purpose, rather, is to remind us of our fragility and, despite our technological capacity for control and manipulation, of how utterly dependent man is on nature. Exactly how this can be the basis for a political engagement with ecology is unclear. Its importance, like so much in Adorno, is anamnestic, aiming to anticipate a new and more responsible way of thinking.

# CONCLUSION

There is no easy way to sum up Adorno's achievement as a political thinker. As we have had ample opportunity to observe, Adorno was a theorist of conceptual conflict. Rather than positing harmonious mediations between what he perceived as flawed alternatives, he preferred to inhabit and explore the tensions between them, and consider them as expressions of deeper social contradictions that ought to be brought to light. Whether between transcendent and immanent critique, a Benjaminian desire for transcendence or a Hegelian emphasis on mediation, or between autonomous art and directly engaged art, he hardly ever sought to resolve the antinomies he detected. His philosophy might thus be said to remain wedded to and also limited by his metaphor of the torn halves of a freedom which does not add up to a whole: the historical moment at which a reconciliation of Adorno's antinomies would have been possible has not yet come about.

I certainly do hope to have shown that the account of Adorno as someone who kept the political at a maximum distance from his theoretical reflection is false. One of his most impressive feats was to have invented a form of philosophical reflection that at every step is politically oriented and critical, yet without eventually relinquishing philosophy altogether. Such work represents a powerful alternative both to Althusser's Marxism, which sought to substitute "science" for philosophy, as well as to Nancy's attempt to ontologize politics and withdraw it from historical mediation. This is not to say, however, that Adorno's writings can be easily applied to contemporary debates around issues such as feminism and deep ecology. While illuminating in some respects, the attempt to extend his work to areas that are not properly mediated by the terms of his dialectic has clear limits.

Adorno's negativism is unhelpful when it comes to analyzing the conscious decision-making processes that must be part of any *collective* political project. The strategically elitist stress on disruption from culturally privileged standpoints prevents a productive understanding of much of the current activity on the Left, especially the anti-globalization movement whose politics has revived the older Marxist interest in questions of justice and solidarity. At worst his politics may amount to a form of subjectivist anarchism that fails to take into account the communal dimension of political struggle and the essential difference between sovereign aesthetic or philosophical meaning and the more down-to-earth process of committing oneself to genuine political decisions and policies. As Lukács hinted at with his vicious yet penetrating remark that Adorno had taken up residence "at the Grand Hotel Abyss," there is always a danger for Adorno's negative dialectic that it becomes a means to secure purity and inner certainty at the expense of engaging with realms in which the acceptance of political responsibility is both costly and unavoidable.

In the conclusion to *Late Marxism*, Jameson (1996: 230) writes that on the basis of Adorno's use of the Marxian law of value and the notion of totality, he feels "able to reassert the essential Marxism of this thinker." As much as I agree with Jameson that these are fundamental theorems in Adorno's social theory, I find his Marxism highly selective and not exactly "essential" to his overall contribution, let alone his thinking about politics. The relative lack of interest in concepts of class struggle, organization, socialist strategy, and revolution suggests rather that Adorno's politics must be sought elsewhere. With reference to his negative dialectics and his account of the sublime modernist art work, I have argued that his real concern politically was to think about the conditions under which a given political order can be resisted and negated without having to adopt the totalitarian myth of the Ideal City. One of Adorno's greatest achievements as a thinker of the Left was precisely to have dismantled its triumphant Jacobin imaginary with its universal subjects and its progressively unfolding History in singular as focal points for social struggle, replacing it with ciphers of reconfigured political spaces coming from testimonies that are scarred by the horrors of history. In order for the project of left-wing thought to survive the pervasive expulsion of utopian thinking from the field of the political that often appears to be its only alternative, however, it must include the possibility of the constitution of a radical imaginary capable of totalizing as negativity a certain social order. On Adorno's view, such an imaginary (which by way of negation points towards "truth" or "reconciliation"), insofar as it is presented in overlapping networks of performative acts of self-expression that seek to authorize themselves as representative, creates a moment of tension, of openness, within the social and reinforces its democratic character. At the core of his vision of politics lies what I have called an ethics of resistance — a readiness to think and act such that the space of the political is liberated from the grasp of identity. The competing extreme, which Adorno never fails to criticize, is the limitation of the field of politics to the management of social positivity. As I have argued, the emphasis on plurality and antagonism, which sets Adorno apart from his successor within the Frankfurt School of Critical

Social Theory, Jürgen Habermas, is meant to ensure that politics never disintegrates into consensually enforced administration.

Adorno's utopian idea of a togetherness of differences provokes the question as to whether it is possible to conceive of a community for which the political is not structured by violence. Desperately unwilling to make it the basis for a historical theodicy, Adorno instead tied it to his categorical imperative of preserving an inappropriable alterity. Only time will tell whether this will continue to be a theme of interest within the tradition of Critical Theory. Its urgency seems in any event never to have been greater.

# NOTES

## INTRODUCTION

1 See Adorno (1991–2: I, 3–23).
2 For alternative accounts of Adorno's recent reception, see Hohendahl (1995: 3–20) and Zuidervaart (1991: 3–43).

## CHAPTER 1

1 Müller-Doohm (2003: 121) suggests that Adorno's early sympathy for socialism was strongly related to his sense that, as a result mainly of the First World War, bourgeois culture, and with it the legitimacy of capitalism, had deteriorated and even collapsed.
2 See the correspondence between Adorno and Berg (1997b: 73–5) in which Adorno explains the philosophical outcome of his 1925 discussions with Walter Benjamin in Naples.
3 Hardt and Negri's (2000) current concept of Empire, which interestingly construes late capitalism as a structure without any outside, a totality which embraces not only companies and consumers down to their very personality but the whole juridical network within which global capitalism unfolds, may vaguely mirror Adorno's idea of a totally administered society, yet without its authoritarian dimension. Whereas Adorno could view late capitalism (in collusion with fascism and Stalinism) as the great obstacle to freedom and democracy, Hardt and Negri consider it as embodying a potential for spontaneity and creation. For Adorno, politics only survives in the negative fringes of social reality — in advanced art and critical-dialectical thinking. For Hardt and Negri, by contrast, politics is made possible by capitalism's inherent unruliness. As in the republican tradition, it becomes equivalent to the exercise of the undelegatable powers of the people, the *demos*.
4 According to Schmucker (1977: 63f.), in his account of the concept of totally administered societies, Adorno keeps wavering between, on the one hand, philosophy of history and, on the other, sociological and economic considerations. While the 1942 "Reflections on Class Theory," for example, makes extensive reference to philosophy of history, explaining the end of liberal capitalism in terms of the self-perpetuating violence and repetition of the human *Urgeschichte* as such, a late essay, such as the 1968 "Is Marx Obsolete?" while not devoid of the problematic extension of a theory of totalitarianism to a democratic context, restricts the analysis to socio-economic considerations. Another equivocation, no less damaging, can be detected as between, on the

181

one hand, claiming that the purposive-rational, organized domination stems exclusively from state agencies, and, on the other, holding that agencies external to the state also partake in this process of integration. Moreover, is the dominating "system" to be interpreted as an autonomous political power, or is it restricted to a one-sided adaptation to technical-administrative imperatives? None of these questions are clearly answered by Adorno.

5 For an alternative account of the same trend, see Beck (1986).

6 See Kraushaar (1998: I, 254): "The students have to some extent taken over the role of the Jews" [*Die Studenten haben so ein wenig die Rolle der Juden übernommen*].

7 Müller-Doohm (2003: 706).

## CHAPTER 2

1 Jay (1984) disputes this claim and argues that what united the Western Marxists was not so much the perceived lack of effective political strategies as the search for a viable concept of social totality.

2 For book-length discussions of Western Marxism, see Anderson (1976), Gouldner (1980), Jacoby (1981), and Jay (1984b).

3 For an account of *Theory of the Novel* which places it in the wider context of Lukács' subsequent social theory, see Bernstein (1984).

4 Wiggershaus (1998: 69) quotes this passage from a newspaper article which Kracauer published in the *Frankfurter Zeitung* in 1922.

5 According to Gillian Rose (1978: 28), "Reification in this context stands for the divisiveness and fragmentation of modern society which is usually dated from the end of Greek antiquity!"

6 Hegel (1975b: 85/6) characterizes the onset of positivity in the following terms: "Even moral doctrines, now made obligatory in a positive sense, i.e., not on their own account, but as commanded by Jesus, lost the inner criterion whereby their necessity is established, and were placed on the same level with every other positive, specific, command, with every external ordinance grounded in circumstances or on mere prudence."

7 For a useful introduction to this issue, see Pippin (1991).

8 Rose (1978: 30) has rightly warned against misattributing the word "reification" (*Verdinglichung*) to Marx in his section in the first volume of *Capital* on the fetishism of commodities. Since Marx doesn't use it, but rather refers to commodification and commodity fetishism, such a misattribution may engender a failure to specify the mode of production in which reification takes place. As Rose points out, Lukács himself is the source of this persistent error.

9 See "Offener Brief an Horkheimer," quoted in Buck-Morss (1977: 67)

10 Buck-Morss (1977) was the first commentator in the English-speaking world to establish beyond doubt the decisive influence Benjamin's work had on the early Adorno.

11 Benjamin (1966: I, 372). Translated by Wolin (1994: 80).

12 For some relatively lucid expositions of Benjamin's early theory of language, see Wohlfart (1989) and Menninghaus (1980). It is worth emphasizing that Benjamin (1978: 321–2) does not base his theory of language on an interpretation of the Bible; rather, he uses the Bible in order to illustrate the theory: "If in what follows the nature of language is considered on the basis of the first chapter of Genesis, the object is neither biblical interpretation, nor subjection of the Bible to objective consideration as revealed truth, but the discovery of what emerges of itself from the biblical text with regard to the nature of

language; and the Bible is only *initially* indispensable for this purpose because the present argument broadly follows it in presupposing language as an ultimate reality, perceptible only in its manifestation, inexplicable and mystical." The problem seems to be that despite the attempt to distance himself from revealed truth, he nevertheless seems to appeal to it to a considerable extent.

13 Consider in this regard Benjamin's (1978: 313) claim, in "Theologico-Political Fragment," that the method of "world politics" is nihilism.

14 See Honneth (2000) for an example of this tendency.

15 According to Rose (1978), the term "instrumental reason" plays no role in Adorno whatsoever. For Habermas (1984) and Wellmer (1991), on the contrary, this notion is the crucial key to unravelling the argument in the *Dialectic of Enlightenment* as a whole. I differ from both of these views. My claim is that it plays a subordinate role.

16 In this respect I see Adorno's project as coherent with Pippin's (1991) call for a "philosophical modernism."

17 According to Demmerling (1994: 156), Adorno employs the term to denote the complex and unstable conjunction of three different moments: mimesis as the imitative disposition of a self toward an other, as a kind of *Sich-Anschmiegen ans Andere*, and finally as gesture, mimicry and expressive behavior. See also Früchtl (1986: 13ff.).

## CHAPTER 3

1 In his lecture-course on metaphysics, Adorno (2000c: 104) writes that "there can be no one, whose organ of experience has not entirely atrophied, for whom the world *after* Auschwitz, that is, the world in which Auschwitz was possible, is the same world as it was before."

2 Berman (2002: 110–31, esp. 111–12) astutely discusses this reply in his account of Adorno's politics.

3 Neither Kraushaar (1998) nor Wiggershaus (1998), the two most detailed accounts of Adorno's political involvement in the 1930s, makes any reference to such underground conspiracy.

4 Adorno (1973–86: XIX, 331–2).

5 Wiggershaus (1998: 157) refers to the incident as "an example of political opportunism."

6 See Heidegger (1990b).

7 In a letter to Benjamin written in April 1934, Adorno (1999a: 46) believes to have seen "signs of collapse" on the part of the Nazi state.

8 It might be added that the reasons to try to hibernate under fascist conditions did not just hinge on his empirical miscalculation of the nature of the regime. There is also — and this is well worth mentioning — a considerable commitment on the part of Adorno to the German language itself. In the 1965 essay "On the Question: 'What is German?' " he (1998b: 212) confesses that in addition to what he calls the subjective reason of homesickness, the objective factor which led to his decision to return to Germany after the war was his ability to write and publish exclusively in German. Following Wilhelm von Humboldt's expressivist notion of language as constitutive of thought and world-view, he argues that the German language "has a special affinity with philosophy and particularly with its speculative element" (212), and hence that writing in German allows him to avoid the trivializing communication of mere thus-ness and positivity that he finds himself disposed to in using a foreign language (in this case English). Adorno's claim is not just that there is an intimacy between a speaker and his or

her native language that encourages and makes possible an uncompromising and exact expression; it is that German, due to its "specific, objective quality" (212), is a better and more exact language for philosophers in general.

However, the evidence he adduces — such as the supreme difficulty of translating Hegel's work into any other language — is unconvincing. Problems of translation may at best point to something like Humboldt's incommensurability thesis: that since a natural language is structured holistically, no single sentence, appearing in a context for its meaning to be determinate, can strictly speaking be translated into any other language. There is no one-to-one match between sentences in different languages. Thus, untranslatability does not show that any one language is expressively better endowed than any other; all it shows, if it is not simply an empirical problem, is that languages are (radically) different. Likewise, Adorno's belief that terms like Geist, Moment, and Erfahrung, rich and suggestive as they no doubt are in for example Hegel's *Phenomenology of Spirit*, are as such privileged conveyors of speculative depth, does nothing to establish their "objective" quality. All we can say is that these are the terms Hegel (and others) use; to think that they are deep because they are German is uninformative; they are deep because (or if) Hegel (and others) is deep, which requires an independent explanation.

9   See "Extorted Reconciliation: On Georg Lukács' *Realism in Our Time*," in Adorno (1991–2: I, 216–40).

10  For a useful account of the different analyses of fascism elaborated by members of the Institute, see Wilson (1982).

11  See also Pollock (1941a).

12  According to Dubiel's (1985:79) gloss on Pollock, "The market, as an indirect instrument coordinating supply and demand, is replaced by a system of direct planning. This planning system rests in the hands of a powerful bureaucracy, itself the product of a fusion of state bureaucracy and top industrial management. The total economic process takes place within the framework of a general plan with guidelines for production, distribution, consumption, savings, and investments."

13  Letter to Horkheimer, June 8, 1941. Cited in Wiggershaus (1998: 282).

14  I owe this observation to Jarvis (1998: 62).

15  Chapter 5 contains a more extended discussion of Adorno's concept of freedom.

16  For his analysis of Freud's metapsychology, see Habermas (1987a).

17  Quoted from Turner (2002: 165).

18  For a more elaborate discussion of this point, see Turner (2002: 150–71, esp. 165).

19  Max Horkheimer to Theodor W. Adorno, December 27, 1944 (Adorno 1973–86: XVII, 614).

20  For an excellent elaboration of this point, see Cohen (2003).

21  This would certainly be an implication of Adorno's (1991–2: I) "Trying to understand *Endgame*," his essay on Beckett.

22  It is worth noticing that the same positions reappeared in the German *Historikerstreit* in 1986/7.

23  I explore this claim further in Hammer (2000a).

## CHAPTER 4

1   See for example the following remark in the *Dialectic of Enlightenment* (1979: 163): "Advertising becomes art and nothing else, just as Goebbels —

with foresight— combines them: *l'art pour l'art*, advertising for its own sake, a pure representation of social power." In Adorno (1991b: 39), the "established conductor" is compared to the "totalitarian Führer." "Like the latter, he reduces aura and organization to a common denominator."

2  In 1937, as the Nationalist Socialist regime seemed stronger and more invincible than ever, Adorno was persuaded by Horkheimer to go to New York in order to work at the Princeton Radio Project, a collaborative research effort aimed at examining the psychological and sociological role of radio transmission. While this introduced Adorno to empirical social science, it turned out to be a chastening experience. In Adorno's view, the positivistic methods that were employed prevented the possibility of any genuinely critical or reflective stance towards the listeners they polled, and the data that were collected eventually found their way into commercial applications. The engagement thus confirmed his already entrenched sense that the autonomy and integrity of science, like any other area of culture, including art, was fundamentally endangered by the systemic intervention of economic and administrative imperatives. In addition, it offered evidence of the purported disintegration of the autonomous bourgeois subject in favor of the forms of pseudo-individuality that he (and Horkheimer) later analyzed in *The Dialectic of Enlightenment*.

3  Adorno (1997a: 13): "For the sake of happiness, happiness is renounced. It is thus that desire survives in art."

4  See also Bourdieu (1977: 214, n. 1).

5  See Althusser (1971: 160): "I say: the category of the subject is constitutive of all ideology, but at the same time and immediately I add that *the category of the subject is only constitutive of all ideology insofar as all ideology has the function (which defines it) of 'constituting' concrete individuals as subjects*."

6  Baudrillard's apocalyptic reference is to Borges' (1974: 67–8) tale "Fauna of Mirrors," printed in *The Book of Imaginary Beings*. Dews (1995: 35–6) considers this evocative tale of a sudden event of collapse into a prelapsarian harmony between the human and the "mirror" worlds with reference to Adorno. Like Dews' Adorno, I see the tale as ultimately expressing some form of conservative illusion.

7  According to Geuss (1981: 2–3), "the very heart of the critical theory of society is its criticism of ideology."

8  In addition to the classic Marxist notion of a conflation between particular and general interest, there are many different types of epistemic properties of an ideological form of consciousness. Other examples would be to naturalize social phenomena or to make a mistake about the epistemic status of a belief. For a useful discussion of these issues, see Geuss (1981: 13–14).

9  Luhmann (1970: 57) prominently represents a purely functional approach.

10  For a similar way of stating the same point, see Hegel (1975c: 237):

> The untruth of the immediate judgment lies in the incongruity between its form and its content. To say 'This rose is red' involves (in virtue of the copula 'is') the coincidence of subject and predicate. The rose however is a concrete thing, and so not red only: it also has an odour, a specific form, and many other features not implied in the predicate red. There are other flowers and objects which are red too. The subject and predicate in the immediate judgment touch, as it were, only in a single point, but do not cover each other.

11  For further elaboration of these claims, see Hammer (2002).

12 In a recently edited letter to Scholem from the *Frankfurter Adorno Blätter*, Adorno (1998: 158) writes the following: "I remain true to the *Phenomenology of Spirit* in my view that the movement of the concept, of the matter at hand, is simultaneously the explicitly thinking movement of the reflecting subject" (quoted in Bozzetti (2002: 296)).

13 For a useful discussion of this thesis, see Cook (2001).

14 Habermas (1984: 382) agrees with Honneth that Adorno, especially as a result of his employment of the notion of mimesis, which is supposed to offer reason a socially transcendent source of authority, tends to opt for a form of transcendent criticism.

15 Zuidervaart quotes from Antonio (1981: 330).

16 See "From Restricted to General Economy: A Hegelianism without Reserve," in Derrida (1978).

17 See Adorno (1997a: 112): "The new art tries to bring about the transformation of communicative into mimetic language. By virtue of its double character, language is a constituent of art and its mortal enemy."

18 I return to the problem of transcendence in Chapter 5.


CHAPTER 5

1 In his critique of Adorno, Habermas (1984: 385) likens the former's concept of mimesis to Heidegger's thinking of Being. It is as though, for Habermas, the mere invocation of the Freiburg thinker is supposed to be sufficient to constitute a valid criticism of someone like Adorno. Bernstein (2001: 26–7n.) goes so far as to hold that "Heidegger's general strategy [in *Being and Time*], and elsewhere, is deeply formative for Adorno."

2 Derrida (2003) returns to Nancy's work and repeatedly praises it for having successfully deconstructed the Cartesian notion of freedom as property, ability, power, or attribute of a subject.

3 See Kant (1985: 54–60).

4 For a good discussion and defense of the incorporation thesis, see Allison (1990: 39–40).

5 See Hegel (1977: 407): "The forgiveness which it extends to the other is the renunciation of itself ..."

6 See Adorno's own critical reference to Schmitt in Adorno (2001b: 325) and (1974a: 132).

7 See Freud (1991: 257–60).


CHAPTER 6

1 The focus on the Adorno–Benjamin debate has shaped much of the English-language reception of Adorno's aesthetics. For commentators who elaborate on this issue, see Buck-Morss (1977), Lunn (1982), and Wolin (1994).

2 The choice between fascist aestheticized politics and communist politicized art hardly does justice to the full complexity of Benjamin's position. According to Caygill (1998: 93), the distinction, rather than suggesting that the only viable response to fascism is to mount a Brechtian production, should be recast in terms of the difference between, on the one hand, an alignment between "fascist monumental self-presentation, aura and aestheticism," which transforms the work of art into an immutable and closed item, and, on the other, a work which is permeable and open, affirmative rather than wary in relation-

ship to its own temporal finitude. In a fine passage, Caygill (1998: 94) relates the latter to Benjamin's concept of experience, "where the future subsists in the present as a contingency which, if realized, will retrospectively change the present." While useful in that it distances Benjamin from a too crude and therefore non-representative position, the problem with Caygill's reading is that it fails to take Brecht's influence adequately into account.

3 Fried (1998: 148–72).

4 Adorno's (1991–2: I, 216–40) critique is mainly directed towards Lukács' 1958 book *The Meaning of Contemporary Realism*, perhaps the major intellectual defense of socialist realism in literature and art.

5 See Brecht (1980).

6 For an interesting elaboration on Adorno's thoughts on film, see Hohendahl (1995: 131–9).

7 Adorno (1997a: 229): "In the age of total neutralization, false reconciliation has of course also paved the way in the sphere of radically abstract art: Nonrepresentational art is suitable for decorating the walls of the newly prosperous."

8 Schoolman (1997) rehearses a similar claim, focusing on Adorno's idea of a "togetherness of differences."

9 See in particular Lyotard (1984).

10 See Foster (1996) and Bois and Krauss (1996).

11 Surprisingly few commentators have fully recognized the importance for Adorno of the category of the sublime. For an exception to this tendency, see Welsch (1990). The problem with Welsch's reading, however, is that he fails to distinguish adequately between Adorno's and Lyotard's projects.

12 For a critical discussion of this aspect of Hegel's theory of the sublime in architecture, see Hollier (1989).

13 Adorno (1993a: 48).

14 It should be emphasized that when I talk of sense and presentation, I am not referring to bare presences or "bits of the given" that would make their impact by causally influencing the subject. In that case we would simply be facing a blind force that thinking could not be responsible for, and which could neither be a necessary nor a sufficient reason to form a given judgment of experience. The point of introducing the vocabulary of "sense" and "presentation" is to suggest that receptivity can be saddled with conceptual content while nonetheless engaging the subject in a manner that is consistent with Adorno's stress on passivity. Sense is a form of intelligibility that communicates with human spontaneity without being a direct outcome of rational activity. It would take a separate book to spell out this claim in detail. Here I can only intimate that I see the late Merleau-Ponty as a thinker who has explored such a notion.

15 My suggestions concerning Adorno's notion of mimesis draw inspiration from Nancy (1998: 123–39).

## CHAPTER 7

1 For the most extensive book-length discussion of this problem, see Blumenberg (1983).

2 See Habermas (1987b: 128):

[Nietzsche] stylizes aesthetic judgment, on the model of a "value appraisal" exiled to irrationality, into a capacity for discriminating beyond good and evil, truth and falsehood. In this way, Nietzsche gains criteria for a critique of culture that unmasks science and morality as being in similar ways ideological expressions of a perverted will to power, just as *Dialectic of Enlightenment* denounces these structures as embodiments of instrumental reason. This confirms our suspicion that Horkheimer and Adorno perceive cultural modernity from a similar experiential horizon, with the same heightened sensibility, and even with the same cramped optics that render one insensible to the traces and the existing forms of communicative rationality.

3 Habermas (1991: 23) claims that Adorno's "norm of knowledge" (*Erkenntnisideal*) is "intuitionistic, based on the appeal to a kind of passive seeing prior to language" (*einen intuitionistischen Erkenntnisideal des sprachlosen Sehenlassens*).
4 See Habermas (1984: 387).
5 For an interpretation of the *Phenomenology* along these lines, see Pinkard (1996).
6 For more on this issue, see Hammer (2000b).
7 See Habermas (1998: 239–52). Habermas' legal and political philosophy is developed in much greater detail in *Between Facts and Norms: Contributions to a Discourse Theory of Law and Democracy* (1996a).
8 Connolly (1993: 156) uses a similar notion — that of a "politics of agonistic respect." According to Connolly, in a genuinely democratic polity a (liberal) passive tolerance and letting be is not enough; it is also necessary to contest identities and self-interpretations by introducing genealogical practices that highlight the contingent, incomplete, relational identity of political selves. For a comparison between Connolly and Adorno in this respect, see Schoolman (1997: 85–90).

## CHAPTER 8

1 See in particular Said (1978).
2 Cavell (1999: 235–46).
3 According to Rorty (1988), if permitted to enter the public sphere, such acts would subvert the fundamental virtues of citizenship, namely commitment to justice, equality, and social progress.
4 Referring to the political dimension of art in particular, Adorno (1991–2: I, 38) — in a passage which I read as deeply perfectionist in its orientation — is equally uncompromising in his view that the, however unassured, articulation of the universal presupposes unconditional individuation:

> For the substance of a poem is not merely an expression of individual impulses and experiences. Those become a matter of art only when they come to participate in something universal by virtue of the specificity they acquire in being given aesthetic form. Not that what the lyric poem expresses must be immediately equivalent to what everyone experiences. Its universality is no *volonté de tous*, not the universality of simply communicating what others are unable to communicate. Rather, immersion in what has taken individual form elevates the lyric poem to the status of something universal by making manifest something not distorted, not grasped, not yet subsumed. It thereby anticipates, spiritually, a situation in which no false universality, that is, nothing profoundly particular, continues to fetter what is other than itself, the human. The lyric work hopes to attain universality through unrestrained individuation. The

danger peculiar to the lyric, however, lies in the fact that its principle of individuation never guarantees that something binding and authentic will be produced.

5 I say more about this in Hammer (2002).
6 Compare Lepenies' (1992: 196) view that Adorno "[raises] elitist claims" and seeks to infuse his writing with "the pathos of the special."
7 See in particular the essays in O'Neill (1999).
8 See Adorno (1998b: 78).
9 Adorno to Marcuse, July 16, 1957 as quoted in Wiggershaus (1998: 498).
10 Marcuse (1966: 168) refers to primary narcissism as "the archetype of another existential relation to *reality*."
11 For a similar reading, see Bernstein (1997: 154–82).
12 I am by no means claiming that the term deep ecology has a fixed, established meaning. On the contrary, there is an ongoing debate about its implications that seek guidance and inspiration from a range of different intellectual sources, including Spinoza, Heidegger, Bergson, and many others. For some representative expressions of the philosophy of deep ecology, see Næss (1973), Sessions (1987), Zimmerman (1983), and Nash (1989).
13 See Marx, *Das Kapital* 3, Zürich 1933, 698 (quoted from Arendt 1958: 156): "Der Wasserfall, wie die Erde uberhaupt, wie alle Naturkraft hat keinen Wert, weil er keine in ihm vergegenständlichte Arbeit darstellt." ["The waterfall, as the earth in general and every natural power, has no value because no objectivized labor is represented in it."] For some useful discussions of the relationship between Marxism and ecology, see Benton (1996).
14 For a contestation of this view, see Alfred Schmidt (1971).
15 For a brilliant discussion of the relationship between subjectivity and utopia in Adorno, see Whitebook (1995: 132–64). Whitebook's position is roughly that Adorno's position is deeply ambiguous, although one of its strengths is that it retains a utopian dimension of subjectivity that gets lost in Habermas' linguistification of Critical Theory. Dews (1995: 19–38) argues that Adorno is indeed closer to counter-enlightenment positions than has often been admitted.
16 Ferry (1995) exemplifies this tendency.

# BIBLIOGRAPHY

## Works by Theodor Adorno

1933. *Kierkegaard. Konstruktion des Ästhetischen.* Tübingen: Mohr.

1947a. (with Hanns Eisler) *Composing for the Films.* New York: Oxford University Press.

1947b. (with Max Horkheimer) *Dialektik der Aufklärung. Philosophische Fragmente.* Amsterdam: Querido.

1949. *Philosophie der neuen Musik.* Tübingen: Mohr.

1950. (with Else Frenkel-Brunswik, Daniel J. Levinson, and Sanford R. Nevitt) *The Authoritarian Personality.* New York: Harper.

1951. *Minima Moralia. Reflexionen aus dem beschädigten Leben.* Berlin: Suhrkamp.

1952. *Versuch über Wagner.* Berlin: Suhrkamp.

1955. *Prismen. Kulturkritik und Gesellschaft.* Berlin: Suhrkamp.

1956a. *Dissonanzen. Musik in der verwalteten Welt.* Göttingen: Vandenhoeck and Ruprecht.

1956b. *Zur Metakritik der Erkenntnistheorie. Studien über Husserl und die phänomenologische Antinomien.* Stuttgart: Kohlhammer.

1957. *Noten zur Literatur I.* Berlin: Suhrkamp.

1959. *Musikalische Schriften I.* Berlin: Suhrkamp.

1960. *Mahler. Eine musikalische Physiognomie.* Frankfurt: Suhrkamp.

1961. *Noten zur Literatur II.* Frankfurt: Suhrkamp.

1962a. *Einleitung in die Musiksoziologie. Zwölf theoretische Vorlesungen.* Frankfurt: Suhrkamp.

1962b. (with Max Horkheimer) *Sociologica II. Reden und Vorträge.* Frankfurt: Europäische Verlagsanstalt.

1963a. *Drei Studien zu Hegel.* Frankfurt: Suhrkamp.

1963b. *Eingriffe. Neun kritische Modelle.* Frankfurt: Suhrkamp.

1963c. *Der getreue Korrepetitor. Lehrschriften zur musikalischen Praxis.* Frankfurt: Suhrkamp.

1963d. *Musikalische Schriften II. Quasi una Fantasia.* Frankfurt: Suhrkamp.

1964a. *Jargon der Eigentlichkeit. Zur deutschen Ideologie.* Frankfurt: Suhrkamp.

1964b. *Moments musicaux.* Frankfurt: Suhrkamp.

1965a. *Noten zur Literatur III.* Frankfurt: Suhrkamp.

1965b. "Offener Brief an Max Horkheimer." *Die Zeit*, February 12, p. 32.

1966. *Negative Dialektik*. Frankfurt: Suhrkamp.

1967. *Ohne Leitbild. Parva Aesthetica*. Frankfurt: Suhrkamp.

1968a. *Alban Berg. Der Meister des kleinsten Übergangs*. Frankfurt: Suhrkamp.

1968b. *Impromptus. Zweite Folge neu gedruckter musikalischer Aufsätze*. Frankfurt: Suhrkamp.

1969a. (with Hans Albert, Ralf Dahrendorf, Jürgen Habermas, Harald Pilot and Karl R. Popper) *Der positivismusstreit in der deutschen Soziologie*. Neuwied: Luchterhand.

1969b. *Stichworte. Kritische Modelle 2*. Frankfurt: Suhrkamp.

1970a. *Ästhetische Theorie*. Ed. Gretel Adorno and Rolf Tiedemann. Frankfurt: Suhrkamp.

1970b. *Aufsätze zur Gesellschaftstheorie und Methodologie*. Frankfurt: Suhrkamp.

1970c. *Erziehung zur Mündigkeit. Vorträge und Gespräche mit Hellmut Becker 1959–1969*. Ed. Gerd Kadelbach. Frankfurt: Suhrkamp.

1970d. *Über Walter Benjamin*. Ed. Rolf Tiedemann. Frankfurt: Suhrkamp.

1971. *Kritik. Kleine Schriften zur Gesellschaft*. Ed. R. Tiedemann. Frankfurt: Suhrkamp.

1973a. *The Jargon of Authenticity*. Trans. Knut Tarnowski and Frederic Will. Evanston: Northwestern University Press.

1973b. *Negative Dialectics*. Trans. E. B. Ashton. New York: Seabury Press.

1973c. *Philosophische Terminologie*, vol. 1. Frankfurt: Suhrkamp.

1973d. *Philosophy of Modern Music*. Trans. Anne G. Mitchell and Wesley V. Blomster. New York: Seabury Press.

1973–86. *Gesammelte Schriften*. Ed. Rolf Tiedemann *et al.*, 20 vols. Frankfurt: Suhrkamp.

1974a. *Minima Moralia: Reflections from Damaged Life*. Trans. Edmund Jephcott. London: Verso.

1974b. *Noten zur Literatur IV*. Frankfurt: Suhrkamp.

1974c. *Philosophische Terminologie*, vol. 2. Frankfurt: Suhrkamp.

1976. *Introduction to the Sociology of Music*. Trans. E. B. Ashton. New York: Seabury Press.

1979. (with Max Horkheimer) *Dialectic of Enlightenment*. Trans. John Cumming. London/New York: Verso.

1981. *In Search of Wagner*. Trans. Rodney Livingstone. London: New Left Books.

1982. *Against Epistemology: A Metacritique. Studies in Husserl and the Phenomenological Antinomies*. Trans. Willis Domingo. Oxford: Blackwell.

1989. *Kierkegaard: Construction of the Aesthetic*. Trans. Robert Hullot-Kentor. Minneapolis: University of Minnesota Press.

1991a. *Berg: Master of the Smallest Link*. Trans. Juliane Brand and Christopher Hailey. Cambridge: Cambridge University Press.

1991b. *The Culture Industry: Selected Essays on Mass Culture*. Trans. collective. Ed. J. M. Bernstein. London: Routledge.

1991–2. *Notes to Literature*. Trans. Shierry Weber Nicholsen, 2 vols. New York: Columbia University Press.

1992a. *Mahler: A Musical Physiognomy*. Trans. Edmund Jephcott. Chicago: University of Chicago Press.

1992b. *Quasi una fantasia: Essays on Modern Music*. Trans. Rodney Livingstone. London: Verso.

1993a. *Beethoven. Philosophie der Musik*. Ed. Rolf Tiedemann. Frankfurt: Suhrkamp.

1993b. *Hegel: Three Studies*. Trans. Shierry Weber Nicholsen. Cambridge, Mass.: The MIT Press.

1994a. *The Stars Look Down to Earth and Other Essays on the Irrational in Culture*. Ed. Stephen Crook. London and New York: Routledge.

1994b. (with Walter Benjamin) *Theodor Adorno–Walter Benjamin: Briefwechsel 1928–1940*. Ed. Henry Lonitz. Frankfurt: Suhrkamp.

1995–8. *Frankfurter Adorno Blätter*, IV and V. Munich: text + kritik.

1997a. *Aesthetic Theory*. Trans. Robert Hullot-Kentor. Minneapolis: University of Minnesota Press.

1997b. (with Alban Berg) *Briefwechsel*. Frankfurt: Suhrkamp.

1997c. *Prisms*. Trans. Samuel and Shierry Weber. Cambridge, Mass.: The MIT Press.

1998a. *Beethoven: The Philosophy of Music*. Ed. Rolf Tiedemann. Trans. Edmund Jephcott. Stanford: Stanford University Press.

1998b. *Critical Models: Interventions and Catchwords*. Trans. Henry W. Pickford. New York: Columbia University Press.

1998c. *Metaphysik. Begriff und Probleme*. Ed. Rolf Tiedemann. Frankfurt: Suhrkamp.

1999a. *The Complete Correspondence, 1928–1940/Theodor W. Adorno and Walter Benjamin*. Trans. Nicholas Walker. Ed. Henri Lonitz. Cambridge, Mass.: Harvard University Press.

1999b. *Sound Figures*. Trans. Rodney Livingstone. Stanford: Stanford University Press.

2000a. *The Adorno Reader*. Ed. Brian O'Connor. Malden, Mass.: Blackwell.

2000b. *Introduction to Sociology*. Ed. Christoph Gödde. Trans. Edmund Jephcott. Stanford: Stanford University Press.

2000c. *Metaphysics: Concept and Problems*. Ed. Rolf Tiedemann. Trans. Edmund Jephcott. Cambridge: Polity Press.

2000d. *Problems of Moral Philosophy*. Ed. Thomas Schröder. Trans. Rodney Livingstone. Cambridge: Polity Press.

2001a. *Kant's Critique of Pure Reason*. Ed. Rolf Tiedemann. Trans. Rodney Livingstone. Stanford: Stanford University Press.

2001b. *Zur Lehre von der Geschichte und von der Freiheit*. Ed. Rolf Tiedemann. Frankfurt: Suhrkamp.

## Works cited in the text

Agamben, Giorgio. 1998. *Homo Sacer: Sovereign Power and Bare Life*. Trans. Daniel Heller-Roazen. Stanford: Stanford University Press.

—— 1999. *Remnants of Auschwitz: The Witness and the Archive*. Trans. Daniel Heller-Roazen. New York: Zone Books.

Allison, Henry. 1990. *Kant's Theory of Freedom*. Cambridge: Cambridge University Press.

Althusser, Louis. 1971. *Lenin and Philosophy and Other Essays*. London: New Left Books.

Anderson, Perry. 1976. *Considerations on Western Marxism*. London: New Left Books.

Antonio, Robert J. 1981. "Immanent Critique as the Core of Critical Theory: Its Origins and Developments in Hegel, Marx and Contemporary Thought," *British Journal of Sociology* 32: 330–45.

Arac, Jonathan, ed. 1986. *Postmodernism and Politics*. Minneapolis: University of Minnesota Press.

Arendt, Hannah. 1958. *The Human Condition*. Chicago: University of Chicago Press.

—— 1965. *Eichmann in Jerusalem*. New York: Viking Press.

—— 1973. *The Origins of Totalitarianism*. New York: Harcourt, Brace & World.

Badiou, Alain. 2001. *Ethics: An Essay on the Understanding of Evil*. London: Verso.

Baudrillard, Jean. 1990. *Seduction*. Trans. Brian Singer. New York: St. Martin's Press.

—— 1996. *The Perfect Crime*. Trans. Chris Turner. London: Verso

Bauman, Zygmunt. 2000. *Liquid Modernity*. Cambridge: Polity Press.

Beck, Ulrich. 1986. *Risikogesellschaft*. Frankfurt: Suhrkamp.

Benhabib, Seyla. 1986. *Critique, Norm, and Utopia: A Study of the Foundations of Critical Theory*. New York: Columbia University Press.

—— 1994. "Deliberative Rationality and Models of Democratic Legitimacy." *Constellations* 1: 26–52.

Benjamin, Walter. 1966. *Briefe*. 2 vols. Eds. Gerschom Scholem and Theodor W. Adorno. Frankfurt: Suhrkamp.

—— 1969. *Illuminations*. Trans. Harry Zohn. New York: Schocken Books.

—— 1977. *The Origin of German Tragic Drama*. Trans. John Osborne. London: New Left Books.

—— 1978. *Reflections: Essays, Aphorisms, Autobiographical Writings*. New York: Schocken Books.

Benton, Ted, ed. 1996. *The Greening of Marxism*. New York: The Guilford Press.

Berman, Russell. 2002. "Adorno's Politics." In *Adorno: A Critical Reader*, eds. Nigel Gibson and Andrew Rubin. Oxford: Blackwell.

Bernstein, Jay. 1984. *The Philosophy of the Novel. Lukács, Marxism and the Dialectics of Form*. Minneapolis: University of Minnesota Press.

—— 1992. *The Fate of Art: Aesthetic Alienation from Kant to Derrida and Adorno*. University Park: Pennsylvania State University Press.

—— 1997. "Fragment, Fascination, Damaged Life: 'The Truth about Hedda Gabler'." In *The Actuality of Adorno: Critical Essays on Adorno and the Postmodern*, ed. Max Pensky. Albany: State University of New York Press.

—— 2001. *Adorno: Disenchantment and Ethics*. Cambridge: Cambridge University Press.

Bloch, Ernst. 2000. *The Spirit of Utopia*. Trans. Anthony A. Nassar. Stanford: Stanford University Press.

Blumenberg, Hans. 1983. *The Legitimacy of the Modern Age*. Trans. Robert Wallace. Cambridge, Mass.: The MIT Press.

Bois, Yve-Alain, and Rosalind Krauss. 1996. *L'informe: mode d'emploi*. Paris: Éditions du Centre Pompidou.

Borges, Jorge Luis. 1974. *The Book of Imaginary Beings*. Trans. Norman Thomas di Giovanni. London/New York: Penguin.

Bourdieu, Pierre. 1977. *Outline of a Theory of Practice*. Trans. Richard Nice. Cambridge: Cambridge University Press.

—— 1984. *Distinction. A Social Critique of the Judgement of Taste*. Trans. Richard Nice. Cambridge, Mass.: Harvard University Press.

Bozzetti, Mauro. 2002. "Hegel on Trial: Adorno's Critique of Philosophical Systems." In *Adorno: A Critical Reader*, eds. Nigel Gibson and Andrew Rubin. Oxford: Blackwell.

Brecht, Bertolt. 1980. "Against Georg Lukács." In *Aesthetics and Politics*, ed. Ronald Taylor. London and New York: Verso.

Brunkhorst, Hauke. 1999. *Adorno and Critical Theory*. Cardiff: University of Wales Press.

Buck-Morss, Susan. 1977. *The Origin of Negative Dialectics: Theodor W. Adorno, Walter Benjamin, and the Frankfurt Institute*. New York: The Free Press.

Butler, Judith. 1997. *The Psychic Life of Power: Theories in Subjection*. Stanford: Stanford University Press.

Cavell, Stanley. 1976. *Must We Mean What We Say? A Book of Essays*. Cambridge: Cambridge University Press.

—— 1979. *The Claim of Reason. Wittgenstein, Skepticism, Morality, and Tragedy*. Oxford: Oxford University Press.

—— 1990. *Conditions Handsome and Unhandsome: The Constitution of Emersonian Perfectionism*. Chicago: The University of Chicago Press.

—— 1999. "Benjamin and Wittgenstein: Signals and Affinities." *Critical Inquiry* 25: 235–46.

Caygill, Howard. 1998. *Walter Benjamin: The Colour of Experience*. London and New York: Routledge.

Cohen, Josh. 2003. *Interrupting Auschwitz. Art, Religion, Philosophy*. London and New York: Continuum.

Collins, Jim. 1987. *Uncommon Cultures: Popular Culture and Post-Modernism*. New York: Routledge.

Connerton, Paul. 1980. *The Tragedy of Enlightenment: An Essay on the Frankfurt School*. Cambridge: Cambridge University Press.

Connolly, William E. 1993. *The Augustinian Imperative: A Reflection on the Politics of Morality*. Newbury Park: Sage.

Cook, Deborah. 1996. *The Culture Industry Revisited: Theodor W. Adorno on Mass Culture*. Lanham: Rowman and Littlefield.

—— 2001. "Adorno, ideology and ideology critique." *Philosophy & Social Criticism* 27 (1): 1–20.

Demmerling, Christoph. 1994. *Sprache und Verdinglichung: Wittgenstein, Adorno und das Projekt einer kritischen Theorie*. Frankfurt: Suhrkamp.

Derrida, Jacques. 1978. *Writing and Difference*. Trans. Alan Bass. Chicago: The University of Chicago Press.

—— 1994. *The Specters of Marx*. Trans. Peggy Kamuf. New York: Routledge.

—— 1999. *Adieu to Emmanuel Levinas*. Trans. P. A. Brault and M. Naas. Stanford: Stanford University Press.

—— 2003. *Voyous. Deux essais sur la raison*. Paris: Éditions Galilée.

Dews, Peter. 1995. *The Limits of Disenchantment: Essays on Contemporary European Philosophy*. London and New York: Verso.

Dubiel, Helmut. 1985. *Theory and Politics: Studies in the Development of Critical Theory.* Trans. Benjamin Gregg. Cambridge, Mass.: The MIT Press.

Eco, Umberto. 1986. *Travels in Hyperreality.* Trans. William Weaver. London: Picador.

Eldridge, Richard. 2002. *The Persistence of Romanticism: Essays in Philosophy and Literature.* Cambridge: Cambridge University Press.

Fackenheim, Emil L. 1982. *To Mend the World: Foundations of Future Jewish Thought.* New York: Schocken.

Ferry, Luc. 1995. *The New Ecological Order.* Trans. Carol Volk. Chicago: Chicago University Press.

Finlayson, Gordon. 2002. "On the Ineffable and the Ethical in Adorno." *European Journal of Philosophy* 10: 1–25.

Foster, Hal. 1996. *The Return of the Real: The Avant-Garde at the End of the Century.* Cambridge, Mass.: The MIT Press.

Foucault, Michel. 1979. *Discipline and Punish: The Birth of the Prison.* Trans. Alan Sheridan. New York: Vintage.

Freud, Sigmund. 1959. *Group Psychology and the Analysis of the Ego.* Trans. James Strachey. New York: Norton.

—— 1972. *Civilization and Its Discontents.* Trans. James Strachey. London: Hogarth Press.

—— 1991. *On Metapsychology.* Trans. James Strachey. London: The Penguin Freud Library, No. 11.

Fried, Michael. 1998. *Art and Objecthood. Essays and Reviews.* Chicago: The University of Chicago Press.

Friedman, George. 1980. *The Political Philosophy of the Frankfurt School.* Ithaca: Cornell University Press.

Früchtl, Joseph. 1986. *Mimesis. Konstellation eines Zentralbegriffs bei Adorno.* Würzburg: Königshausen & Neumann.

Geuss, Raymond. 1981. *The Idea of a Critical Theory: Habermas and the Frankfurt School.* Cambridge: Cambridge University Press.

Gibson, Nigel, and Andrew Rubin, eds. 2002. *Adorno: A Critical Reader.* Oxford: Blackwell.

Gouldner, Alvin W. 1980. *The Two Marxisms: Contradictions and Anomalies in the Development of Theory.* New York: Seabury Press.

Grenz, Friedemann. 1974. *Adornos Philosophie in Grundbegriffen.* Frankfurt: Suhrkamp.

Guzzoni, Ute. 1981. *Identität oder nicht: Zur kritischen Theorie der Ontologie.* Freiburg: Alber.

Habermas, Jürgen. 1984. *The Theory of Communicative Action, Volume One: Reason and the Rationalization of Society.* Trans. Thomas McCarthy. London: Heinemann.

—— 1987a. *Knowledge and Human Interests.* Trans. Jeremy Shapiro. New York: Beacon Press.

—— 1987b. *The Philosophical Discourse of Modernity.* Trans. Frederick Lawrence. Cambridge: Polity Press.

—— 1991. *Texte und Kontexte.* Frankfurt: Suhrkamp.

—— 1996a. *Between Facts and Norms: Contributions to a Discourse Theory of Law and Democracy.* Trans. William Rehg. Cambridge, Mass.: The MIT Press.

—— 1996b. *Postmetaphysical Thinking*. Trans. W. M. Hohengarten. Cambridge, Mass.: The MIT Press.

—— 1998. *The Inclusion of the Other. Studies in Political Theory*. Cambridge, Mass.: The MIT Press.

Hammer, Espen. 1997. "Romanticism Revisited." *Inquiry* 40 (2): 225–42.

—— 1998. "Verwandlung des Alltäglichen." *Deutsche Zeitschrift für Philosophie* 46 (2): 267–81.

—— 2000a. "Adorno and Extreme Evil." *Philosophy and Social Criticism* 26 (4): 75–93.

—— 2000b. "Minding the World: Adorno's Critique of Idealism." *Philosophy and Social Criticism* 26 (2): 71–92.

—— 2002. *Stanley Cavell: Skepticism, Subjectivity, and the Ordinary*. Oxford: Polity Press.

—— 2006. "Cavell and Political Romanticism." In *The Claim to Community: Essays on Stanley Cavell and Political Theory*, ed. Andrew Norris. Stanford: Stanford University Press.

Hardt, Michael, and Antonio Negri. 2000. *Empire*. Cambridge, Mass.: Harvard University Press.

Hegel, G. W. F. 1975a. *Aesthetics: Lectures on Fine Art*, vol. 1. Trans. T. M. Knox. Oxford: Clarendon Press.

—— 1975b. *Early Theological Writings*. Trans. T. M. Knox. Chicago: Chicago University Press.

—— 1975c. *Encyclopaedia Logic*. Trans. William Wallace. Oxford: Clarendon Press.

—— 1977. *Phenomenology of Spirit*. Trans. A. V. Miller. Oxford: Oxford University Press.

—— 1991. *Elements of the Philosophy of Right*. Trans. H. B. Nisbet. Cambridge: Cambridge University Press.

—— 1992. *Early Theological Writings*. Trans. T. M. Knox. Philadelphia: University of Pennsylvania Press.

Heidegger, Martin. 1962. *Being and Time*. Trans. John Macquarrie and Edward Robinson. New York: Harper & Row.

—— 1990a. *Kant and the Problem of Metaphysics*. Bloomington: Indiana University Press.

—— 1990b. "The Self-Affirmation of the German University." In *Martin Heidegger and National Socialism*. Trans. Karsten Harries. New York: Paragon House.

—— 1999. *Contributions to Philosophy (From Enowning)*. Trans. Parvis Emad and Kenneth Maly. Bloomington: Indiana University Press.

Hewitt, Andrew. 1992. "A Feminine Dialectic of Enlightenment? Horkheimer and Adorno Revisited," *New German Critique* 56: 143–70.

Hohendahl, Peter Uwe. 1995. *Prismatic Thought: Theodor W. Adorno*. Lincoln: University of Nebraska Press.

Hollier, Denis. 1989. *Against Architecture*. Cambridge, Mass.: The MIT Press.

Honneth, Axel. 1991. *The Critique of Power: Reflective Stages in a Critical Social Theory*. Trans. Kenneth Baynes. Cambridge, Mass.: The MIT Press.

—— 1994. *Struggles for Recognition*. Trans. J. Andersen. Cambridge, Mass.: The MIT Press.

—— 2000. "The Possibility of a Disclosing Critique of Society: The Dialectic of Enlightenment in Light of Current Debates in Social Criticism." *Constellations* 7 (1): 116–27.

Horkheimer, Max. 1947. *Eclipse of Reason*. New York: Oxford University Press.

Huhn, Tom and Lambert Zuidervaart, eds. 1997. *The Semblance of Subjectivity: Essays in Adorno's Aesthetic Theory*. Cambridge, Mass.: The MIT Press.

Hullot-Kentor, Robert. 1989. "Back to Adorno." *Telos* 81: 5–29.

Huyssen, Andreas. 2002. "Adorno in Reverse: From Hollywood to Richard Wagner." In *Adorno: A Critical Reader*. Oxford: Blackwell.

Jacoby, Russell. 1981. *Dialectic of Defeat: Contours of Western Marxism*. Cambridge: Cambridge University Press.

Jameson, Fredric. 1971. *Marxism and Form: Twentieth Century Dialectical Theories of Literature*. Princeton: Princeton University Press.

—— 1996. *Late Marxism: Adorno, or the Persistence of the Dialectic*. London and New York: Verso.

Jarvis, Simon. 1998. *Adorno: A Critical Introduction*. Cambridge: Polity Press.

Jay, Martin. 1984a. *Adorno*. Cambridge, Mass.: Harvard University Press.

—— 1984b. *Marxism and Totality: The Adventures of a Concept from Lukács to Habermas*. Berkeley: University of California Press.

—— 1996. *The Dialectical Imagination: A History of the Frankfurt School and the Institute of Social Research, 1923–1950*. Berkeley: University of California Press.

Kant, Immanuel. 1960. *Religion within the Limits of Reason Alone*. Trans. Theodore M. Greene and Hoyt H. Hudson. New York: Harper & Row.

—— 1975. *Critique of Practical Reason*. Trans. Lewis White Beck. Indianapolis: Bobbs-Merrill.

—— 1985. *Political Writings*. Ed. H. Reiss. Trans. H. B. Nisbet. Cambridge: Cambridge University Press.

—— 1986. *Critique of Pure Reason*. Trans. Norman Kemp Smith. New York: Macmillan.

—— 1987. *Critique of Judgment*. Trans. Werner S. Pluhar. Indianapolis: Hackett.

Kellner, Douglas. 1989. *Critical Theory, Marxism and Modernity*. Cambridge: Polity Press.

—— 2002. "Adorno and the Dialectics of Mass Culture." In *Adorno: A Critical Reader*. Oxford: Blackwell.

Kraushaar, Wolfgang, ed. 1998. *Frankfurter Schule und Studentenbewegung: von der Flaschenpost zum Molotowcocktail 1946–1995*. 3 vols. Frankfurt: Rogner & Bernhard bei Zweitausendeins.

Lasch, Christopher. 1991. *The Culture of Narcissism: American Life in the Age of Diminishing Expectations*. New York: Norton.

Lefort, Claude. 1988. *Democracy and Political Theory*. Trans. David Macey. Minneapolis: University of Minneapolis Press.

Lepenies, Wolf. 1992. *Melancholy and Society*. Trans. Jeremy Gaines and Doris Jones. Cambridge, Mass.: Harvard University Press.

Levinas, Emmanuel. 1969. *Totality and Infinity*. Trans. Alphonso Lingis. Pittsburgh: Duquesne University Press.

Luhmann, Niklas. 1970. *Soziologische Aufklärung*. Köln: Opladen.

Lukács, Georg. 1963. *The Meaning of Contemporary Realism*. London: Merlin.

—— 1971a. *The Theory of the Novel. A Historical-Philosophical Essay on the Forms of Great Epic Literature.* Trans. Anna Bostock. Cambridge, Mass.: The MIT Press.

—— 1971b. *History and Class Consciousness: Studies in Marxist Dialectics.* Trans. Rodney Livingstone. London: Merlin.

Lunn, Eugene. 1982. *Marxism and Modernism: A Historical Study of Lukács, Brecht, Benjamin, and Adorno.* Berkeley: University of California Press.

Lyotard, Jean-François. 1971. *Discours, figure.* Paris: Klincksieck.

—— 1974. "Adorno as Devil." *Telos* 19: 127–37.

—— 1984. "Answering the Question: What Is Postmodernism." In *The Postmodern Condition: A Report on Knowledge.* Manchester: Manchester University Press.

—— 1988. *The Differend: Phrases in Dispute.* Minneapolis: University of Minnesota Press.

Marcuse, Herbert. 1964. *The One-dimensional Man: Studies in the Ideology of Advanced Industrial Society.* London: Routledge.

—— 1966. *Eros and Civilization: A Philosophical Enquiry into Freud.* Boston: Beacon Press.

Marx, Karl. 1968. *Writings of the Young Marx on Philosophy and Society.* Trans. and eds. L. Easton and K. Guddat. Garden City, NY: Doubleday.

—— 1969. *Theories of Surplus Value.* Trans. Renate Simpson. London: Lawrence & Wishart.

—— 1971. *A Contribution to the Critique of Political Economy.* Trans. S. W. Ryazanskaya. London: Lawrence & Wishart.

—— 1973. *Grundrisse.* Trans. Martin Nicolaus. London: Penguin.

—— 1976. *Capital,* vol. 1. Trans. Ben Fowkes. Harmondsworth: Penguin.

McDowell, John. 1994. *Mind and World.* Cambridge, Mass.: Harvard University Press.

Menninghaus, Winfried. 1980. *Walter Benjamins Theorie der Sprachmagie.* Frankfurt: Suhrkamp.

Modleski, Tania, ed. 1986. *Studies in Entertainment: Critical Approaches to Mass Culture.* Bloomington: Indiana University Press.

Mörchen, Hermann. 1981. *Adorno und Heidegger: Untersuchung einer philosophischen Kommunikationsverweigerung.* Stuttgart: Klett-Cotta.

Mouffe, Chantal. 2000. *The Democratic Paradox.* London and New York: Verso.

Müller-Doohm, Stefan. 2003. *Adorno. Eine Biografie.* Frankfurt: Suhrkamp.

Næss, Arne. 1973. "The Shallow and the Deep, Long-Range Ecology Movement. A Summary." *Inquiry* 16: 95–100.

Nägele, Rainer. 1986. "The Scene of the Other: Theodor W. Adorno's Negative Dialectic in the Context of Poststructuralism." In *Postmodernism and Politics,* ed. Jonathan Arac. Minneapolis: University of Minnesota Press, 91–111.

Nancy, Jean-Luc. 1991. *The Inoperative Community.* Minneapolis: University of Minnesota Press.

—— 1993. *The Experience of Freedom.* Stanford: Stanford University Press.

—— 1998. *The Sense of the World.* Minneapolis: University of Minnesota Press.

Nash, Roderick F. 1989. *The Rights of Nature. A History of Environmental Ethics.* Madison: The University of Wisconsin Press.

Neumann, Franz. 1942. *Behemoth: The Structure and Practice of National Socialism*. London: Gollancz.

Nicholsen, Shierry Weber. 1997. *Exact Imagination, Late Work: On Adorno's Aesthetics*. Cambridge, Mass.: The MIT Press.

—— 2003. *The Love of Nature and the End of the World: The Unspoken Dimensions of Environmental Concern*. Cambridge, Mass.: The MIT Press.

O'Neill, Maggie, ed. 1999. *Adorno, Culture and Feminism*. London: Sage Publications.

Pels, Richard H. 1985. *The Liberal Mind in a Conservative Age*. New York: Harper & Row.

Pensky, Max, ed. 1997. *The Actuality of Adorno: Critical Essays on Adorno and the Postmodern*. Albany: State University of New York Press.

Pinkard, Terry. 1996. *Hegel's Phenomenology: The Sociality of Reason*. Cambridge: Cambridge University Press.

Pippin, Robert. 1989. *Hegel's Idealism: The Satisfactions of Self-Consciousness*. Cambridge: Cambridge University Press.

—— 1991. *Modernity as a Philosophical Problem: On the Dissatisfactions of European High Culture*. Cambridge, Mass.: Blackwell.

—— 1997. *Idealism and Modernism: Hegelian Variations*. Cambridge: Cambridge University Press.

Pollock, Friedrich. 1941a. "Is National Socialism a New Order?" *Studies in Philosophy and Social Science* 9: 440–55.

—— 1941b. "State Capitalism: Its Possibilities and Limitations." *Studies in Philosophy and Social Science* 9: 200–25.

Popper, Karl. 1967. *The Open Society and Its Enemies*. New York: Harper & Row.

Rabinbach, Anson. 2002. " 'Why Were the Jews Sacrificed?' The Place of Antisemitism in Adorno and Horkheimer's *Dialectic of Enlightenment*." In *Adorno: A Critical Reader*, 132–49. Oxford: Blackwell.

Rawls, John. 1971. *A Theory of Justice*. Cambridge, Mass.: Harvard University Press.

Ricoeur, Paul. 1970. *Freud and Philosophy: An Essay on Interpretation*. Trans. Denis Savage. New Haven: Yale University Press.

Rorty, Richard. 1988. *Contingency, Irony, and Solidarity*. Cambridge: Cambridge University Press.

—— 2000. "The Overphilosophication of Politics." *Constellations* 7 (1): 128–32.

Rose, Gillian. 1978. *The Melancholy Science. An Introduction to the Thought of Theodor W. Adorno*. London: The Macmillan Press.

Safranski, Rüdiger. 1998. *Martin Heidegger: Between Good and Evil*. Trans. Ewald Osers. Cambridge, Mass.: Harvard University Press.

Said, Edward. 1978. *Orientalism*. New York: Vintage.

Sartre, Jean-Paul. 1965. *Anti-Semite and Jew*. New York: Schocken Books.

Schmidt, Alfred. 1971. *The Concept of Nature in Marx*. Trans. Ben Fowkes. London: New Left Books.

Schmucker, J. F. 1977. *Adorno – Logik des Zerfalls*. Stuttgart: Frommann-Holzboog.

Schoolman, Morton. 1997. "Toward a Politics of Darkness: Individuality and Its Politics in Adorno's Aesthetics." *Political Theory* 25 (1): 57–92.

Sennett, Richard. 1998. *The Corrosion of Character: The Personal Consequences of Work in the New Capitalism.* New York: Norton.

Sessions, George. 1987. "The Deep Ecology Movement: a Review." *Environmental Review* 11: 105–25.

Sloterdijk, Peter. 1987. *Critique of Cynical Reason.* Trans. Michael Eldred. Minneapolis: University of Minnesota Press.

Taylor, Ronald, ed. 1980. *Aesthetics and Politics.* London and New York: Verso.

Turner, Lou. 2002. "Demythologizing the Authoritarian Personality: Reconnoitering Adorno's Retreat from Marx." In *Adorno: A Critical Reader.* Oxford: Blackwell.

Weber, Max. 1974. *From Max Weber: Essays in Sociology.* Eds. and trans. H. H. Gerth and C. W. Mills. New York: Oxford University Press.

Wellmer, Albrecht. 1991. *The Persistence of Modernity: Essays on Aesthetics, Ethics, and Postmodernism.* Trans. D. Midgley. Cambridge, Mass.: The MIT Press.

—— 1997. "Adorno, Modernity, and the Sublime." In *The Actuality of Adorno.* Albany: State University of New York Press.

Welsch, Wolfgang. 1990. *Ästhetisches Denken.* Stuttgart: Reclam.

Whitebook, Joel. 1995. *Perversion and Utopia: A Study in Psychoanalysis and Critical Theory.* Cambridge, Mass.: The MIT Press.

Wiggershaus, Rolf. 1998. *The Frankfurt School: Its History, Theories, and Political Significance.* Trans. Michael Robertson. Cambridge, Mass.: The MIT Press.

Wilke, Sabine, and Heidi Schlipphacke. 1997. "Construction of a Gendered Subject: A Feminist Reading of Adorno's *Aesthetic Theory.*" In *The Semblance of Subjectivity*, eds. Tom Huhn and Lambert Zuidervaart. Cambridge, Mass.: The MIT Press.

Wilson, Michael. 1982. *Das Institut für Sozialforschung und seine Faschismusanalyse.* Frankfurt: Campus Verlag.

Wohlfahrt, Irving. 1989. "On Some Jewish Motifs in Benjamin." In *The Problems of Modernity*, ed. Andrew Benjamin. London and New York: Routledge.

Wolin, Richard. 1994. *Walter Benjamin: An Aesthetic of Redemption.* Berkeley and Los Angeles: University of California Press.

Zimmerman, Michael E. 1983. "Toward a Heideggerian Ethos for Radical Environmentalism." *Environmental Ethics* 5: 101–19.

Zuidervaart, Lambert. 1991. *Adorno's Aesthetic Theory: The Redemption of Illusion.* Cambridge, Mass.: The MIT Press.

# INDEX